WOMAN'S BODY, WOMAN'S WORD

WOMAN'S BODY, WOMAN'S WORD

GENDER AND DISCOURSE IN
ARABO-ISLAMIC WRITING

Fedwa Malti-Douglas

PRINCETON UNIVERSITY PRESS   PRINCETON, NEW JERSEY

Library of Congress Cataloging-in-Publication Data

Malti-Douglas, Fedwa.
Woman's body, woman's word : gender and discourse in Arabo-
Islamic writing / Fedwa Malti-Douglas.
p.   cm.
Includes bibliographical references (p.   ) and index.
ISBN 0-691-06856-9 (CL)—ISBN 0-691-01488-4 (PB)
1. Women in literature. 2. Sex in literature. 3. Arabic literature—750-
1258—History and criticism. 4. Islamic literature, Arabic—History
and criticism. 5. Arabic literature—Women authors—History and
criticism. I. Title.
PJ7519.W66M34   1992
892'.709352042—dc20   91-12804   CIP

_____ To the memory of my father _____

ARAB PHYSICIAN AND WRITER,

WHOSE LIFE WAS DEDICATED TO HUMAN DIGNITY

Contents

Acknowledgments

UNEARTHING the seeds that lead to a book's fruition is a long and pleasurable task. Innumerable trips to the Middle East, papers at professional conferences, days spent in manuscript collections: these tell only part of the story, the raw material, as it were. The rest is made up of concrete names, of friends and colleagues, without whose presence a project such as this one would never have materialized. Every chapter has its own saga, each mixes the personal and the professional.

How can I forget the generosity of my dear friend, the late poet Salâh ʿAbd al-Sabûr, when he was the Director of Dâr al-Kutub in Cairo, in providing me with a copy of the manuscript of Ibn al-Batanûnî's work? I will never forget his wonderful laugh when he realized what the medieval book was about. If it were not for Lawrence I. Conrad's invitation to participate in an interdisciplinary conference on *Hayy ibn Yaqzân* at the Wellcome Institute for the History of Medicine in London, I doubt that I would have walked the gender path in the analysis of philosophical and mystical treatises. The international list of specialists he gathered in Islamic science, medicine, philosophy, and mysticism was most impressive, and a better environment for honing my ideas could have not been found. It was at Nawâl al-Saʿdâwî's urging that I then presented my research on Ibn Tufayl at a meeting of the Jamʿiyyat Tadâmun al-Marʾa al-ʿArabiyya (Arab Women's Solidarity Association) in Cairo. The Egyptian audience was most lively, the discussions were extremely fruitful, and, as always, al-Saʿdâwî's enthusiasm was infectious. Leila Ahmed, Ann Kibbey, William Brinner, Laurence Michalak, and Piotr Michalowski provided me with forums in which to try out my ideas on Nawâl al-Saʿdâwî and benefit from the comments of students and colleagues. Salma Khadra Jayyusi opened my eyes to Fadwâ Tûqân's autobiography, and it was Yûsuf al-Qaʿîd who generously offered to bring me a copy of the text from Jordan, when it was unobtainable in Cairo. The U.C.L.A. Twelfth Levi Della Vida Award Conference honoring André Miquel was a great occasion for me to put into shape my thoughts on Shahrazâd. It is to André Miquel, Georges Sabagh, and Speros Vryonis that I owe a debt of gratitude for that opportunity.

Time seems to always be in short supply for academics. How grateful I am, therefore, to the numerous colleagues and friends who sacrificed this precious commodity to read and comment on the whole manuscript or parts of it: Roger Allen, Christoph Bürgel, Charles Butterworth, Miriam Cooke, Sherman Jackson, Jane Marcus, Susan Napier, James Piscatori,

Denise Spellberg, Suzanne Stetkevych. Some of their suggestions will be recognizable, others not. Nevertheless, the book has only been improved by their careful and painstaking readings.

Princeton University Press has, to put it simply, spoiled me. From the initial conception of this project, friends and editors like Margaret Case and Robert E. Brown have been guardian angels. Margaret Case eliminated any preliminary hesitations I might have had and gave me faith to continue with the proposed book. Robert E. Brown, with his customary diplomacy and skill, guided the work through the usual publishing intricacies to safe harbor. The enthusiasm of my copy editor, Lauren Lepow, went far beyond the call of duty. Excited yet exacting, she meticulously polished the rough edges of the book with her judicious readings.

The intellectual and professional path of an Arab woman is never an easy one. I have been fortunate to have enjoyed the example and, more important, the friendship of prominent Arab women intellectuals and artists: Evelyne Accad, Etel Adnan, Amel Ben Aba, Assia Djebar, Simone Fattal, Salma Khadra Jayyusi, Wisâl Khâlid, Samîra al-Mâniʿ, Hudâ al-Naʿmânî, ʿAbla al-Ruwaynî, Nawâl al-Saʿdâwî, Hanân al-Shaykh. Be it in London, Paris, the United States or the Middle East, our meetings have served as injections of new blood for me. Always willing to share their experiences, always encouraging, their mere presence has sustained me through the years, teaching me that mine was not a solitary voice.

Allen Douglas. I cannot express in words what his presence has meant for me as I conceived and composed this work. We discussed its ideas, we debated its premises. He read and reread it. An intellectual magician, he is always able to dose criticism and encouragement in perfect measure.

And what do I say about S. P.-T.? Born alongside the first chapter of this book, she has patiently seen it through. It is the moments of calm and serenity spent with her that have made those otherwise unbearable moments of life bearable.

Austin, Texas
February 1991

Note on Translation, Transcription, and Abbreviation

ALL TRANSLATIONS in the text are my own, unless otherwise indicated, and all references are to the Arabic originals. When English or other European translations are available, these are noted in the first citation of the text.

I have used a simplified transcription system in which the lengtheners on lowercase vowels are indicated with the French circumflex accent. The ʿayn and the _hamza_ are represented by the conventional symbols. Specialists should be able to easily identify the Arabic words.

_EI_² refers to the _Encyclopaedia of Islam_, 2d ed. (Leiden: E. J. Brill, 1960–).

WOMAN'S BODY, WOMAN'S WORD

Introduction

THE ARAB WOMAN is a most fascinating creature. Is she veiled? Is she not veiled? Is she oppressed? Is she not oppressed? Were her rights greater before Islam? Are her rights greater after Islam? Does she have a voice? Does she not have a voice? Book titles and book covers in the West tell part of the tale: behind the veil, beyond the veil, veiled women, partially veiled women, voices that have been heard, voices that are waiting to be heard, and on and on.[1] Advocates of opposing sides unceasingly cheer one view or another. From the East, writings emerge to support one or another of these positions. Arab feminists rally with their Western counterparts; Muslim apologetic materials provide fodder for the equivalent Western stance.

This futile dialogue on gender and women has long attracted the West. The image of women languishing under the yoke of Islam titillates the Western observer and permits him to place himself in the superior position. Women and their role become a stick with which the West can beat the East. More than that, the liberation of women in the East poses its own special dilemmas, complicating and aggravating this dialogue. Since, as Fatima Mernissi eloquently argues, women's liberation in the modern Middle East is associated with westernization, the entire subject, willy-nilly, becomes enmeshed in political and civilizational debates.[2]

The parallel literary critical dialogue on women in the Arab world is still in its infancy. The "images of women" tradition still dominates. This, as Toril Moi has shown for Western feminist criticism, is a stage that, though necessary, must be transcended.[3] In the study of contemporary Arabic literature, the process has begun, particularly in the areas of war, violence, and gender. The book-length studies by Miriam Cooke and Evelyne Accad are breaking ground and paving the way for more complex literary and cultural questions.[4] For the body, and for all of classical

[1] For some examples of this phenomenon, see Fedwa Malti-Douglas, "Views of Arab Women: Society, Text, and Critic," *Edebiyât* 4 (1979): 256–273.

[2] Fatima Mernissi, *Beyond the Veil: Male-Female Dynamics in a Modern Muslim Society* (Cambridge, Mass.: Schenkman Publishing Company, 1975), pp. 99–102. See, also, the pamphlet by Muhammad Fahmî 'Abd al-Wahhâb, *al-Harakât al-Nisâ'iyya fî al-Sharq wa-Silatuhâ bil-Isti'mâr wal-Sahyûniyya al-'Alamiyya* (Cairo: Dâr al-I'tisâm, 1979).

[3] Toril Moi, *Sexual/Textual Politics: Feminist Literary Theory* (London: Methuen, 1985), pp. 42–49.

[4] Miriam Cooke, *War's Other Voices: Women Writers on the Lebanese Civil War* (Cambridge: Cambridge University Press, 1987); Evelyne Accad, *Sexuality and War: Literary Masks of the Middle East* (New York: New York University Press, 1990).

Arabo-Islamic letters, the territory remains, if I may use this word, virgin.[5]

Woman's Body, Woman's Word: Gender and Discourse in Arabo-Islamic Writing proposes to investigate precisely those intersections found in its title. The work is both revolutionary and heterodox in more than one way. It is not restricted chronologically, transcending the traditional critical divisions in Arabic letters that permit scholars to speak, on the one hand, of classical or medieval Arabic literature, and, on the other hand, of modern literature. It argues that, in the centuries-old Arabic textual tradition, a dialectic operates between mental structures involving women and sexuality in the modern age and their antecedents in the classical period, that modern literature must also be seen against its classical background. The breaking of chronological boundaries is coupled with a breaking of textual or generic limits. The Arabo-Islamic writing of this book's title will not be isolated simply in belletristic works. Philosophy, mysticism, geography, cosmography, biography: all are essential players in the gender game and in the propagation of cultural ideas and values. Religio-theological conceptions find their way into the world of lexicography and philology. That is why this discourse is Arabo-Islamic. Some of the texts under discussion are among the most profane possible; others are classics of Islamic religious writing. But in even the most profane locations, religious referents abound, especially when the subject is women. Historically, Arabic culture has been, and remains, an essentially Islamic one, though there are, of course, non-Arabic Islamic cultures. But the Arabo-Islamic discourse is not the statement of the religion Islam in ideal terms, or even as most Muslims today might wish to understand it. It is the reflection of a civilizational reality in which religious values and ideals become embodied in the literary and cultural expressions of historical Middle Eastern societies. All of the texts analyzed are, or were, influential. But many are not in the canon. Breaking down this barrier is as important as breaking down the chronological one.

The cultural world of this Arabo-Islamic discourse is that of prose, and in the classical period, that of the male scriptor. This is not entirely a coincidence. Prose by its nature permits a clearer representation, a more elaborate reformulation and restructuring of the world. Mimesis is tied to its essence. This is especially clear when prose is compared to traditional Arabic poetry, a highly conventionalized form. While certain carefully defined poetic subgenres were assigned to women, the world of

---

[5] A recent article by Leila Ahmed, "Arab Culture and Writing Women's Bodies," *Feminist Issues* (Spring 1989): 41–55, seeks to understand a story by Alifa Rif'at against the context of classical Arabic medical lore. These issues, I expect, will be given fuller treatment in Ahmed's forthcoming book.

prose was effectively closed to them.[6] Hence, it is on prose that we shall concentrate, though it must be remembered that certain forms of classical Arabic prose include and effectively subordinate verse selections within their discourse.[7]

Little did Shahrazâd[8] know when she stepped into the textual world of *The Thousand and One Nights* that she would one day become a pawn in this game of gender politics. Little did she know that she would engender (in both senses) modern texts that would recast her own story. Little did she know that her control of narration (alas, but a fleeting phenomenon) would be used to argue in favor of the Arab woman's access to discourse.[9] This symbol of storytelling, this mistress of narrators East and West has a saga so dramatic that it overshadows the true gender dynamics in the text (chapter 1). Her entrance into the world of Arabo-Islamic discourse is much discussed, her exit not. Pitted against a royal serial murderer, she exploits her body and her words to lead him back to normality. Her attempts to create a functioning heterosexual couple are played out against a greater civilizational pull for a male homosocial couple. Shahrazâd herself will open the door for us. She will lead us not into her own nights of storytelling but into an investigation of the explosive relationship among sexuality, the body, and woman's voice in the Arabo-Islamic sphere. The gender dynamics her odyssey (in its largest possible meaning) creates will have an uncanny tendency to recur throughout the present book.

Shahrazâd then speaks. But woman's voice is more than a physiological faculty. It is the narrative instrument that permits her to be a literary medium, to vie with the male in the process of textual creation. To control the narrative process, however, is no small task. Shahrazâd demonstrates to her literary cousins and descendants that an intimate relationship must

---

[6] In her book, *al-Mar'a fî Adab al-'Asr al-'Abbâsî* (Baghdad: Dâr al-Rashîd lil-Nashr, 1981), Wâjida Majîd 'Abd Allâh al-Atraqjî includes examples of what she considers "women's literature." But, except for poetry, which she also treats separately, her examples consist essentially of either the remarks of women quoted in works by men (which I deal with, for example, in chapter 2) or of incidental writings, like personal letters that sometimes made their way into histories or male writings. They do not constitute socially sanctioned literary production.

[7] A study of the gender politics of Arabic poetry would be a book of its own. Poetry as well as some other topics are treated in a chapter in the forthcoming book by J. C. Bürgel, *Allmacht und Mächtigkeit* (Munich: Beck, forthcoming).

[8] The names of the four leading characters from the frame of *The Thousand and One Nights* vary slightly from one edition to another. I have decided to follow the forms found in the Bûlâq edition, cited in chapter 1 below, because they are closest to the most common forms used in the Middle East and the West.

[9] See, for example, Barbara Harlow, "The Middle East," in *Longman Anthology of World Literature by Women*, compiled by Marian Arkin and Barbara Shollar (New York: Longman, 1989), p. 1165.

be created between writing and the body. This mistress of the word is a mistress of the ruse as well.

In *Woman's Body, Woman's Word*, some of the most quasi-sacred texts of the Arabo-Islamic sphere will be made to stand alongside *The Thousand and One Nights*, subject to the gender microscope. As the editors of, and the contributors to, *Rewriting the Renaissance* eloquently demonstrate, the reexamination of cherished texts from different angles, principally feminist ones, is a most enriching experience.[10] After the work of Caroline Walker Bynum, Claudine Herrmann, Margaret R. Miles, and Elaine Pagels, how can one leave the Arabo-Islamic stones unturned?[11]

An objection can be raised, however. Are feminist or gender-conscious approaches appropriate to a non-Western society, especially if feminism is considered an ideology of Western origin? Are not gender relations different in non-Western societies? Of course, they are; and we shall see some of the ways. Gender-conscious analyses are vital when the culture in question uses gender as a major organizing principle, in social organization, in *mentalités*, or, as is most usual, in both. Who would deny that this has been the case in the Arabo-Islamic cultural sphere, as it has been in the world of the Christian and post-Christian West? The fact that such struggles and ideologies combine with other kinds of issues in many Third World contexts, and whether one wishes to consider the resulting amalgams sufficiently distinct to apply neologisms like *postfeminism*, changes nothing in this fundamental reality.[12] Consciousness of gender and arguments about the roles of men and women were not brought to the Arab world by Western feminists, like serpents in the Garden of Eden. These issues have always been major and fully conscious preoccupations of Arab writers who have filled their literature with chapters and books on women, their roles, their problems, and the like.

Medieval Arab critics did not consider *The Thousand and One Nights* serious literature. More respectable, because linguistically more sophisticated, was the largely anecdotal prose genre referred to by Western scholars as *adab*. The rich medieval adab corpus that gave birth to those delightful trickster character types also begat the "woman" as character type (chapter 2). The female, defined by her gender, is made to enter the

[10] Margaret W. Ferguson, Maureen Quilligan, and Nancy J. Vickers, *Rewriting the Renaissance: The Discourses of Sexual Difference in Early Modern Europe* (Chicago: University of Chicago Press, 1986).

[11] Caroline Walker Bynum, *Jesus as Mother: Studies in the Spirituality of the High Middle Ages* (Berkeley: University of California Press, 1982); Claudine Herrmann, *Les voleuses de langue* (Paris: éditions des femmes, 1976); Margaret R. Miles, *Carnal Knowing: Female Nakedness and Religious Meaning in the Christian West* (Boston: Beacon Press, 1989); Elaine Pagels, *Adam, Eve, and the Serpent* (New York: Vintage Books, 1989).

[12] See, for example, Trinh T. Minh-ha, *Woman, Native, Other: Writing Postcoloniality and Feminism* (Bloomington: Indiana University Press, 1989).

pantheon of adab character types largely through her witty manipulation of the body. Her ruse is thus close, if not identical, to that of Shahrazâd.

The dangers inherent in this female body are never far away, however. Ibn al-Batanûnî's (ca. 900/1494) vision seems at the outset to vie with the more profane adab one (chapter 3). But his misogynist recasting of sacred history can only operate because the cultural forces behind it are extremely strong. The Qur'ânic phrase that serves him as an antifemale refrain centers on woman's guile and is evoked in *The Thousand and One Nights*. These literary worlds may seem superficially distant, but their gender dynamics are most certainly not.

Perhaps the best solution to this ever-present threat in woman's body is that of the Andalusian philosopher-physician, Ibn Tufayl (d. 581/ 1185–1186) (chapter 4). His mystico-philosophical allegory, *Hayy ibn Yaqzân*, is one of the monuments of classical Arabo-Islamic civilization to weather the test of time. The story has the makings of a fairy tale: a young boy on a desert island is nurtured by a gazelle and grows up learning all he needs to learn, eventually turning to the mystic way of life, which he shares with another male. A disturbing negation, when not an absence, of sexuality characterizes this text. *Hayy ibn Yaqzân* vies with *The Thousand and One Nights* in popularity: modified versions of the story turn up in the contemporary Middle East in children's books, in comic-strip form, and as subjects of paintings.

Ibn Tufayl sets up his ideal male world on the island of al-Waqwâq, a legendary and phantasmagoric locus where women grow on trees. Medieval geographers and cosmographers will flesh this out, demonstrating that more is at stake in Ibn Tufayl's male utopian vision than simply an occultation of the female. Societies of women that propagate themselves, cities of women: these all become part of the fantasy world of the medieval Arabic male narrator (chapter 5).

Though Ibn Tufayl's text has one foot in geographical and cosmographical works, its other foot is just as solidly planted in the Arabo-Islamic philosophical consciousness. Hence it is that woman's body and woman's word enter a different realm, that of the flight from sex, the female, and corporeality. Asexual philosophy and sexual geography are but two facets of the same phenomenon (chapter 5).

From classical Arabo-Islamic prose, some of which dates to the ninth century, to contemporary Arabic prose—quite a chronological leap! And chronology is only part of the issue. How is this possible? How can such a radical analytical step be justified? True, there are essential differences between classical Arabo-Islamic prose and its modern descendant. Some twentieth-century literary forms, such as the novel and the short story, do not have classical antecedents. Their external form is influenced by the parallel developments in modern Western prose. Problems of literary closure differ between classical and modern Arabic prose: the adab work, for example, is composed of a great number of independent literary units ranging from the anecdote to a verse from the Muslim holy book. The spirit of classical Arabic texts diverges from the modern counterparts with their greater emphasis on the individual. But there are essential points of convergence, areas of mental structures that link modern Arabic prose to its literary predecessors.

Western cultural critics have shown the continuing influence of age-old paradigms, despite momentous social and economic changes. I shall show the same for the dominant civilization of the Middle East. *Longue durée* cultural perspectives must be explored, especially in areas so closely intertwined at once with the most intimate of values and the most sacred of texts. Most of the medieval texts that we shall consider have their versions or their echoes in the books sold on the street corners of Arab cities today. At the present moment, when some of the most important intellectuals and political organizers of the region are seeking their models in either the Islamic Middle Ages or the time of the Prophet, one cannot deny this culture its profound sense of historical continuity.

But dramatic is the difference when modern texts are the responsibility of female scriptors. What *Woman's Body, Woman's Word* is proposing is not a survey of the images of women in classical and modern Arabic prose but rather the analytical confrontation of classical prose texts by male scriptors and modern prose texts by female scriptors. Linking the two are woman's body and woman's word. Rather than a direct continuation, we have a response. Classical male scriptors warned of the tricks of women. Modern women writers challenge them with tricks of their own.

The modern feminist response to the predominant classical mental structures is conditioned by two new circumstances. The first is a greater access to print for Arab women, especially in the narrative and descriptive genres hitherto closed to them. The second is the emergence of feminism itself, permitting the modern female writer to challenge the sexist and patriarchal assumptions of the Arabic literary canon. Nevertheless, she must work through this complex of inherited values, even when subverting them. The woman Arab writer of the late twentieth century achieves her literary voice, but she too must do so through the body.

Modern Arabic women's literature was not born in the last decade. Its germs were already present in the nineteenth century. Parallel with, yet somewhat behind, male Arabic literature, its development increased in the twentieth century, accelerating even faster after the Second World War.[13] In our days, "the literature of long finger nails," as one male critic

[13] For the early history of modern Arabic women's writing, see Miriam Cooke, "Telling

has called it,[14] has become increasingly ubiquitous. Nevertheless, it is only in the last few decades that modern Arabic literature, and with it modern Arabic women's literature, has achieved a level of relative frankness on questions of corporality and sexuality.[15] Even now, however, neither has achieved the sexual openness that characterized virtually all of classical Arabic letters.[16] Hence, it is from the women writers of our own day that we must seek responses to the challenges of the classical male scriptors.

It is perhaps not coincidental that the most uncompromisingly feminist of all modern Arabic authors should be a female physician. The Egyptian Nawâl al-Sa'dâwî has made her mark on the international feminist movement with her outspoken opinions on woman's sexuality and position in the Middle East. *The Hidden Face of Eve* has been widely translated.[17] More than any other contemporary writer, it is al-Sa'dâwî whose concerns with the body are unquestioned. Her first novel, *Mudhakkirât Tabîba* (Memoirs of a female physician) is a feminist response to that male classic of modern Arabic autobiography, *al-Ayyâm* (The days), by the twentieth-century Arab world's leading modernizer, Tâhâ Husayn (chapter 6). The literary dialogue she undertakes with the male text is articulated through a complex relationship among blindness (Tâhâ Husayn was blind), sexuality, and woman's physicality. This nexus of mutually defined physicality is a classical Arabo-Islamic mental construct, existing in literary, legal, and theological sources.

Yet the narrator of *Memoirs* manages to transcend her body, to go beyond its social and physical constraints. The catalyst is medicine—itself, of course, a science of the body. The social power of the physician exorcizes the weakness of the female (chapter 7). Science, however, cannot be the sole balm; it must be combined with art. And this for Nawâl al-Sa'dâwî is in a larger sense the act of writing, the act of textual creation.

Their Lives: A Hundred Years of Arab Women's Writings," *World Literature Today* 60 (Spring 1986): 212–216.

[14] Mahmûd Fawzî, *Adab al-Azâfir al-Tawîla* (Cairo: Dâr Nahdat Misr lil-Tab' wal-Nashr, 1987).

[15] Turn-of-the-century women writers, by comparison, are in a different mental universe. See, for example, Bâhithat al-Bâdiya [Malak Hifnî Nâsif], *al-Nisâ'iyyât* (Cairo: Dâr al-Hudâ lil-Tab' wal-Nashr wal-Tawzî', n.d.); Irène Fenoglio-Abd el Aal, *Défense et illustration de l'Egyptienne: Aux débuts d'une expression féminine* (Cairo: Centre d'Etudes et de Documentation Economique, Juridique, et Sociale, 1988).

[16] See, for example, the bowdlerizations of the editor of al-Suyûtî, *Nuzhat al-Julasâ' fî Ash'âr al-Nisâ'*, ed. 'Abd al-Latîf 'Ashûr (Cairo: Maktabat al-Qur'ân, 1986), p. 10.

[17] The original Arabic title is: *al-Wajh al-'Arî lil-Mar'a al-'Arabiyya*, which translated literally means: The naked face of the Arab woman. See Nawâl al-Sa'dâwî, *al-Wajh al-'Arî lil-Mar'a al-'Arabiyya* (Beirut: al-Mu'assasa al-'Arabiyya lil-Dirâsât wal-Nashr, 1977). For the English translation, see Nawal el-Saadawi, *The Hidden Face of Eve: Women in the Arab World*, trans. Sherif Hetata (Boston: Beacon Press, 1982).

The ability of her female narrators to control discourse, to utter words, becomes a major issue in her fiction. Many of them can do so only through the intervention of a female physician, in an interesting framing technique of narration within narration: feminist and subverted echoes of Shahrazâd. The initial Foucauldian power relationship has not substantially changed. As the physician is in a subject-object relationship with her patient, so the physician as purveyor of discourse is in a similar power relationship with her enframed narrator. Writing, like medicine, is articulated through the body. Though medicine becomes the key that unlocks gender boundaries, it brings one, in an ironic way, back to the body.

If medicine as linked to corporality is what gives much of Nawâl al-Saʿdâwî's fiction its feminist raison d'être, it is corporality of a different but related kind that proves to be important in ʿAbla al-Ruwaynî's subversive biography of her dead husband, Amal Dunqul (chapter 8). Until his tragic death from cancer, the young Amal Dunqul was Egypt's leading poet. The supposed biography of the poet represents a rebirth for his widow, permitting her to take control of the discourse. A poet lives through his verbal art, and it is this that ʿAbla al-Ruwaynî must subvert to have the right to her own narrative. In the process, sexual roles are inverted and the corporality of the male redefined. But ʿAbla al-Ruwaynî's postmortem text is also dialectically reacting with the tradition, especially the classical *rithâ'*, that elegiac poetry most often reserved for women. Much like her narrative sisters, she ties herself to the tradition while pulling away from it.

It is perhaps no literary accident that it should be a female poet, the Palestinian Fadwâ Tûqân, who best redefines the classical (chapter 9). Her prose medium is the autobiography, a revered and established form, even in classical Arabic letters. But hers is an account that exploits a non-linear form, that redefines a life story. At the same time, Tûqân's odyssey is a revolt against the central physical image of giving birth, as it is a seizure of woman's right to speak. Her *Mountain Journey, Difficult Journey* reformulates issues that will have proven so central in *Woman's Body, Woman's Word*, from Shahrazâd to Nawâl al-Saʿdâwî.

Classical or modern, woman's voice in Arabo-Islamic discourse is indissolubly tied to sexuality and the body. Whether a woman must speak through the body (as in the classical) or in reaction to it (as in the modern), the conclusion remains the same. For woman, the word remains anchored to the body.

CHAPTER 1

Narration and Desire: Shahrazâd

SHAHRAZÂD, the female spinner of tales in *The Thousand and One Nights*, queen of narrators East and West, has long been the symbol of storytelling. Her power over words and her perceived ability to control discourse have provoked the envy of male writers from Edgar Allan Poe to John Barth.[1]

In his delightful and critically conscious novel, *La lectrice* (now also a film), Raymond Jean blends sexual and literary desire, feminine seductiveness and narration. Like a modern-day Shahrazâd, his comely heroine narrates texts (actually she reads aloud) to a series of listeners who readily confuse literature and sexuality. What most distinguishes the twentieth-century French heroine from her Arabo-Persian predecessor is her lack of control. Desire swirls around her, while she has little hold on it.[2] All the more striking by contrast is Shahrazâd's mastery. It is she who controls the relation between desire and the text, at least up to a point.

The Shahrazâd we shall examine is also a sexual being, who manipulates discourse (and men) through her body. It is the latter that permits her to speak, as male violence is met with her sexuality, articulated through her body and her words. At the same time, Shahrazâd uses narrative to redirect desire and, hence, sexuality.

The frame story of *The Thousand and One Nights*—that is, the work's prologue and epilogue, as they are usually termed—is without doubt one of the most powerful narratives in world literature. It is not simply from its mixture of sex and violence that the frame of the *Nights* draws its enduring appeal. Rather, this lies in the unique relationship it forges between sexual and narrative desire.

Innumerable critics have written on *Alf Layla wa-Layla*. (A "thousand and one" might not be an exaggeration.) And the frame story is mentioned in much of the criticism. Most of the interpretations divide themselves into two schools: the time-gaining, on the one hand, and the healing, on the other. From Shahrazâd's perspective, the frame becomes a "time-gaining" technique, similar to other time-gaining or lifesaving acts

[1] Edgar Allan Poe, "The Thousand-and-Second Tale of Scheherazade," in *Edgar Allan Poe, Greenwich Unabridged Library Classics* (New York: Chatham River Press, 1981), pp. 491–502; John Barth, *Chimera* (New York: Fawcett Crest, 1972), pp. 9–64.

[2] Raymond Jean, *La lectrice* (Paris: Actes Sud, 1986).

of narration in the body of the *Nights* themselves. To quote Mia Gerhardt, "Shehrezâd temporizes by making one story follow another, until at last she has gained her victory."[3] Likewise, Bruno Bettelheim notes that "delivery from death through the telling of fairy tales is a motif which starts the cycle."[4] But Bettelheim is representative, indeed probably the best representative, of the "healing" school. For the psychoanalytic critic, there are two protagonists, Shâhriyâr and Shahrazâd. She is the ego, while her male counterpart is dominated by the id, and the entire text functions as an "integration of the king's personality."[5] Integration of personality, now translated into Jungian terms, is also central to Jerome Clinton's discussion.[6] The interpretive arguments of time-gaining and healing are clearly interrelated.

A different sort of approach to the frame is embodied in some recent French criticism, an attention to the idea of desire. Desire in connection with Shahrazâd is invoked by André Miquel.[7] But the linking of Shahrazâd to desire is no doubt clearest in the work of Jamel Eddine Bencheikh, for whom the master storyteller represents "tout être de désir" (all beings of desire).[8] It is perhaps Edgard Weber in his *Le secret des mille et une nuits: L'inter . . . dit de Shéhérazade* (which despite its quasi-cinematic title and provocative cover is well worth reading) who takes the most psychoanalytical approach when examining the position of desire in this classic of world literature.[9] Here, again, however, many textual strategies go unnoticed. Subordinated as well is Shahrazâd herself, who becomes,

[3] Mia I. Gerhardt, *The Art of Storytelling: A Literary Study of the Thousand and One Nights* (Leiden: E. J. Brill, 1963), pp. 397–398. Cf. Edgard Weber, *Le secret des Mille et une nuits: L'inter . . . dit de Shéhérazade* (Toulouse[?]: Eché, 1987), pp. 61–62. It is with this group that we should associate the "lifesaving" interpretations of Tzvetan Todorov, "Les hommes-récits," in Tzvetan Todorov, *Poétique de la prose* (Paris: Editions du Seuil, 1971), pp. 78–91, and Abdelkebir Khatibi, "De la mille et troisième nuit," in *La séduction,* ed. Maurice Olender and Jacques Sojcher (Paris: Editions Aubier Montaigne, 1980), pp. 131–147.

[4] Bruno Bettelheim, *The Uses of Enchantment: The Meaning and Importance of Fairy Tales* (New York: Vintage Books, 1977), p. 87.

[5] Ibid., pp. 87–90.

[6] Jerome W. Clinton, "Madness and Cure in *The 1001 Nights*," *Studia Islamica* 61 (1985): 107–125.

[7] See, for example, André Miquel, "Mille nuits, plus une," *Critique, littératures populaires* 36 (March 1980): 243.

[8] Jamel Eddine Bencheikh, "Le roi, la reine et l'esclave noir," special issue on *Itinéraires d'écritures, Peuples méditerranéens* 30 (1985): 154. This article has been reprinted in Jamel Eddine Bencheikh, *Les Mille et Une Nuits ou la parole prisonnière* (Paris: Editions Gallimard, 1988), pp. 21–39.

[9] Weber, *Secret.* Naïm Kattan in "Du récit du désir dans les Mille et une Nuits," in Olender and Sojcher, *La séduction,* pp. 173–179, seeks to link desire, seduction, and the text. But rather than developing this argument, he severely abbreviates the story itself and instead shifts to a series of reductionist generalizations about the corpus of the *Nights.*

in fact, the very embodiment of speech (the title of one section is "Shé-hérazade ou la parole").[10]

All these views of Shahrazâd and the frame have one overriding characteristic in common: they are prefeminist and pre–gender conscious, in the intellectual, not the chronological sense. Making Shahrazâd represent beings of desire (or equating her with speech), confining her to the role of healer, draws attention away from both the strength of her personality and her mastery of the situation, while occulting male-female power dynamics.

Striking in this nonfeminism is its articulation, even exaggeration, in the writings of the noted Moroccan feminist, Fatima Mernissi, for whom Shahrazâd is "an innocent young girl whom a fatal destiny led to Chahrayar's bed," and her achievement, "the miraculous triumph of the innocent."[11] Such a view belittles Shahrazâd's wisdom and cleverness, on the one hand, and her initiative and mastery, on the other. She is not led by a fatal destiny to the king's bed, nor is her triumph due to miraculous chance.

Ironically, it has been male creative writers themselves who have most clearly perceived, and most forcibly reacted against, the feminist implications of the frame story, with its image of mastery through narration. That is why authors like Poe and Barth, for example (aided in this by a slightly misplaced professional jealousy—after all, Shahrazâd is not the work's author, only its principal narrator), feel the need to conjure away either Shahrazâd's literary or her sexual and interpersonal achievements.[12]

The frame, despite the literary interludes of the Shahrazâdian-narrated nights, is a complete literary unit, and its prologue should not be separated and considered a "pré-texte" (or fore-text), as Bencheikh argues.[13] The epilogue of the frame—usually dismissed cavalierly, when not overlooked completely—is an integral part of the story, redefining through its literary closure the meaning of the prologue itself. Many critics, beginning at least with Mia Gerhardt, have called attention to what they consider an incongruity between the ostensible purpose of Shahrazâd's storytelling and the contents of many of the stories told, providing as they do examples of evil women.[14] Such a line of argument runs a double danger: either an overreliance on a mechanistic type of psychological expla-

[10] Weber, *Secret*, pp. 96–100.

[11] Fatima Mernissi, *Chahrazad n'est pas marocaine* (Casablanca: Editions Le fennec, 1988), p. 9.

[12] Poe, "The Thousand-and-Second Tale"; Barth, *Chimera*.

[13] Bencheikh, "Le roi," pp. 151–154.

[14] See, for example, Gerhardt, *Art*, p. 399; Bencheikh, "Le roi," p. 151.

nation (Clinton has shown one of its pitfalls),[15] or a tendency to judge the significance and impact of individual stories outside the larger corpus of the *Nights* as a whole. In either case, the entire issue is, in a certain sense, irrelevant, since the storytelling frame has, as will become clear, properties independent of the content of the stories told.

For analytical purposes, the frame can be divided into six sections:

1. The first section opens with Shâhriyâr's desire to see his younger brother Shâhzamân, from whom he has been separated for twenty years. This desire instigates Shâhzamân's voyage to his brother, which in turn becomes the occasion for the discovery of his own wife's infidelity. It is also while visiting Shâhriyâr that he discovers the perfidy of the older monarch's wife.

2. The second section consists of a voyage as well. This one involves both brothers, who abandon their kingdoms because of their wives' adulterous behavior. On this journey, they encounter the *'ifrît* and the young woman, who forces them under threat of death to copulate with her. At the end of this experience, they decide to return to their kingdom, and to abandon the permanent company of women.

3. The third section, embodying Shâhriyâr's violent reaction to the past events in the frame, narrates his one-night sexual encounters that culminate in each case with the murder of his female partner.

4. With section four, Shahrazâd enters the scene. Despite her father's protests, she insists on being offered to the monarch and enlists the help of her sister, Dunyâzâd, in her act. Here begins the narration.

5. The frame does not stop at this point; and its fifth section is its continuation during Shahrazâd's thousand and one nights of storytelling. The storytelling must not be equated with the contents of the stories told. If the stories that Shahrazâd tells are outside the frame (or might one better say inside?), the act of telling them is the continuation of the frame. It should be remembered that once she has begun, Shahrazâd does not disappear like some now-obsolescent literary device. She is a most intrusive narrator, who appears at a minimum at the beginning and end of every night. Shâhriyâr and Dunyâzâd, also characters from the frame story, make occasional appearances as well.

6. The last part of the frame is its closure with the happy ending. Shâhriyâr is told that he has meanwhile fathered three sons (fortunate conceptions, indeed) and Shahrazâd is rewarded in a wedding ceremony. In a longer version, Shahrazâd weds Shâhriyâr, Dunyâzâd weds Shâhzamân, and the text of the *Nights* is set down in writing. All live happily till death do them part.

---

[15] Clinton, "Madness," pp. 120–124.

Desire is at the root of the frame of the *Nights*, but desire as a problem. There are proper desires as there are improper ones. Or, to speak more precisely, there are proper and improper patterns of desire, and ways of using and fulfilling desire. Proper and improper, here, are more than moral antinomies: they reach beyond the relatively restricted domain of the just and the unjust to the more worldly regions of the appropriate and the ultimately satisfying.

The importance of desire is clear from the first events of the frame. Shâhriyâr longs for his brother (*ishtâqa ilâ*). This longing, seemingly at the outset quite natural, is, however, problem-generating, since it sets in motion the events that will follow. The fulfillment of this desire, i.e., Shâhzamân's voyage to visit his brother, permits the younger monarch to discover the perfidy of his wife, only the first in a series of such discoveries. More than simply a wish to see the brother, Shâhriyâr's desire can be defined as a need for another, in this case, a male. What we are observing in the opening events of the text is an allusion to the formation of a homosocial desire and coupling that will prove crucial in subsequent events in the *Nights*. *Homosocial* must be distinguished from *homosexual* and by no means implies a sexual relationship, but rather a social relationship between two individuals of the same gender. This construct has been studied in a brilliant work by Eve Kosofsky Sedgwick.[16] There is a tendency in the West to interpret examples of homosociality as indexes of latent or overt homosexuality. But this is really a reflection of the obsessional relationship of Western culture with homosexuality, and the culture's homophobia, since the later Middle Ages.[17] In the Arabo-Islamic cultural sphere, true homosexuality, while certainly present, poses less of a psychological problem for the culture. Classical Arabic authors felt no embarrassment in discussing male homoeroticism, occasionally in the context of heterosexual eroticism.[18] The crisis with which the *Nights* begins is one that is itself initiated by male homosocial desire. The resulting problematic male couple is, in its own way, as important as the pair Shâhriyâr-Shahrazâd. As we shall see, the male couple is a crucial phenomenon in the gender dynamics of classical Arabic literature.[19]

For the frame of the *Nights*, the male couple is a central problem. This relationship, a constant in all versions, seems superficially anomalous and has been effectively ignored by most critics (we are usually told what

[16] Eve Kosofsky Sedgwick, *Between Men: English Literature and Male Homosocial Desire* (New York: Columbia University Press, 1985).

[17] John Boswell, *Christianity, Social Tolerance, and Homosexuality* (Chicago: University of Chicago Press, 1980).

[18] See, for example, Ibn Qayyim al-Jawziyya, *Hukm al-Nazar lil-Nisâ'* (Cairo: Maktab al-Turâth al-Islâmî, 1982), pp. 17–18.

[19] See chapter 4 below.

Shâhriyâr stands for, not Shâhzamân, still less their relationship).[20] After all, the story could seem to function without the couple: a king sets off on a journey, comes back suddenly to discover his wife's infidelity, dispatches her, sets out again with a heavy heart, and meets the 'ifrît and his young woman, after which he turns against all womankind, deciding to sleep with and kill a new partner each night (this is indeed the way the story is related by Fatima Mernissi).[21] Clearly then, the male couple must be fulfilling some other function.

It is as a homosocial couple that Shâhriyâr and Shâhzamân decide to flee from the world after the older brother has seen his wife copulating with the black slave. The repeated use of the Arabic *dunyâ* is not without significance.[22] Etymologically the basest of places, it represents the world negatively, as the opposite of spirituality, and is often associated, again negatively, with sex and the female.[23] But it is precisely when the homosocial couple of the two brothers goes off together that things turn topsy-turvy in the text.

The homosocial couple is contrasted with the heterosexual one, the latter not merely problematic, but in a state of crisis. It is perhaps the coexistence of the two types of couples that is most explosive and unleashes unnatural events. It is when Shâhzamân goes to bid farewell to his wife—that is, when he is about to fulfill Shâhriyâr's homosocial desire—that he discovers her adulterous act. Her perfidy is all the more vile, not only because of her choice of mate (a cook), but also when set against the king's devotion. And it is when Shâhriyâr and Shâhzamân go off on their homosocial voyage that they encounter the 'ifrît and the young woman, an encounter which, as we shall see, dramatically alters the rest of the narrative.

Homosocial desire is intricately linked in the frame of the *Nights* with the idea of voyage. Travel is normally a learning and maturing experience, as are, for example, the voyages of Sindibâd. The implications of the term *dunyâ* and Shâhriyâr's statement that they should go forth "in the love of God"[24] even add the flavor of a spiritual quest. When seen in

---

[20] An exception is Ferial Jabouri Ghazoul, who uses it as an example of what she considers to be frequent binary structures in the text. Ferial Jabouri Ghazoul, *The Arabian Nights: A Structural Analysis* (Cairo: Cairo Associated Institution for the Study and Preservation of Arab Cultural Values, 1980), pp. 41–44.

[21] Mernissi, *Chahrazad*, pp. 9–12. Cf. Ghazoul, *Arabian Nights*, p. 55, who writes that "*The Arabian Nights* is the story of a conjugal union ruptured by one female and restored by another."

[22] *Kitâb Alf Layla wa-Layla*, ed. Muhsin Mahdi (Leiden: E. J. Brill, 1984), 1:62–63.

[23] A. S. Tritton, "Dunyâ," *EI*². See, also, for example, al-Qurtubî, *Bahjat al-Majâlis wa-Uns al-Mujâlis*, ed. Muhammad Mursî al-Khawlî (Beirut: Dâr al-Kutub al-'Ilmiyya, 1982), 3:278ff. See, also, chapter 5 below.

[24] *Alf Layla*, ed. Mahdi, 1:63.

the context of the frame story as a whole, however, the voyages turn out to be a mislearning experience. Both voyages were instigated by the older king, Shâhriyâr. The first voyage, that of Shâhzamân to Shâhriyâr, taught both monarchs that their wives were adulterous females.

The second voyage, the one undertaken by the two brothers as a full male couple, brings together the problematics of the first three sections of the frame, both resuming earlier and prefiguring later events. This voyage is suggested by Shâhriyâr as a response to his discovery that his wife is, indeed, as Shâhzamân told and showed him, a perfidious female getting her sexual pleasure in an interracial orgy. Harlow elegantly refers to "the multiple transgressions of family, race and class."[25] The two brothers then go off and meet the ʿifrît and the young woman. The centrality of this encounter for our argument dictates its presentation in some detail.

Arriving on a seashore, the two brothers hear a great yell from the middle of the water. The sea suddenly parts, and a black column rises from it and keeps rising. The two are very afraid and climb up a tree to hide among its leaves. The column turns out to be a black ʿifrît who comes out carrying a big glass trunk. He proceeds to unlock the trunk, and out comes a beautiful young woman, whom he then places under the tree. The ʿifrît addresses the woman, making it clear that he had kidnapped her on her wedding night. He then falls asleep with his head on the young woman's lap. But she, looking up and seeing our two heroes in the tree, lifts up the ʿifrît's head and beckons to the two kings to come down. They refuse, she insists, they refuse again, and she threatens them with death at the hands of the ʿifrît. The two descend slowly until they are in front of her, at which point she raises her legs and tells them to have sexual intercourse with her, again under threat of death. They beg her to let them off, but she repeats her threats. So the older brother has intercourse with her and is followed by the younger one. The Bûlâq edition of the Nights adds that the two debate as to which of them should precede the other in this act.[26] She then asks for their rings, explaining that she will add them to the rings of all the men who had had intercourse with her, making a total of a hundred. After the two kings listen to the young woman's explanations, they exclaim: "Allâh. Allâh. Lâ hawla wa-lâ quwwa illâ bil-lâhi al-ʿalî al-ʿazîm. Inna kaydakunna ʿazîm" (God. God. There is no power and no strength save in God, the High, the Great. Indeed your guile is great).[27] The two men surrender their rings; she adds them to her collection and dismisses the brothers, once again under threat of death.

This episode is at the heart of the second voyage, at the heart of the

[25] Harlow, "The Middle East," p. 1165.

[26] Alf Layla wa-Layla (Cairo: Matbaʿat Bûlâq, 1252 A.H.), 1:4.

[27] Alf Layla, ed. Mahdi, 1:64.

mislearning experience of the two brothers, and thus at the heart of what Shahrazâd must undo in her own lessons. Weber has already analyzed the sexual imagery in this incident: the black column and the box.[28] The French critic also notes that this episode presents a change of roles: we watch as the two kings do unto the 'ifrît as was done unto them.[29] But the reversal goes further. This encounter is a sort of reverse reflection and refraction of the earlier adventures of the adulterous queens. There, the queens cheated on their royal husbands: in Shâhzamân's case with a loathsome cook and in Shâhriyâr's with a black slave. Here, the woman cheats on her loathsome 'ifrît mate with the royal male couple. Sexual roles are reversed, but so are social ones. More significant, Shâhriyâr's wife, in her adulterous interlude, called out to the black slave, and he jumped down from the tree to perform his sexual act. The two kings, in a structurally parallel fashion, are similarly called down from a tree to do their deeds. On one level, their role has been assimilated to that of the slave. But the trees are not accidental. If the black slave descending from the tree can be thought of as an ape, so too now can the royal brothers. They have been reduced to the level of animality, perhaps their ultimate degradation, and a potent symbol of the meaning of becoming a sexual object.

Here, thus, the completed male couple is juxtaposed with the most problematic possible heterosexual couple, that of the 'ifrît and the young woman. Indeed, the 'ifrît and the woman are the image of a flawed couple: he holds her prisoner; she cheats on him anyway.

The young woman's position is certainly, at least at the outset of the incident, more morally ambiguous than that of the royal queens. When the 'ifrît calls out to her, "O you whom I kidnapped on her wedding night," the reader initially feels pity for her plight. What worse fate than to be kidnapped by no less than an 'ifrît and—more dreadful still—on her wedding night, her night of sexual union with her normal spouse? In theory, one could justify her sexual wanderings as a reaction against her violation and imprisonment. She has been unjustly treated, and her exploitive behavior is a response to the male gender for this treatment. If, as an adulteress, she partakes of the earlier roles of the royal queens, as an injured party taking revenge on the sex that has wronged her, she prefigures the behavior of Shâhriyâr (and, in some versions, Shâhzamân).[30] It is this double aspect of the woman's role which casts doubt on Clinton's judgment that not only is she in the right but her justification extends backward by implication to Shâhriyâr's wife.[31] Plainly exploitive behav-

[28] Weber, *Secret*, p. 86.
[29] Ibid., p. 87. This point is also echoed by Ghazoul, *Arabian Nights*, p. 45.
[30] Cf. Weber, *Secret*, p. 87, who notes the similarity without its moral implications.
[31] Clinton, "Madness," pp. 111–112.

ior, like that of the young woman imprisoned by the ʿifrît, whatever its origin, is fundamentally unjustified within the moral system of the frame of *The Thousand and One Nights*.

It is only when she has revealed her trickery that Shâhriyâr and Shâhzamân respond in unison with their "Allâh. Allâh. . . . Inna kaydakunna ʿazîm" (God. God. . . . Indeed, your guile is great). The univocal response is crucial: no doubt can be cast on the nature of the male judgment of the situation. "Inna kaydakunna ʿazîm" is a Qurʾânic quote from the twelfth chapter, the *sûra* of Joseph.[32] But the intertextual presence of this verse does more than simply call up the prototypical story of the Egyptian ruler's wife, her infatuation with Joseph, and the familiar subsequent events. The formula served in the medieval period as a sort of literary catchall for evoking the tricks of women;[33] and it continues to this day in modern Arabic literature, as seen in a short story by Najîb Mahfûz and another by Naʿîm ʿAtiyya.[34] The use of this phrase brings the young woman in the *Nights* in league with her ancient Egyptian cousin, if not with all females. The lesson has also been couched in Islamic terms. The two males have, thus, cast their judgment on the entire female gender, including, of course, their own wives.

The univocal aspect of the two kings' declarations has still deeper literary implications. A narrative voice normally defines a character. Here, the two kings are speaking as one. Their narrative voices have become fused; they have been turned into one character. What better way to portray the male couple than by permitting its two members to express simultaneously the same opinion? The male couple has reached its full literary apex. The narrative voice is, however, both an expression (in both senses of the terms) and a culmination of a coupling that in fact had matured earlier in the text. Did not both Shâhriyâr and Shâhzamân perform the same sexual act with the same woman, under the same circumstances, and within the same narrative time frame? They share the same adventure, the same woman, and react orally and simultaneously in the same fashion.

The episode with the young woman foregrounds another central element in the frame: the nexus of sex and death. It is by threatening the royal duo with death that she is able to lure them out of the tree. Only further death threats can lead them to copulation with the beautiful

---

[32] *Al-Qurʾân*, Sûrat Yûsuf, verse 28.

[33] For a fuller discussion of this problem, see chapters 2 and 3 below.

[34] Najîb Mahfûz, "Kayduhunna," in Najîb Mahfûz, *Hams al-Junûn* (Beirut: Dâr al-Qalam, 1973), pp. 79–89; Naʿîm ʿAtiyya, "Kayduhunna ʿAzîm," in Naʿîm ʿAtiyya, *Nisâʾ fî al-Mahâkim* (Cairo: Dâr al-Maʿârif, 1980), pp. 82–88. Cf. the lines by Ghazi A. Algosaibi, "Here, life is a virgin still / who did not learn deceit / or woman's clever wiles." Ghazi A. Algosaibi, *From the Orient and the Desert* (London: Oriel Press, 1977), p. 1.

young woman. By its central position, this episode manipulates this explosive nexus in such a way that it refers to both preceding and future
events. After all, Shâhzamân killed his wife and her sexual partner when
he discovered them *en flagrant délit*. This violent punishment inflicted on
the spur of the moment can be seen as a result of his anger; nevertheless,
it establishes the sex/death nexus. And we know that Shâhriyâr will in-
dulge in the repeated killing of his female sexual partners after each night
of pleasure. Although his premeditated act differs from Shâhzamân's
spontaneous reaction, it still operates around the same nexus.

Shâhriyâr's premeditated act is linked directly to his/their experience
with the young woman. Back on the road, he notes to Shâhzamân that
the 'ifrît's misfortune is certainly greater than theirs, recounts in summary fashion their run-in with the ill-fated couple, and tells Shâhzamân
that they will return to their kingdoms, never to marry a woman again.
He concludes, "As for me, I will show you what I will do."[35] Shâhriyâr
has his vizier kill his wife, and he himself executes the slave girls. It is then
that he makes his decision to take a woman for one night and kill her.
Shâhzamân is sent off to his own kingdom, and he exits the scene. Then
begins the cycle of one-night stands, going through a descending social
hierarchy, followed by the ritual killing of the women.[36]

Shâhriyâr has certainly mislearned his lesson well. Like the 'ifrît's
young woman who was kidnapped on her wedding night, he has been
deeply wounded. Unlike his brother Shâhzamân, however, he does not
kill his adulterous wife immediately. Instead, he allows himself to be
guided by the actions/reactions of the young woman. Like her, he will
take an exploitive approach to the opposite sex. It is she who demonstrates a new rhythm to him, one based on individual revenge against the
entirety of the opposite sex. Her female behavior is clearly explained as
she collects the two rings from the duo to add to her collection: she has
enjoyed the pleasure of ninety-eight men, the latest two bringing the number to one hundred. Her pattern is: (1) threat of death; (2) copulation;
and with it (3) end of relationship. Shâhriyâr's male pattern and response
will be a reverse reflection of hers: (1) copulation; (2) death; and (3) end
of relationship. She is one woman who will exploit a multiplicity of
males; he is one man who will exploit a multiplicity of females. In both
cases, relationships are short and shallow. Time is fractured, discontinu-
ous.

Shâhriyâr's institution of the sequel of death for each sexual act has
numerous reverberations. On the simplest level, it is clear violence against
women. He is a serial murderer who is able to continue his acts unharmed

---

[35] *Alf Layla*, ed. Mahdi, 1:65.

[36] In the Bûlâq edition, the king himself does the killing. *Alf Layla*, Bûlâq edition, 1:4.

because of his royal status.[37] His subjects may be unhappy with the continued killing, but they are powerless in the face of his sovereignty.

From another point of view, death immediately following the sex act resembles *la petite mort*, that is, orgasm. Seen this way, Shâhriyâr's action functions like a caricature of immature male sexual behavior. Desire never has the opportunity to develop in time, cut off by death/orgasm. Relationships have been forced into the rhythms of an unsophisticated sexuality. This is desire and sexuality gone awry. It is hardly a coincidence, therefore, that it is a woman who must break this rhythm, substituting for it a new pattern of desire which, when transposed to the terrain of sexuality, can be seen as a more female approach to pleasure.

This woman is Shahrazâd: an intellectual wonder, who has memorized books, poetry, wisdom, and more. She is knowledgeable, intelligent, wise, and an *adîba* (woman learned in the arts of literature and society). Her desire is initially expressed to her father: she wishes him (*ashtahî minka*) to marry her to the king. She will liberate everyone or die. Her father gets angry and tries to discourage her by explaining the situation to her, going so far as to tell her an "exemplary tale,"[38] but to no avail. So her father informs the king of her desire. The latter is happy (*fariha*) and tells the vizier to bring her that night. The vizier then tells Shahrazâd, who is also very pleased (*farihat*). She explains to Dunyâzâd that she will send for her and that she should ask for a story after she has seen that the king has performed the act. Dunyâzâd patiently waits under the bed for the king to perform his act (*gharad*).[39] This virtual ménage à trois posits Dunyâzâd and Shahrazâd as potential counterweight to the male pair, Shâhriyâr/ Shâhzamân. Then the younger sister asks for the story, as she was told, the king approves, and Shahrazâd's role in world literature is launched. Yet it is Dunyâzâd who links sex and narration by first witnessing the act, then requesting the story.

The parallel happiness of Shâhriyâr and Shahrazâd (expressed by the same Arabic verb—*fariha*) puts the two on an equal footing. The relationship has been created. Shahrazâd is unlike all the previous females presented in the text. They embodied physical desire that was purely sexual, expressed in the most direct manner possible. Shâhriyâr's wife calls out to the black slave, "O Mas'ûd, O Mas'ûd."[40] Even the 'ifrît's young woman simply raises her legs in an open invitation to copulation.[41] The

---

[37] A contemporary Arab poet has already compared Shâhriyâr to Charles Manson. See Muhyî Mahmûd, *Nubû'a Shârida* (Cairo: Matâbi' Dâr al-Sha'b, 1978), pp. 53–59.

[38] Muhsin Mahdi, "Exemplary Tales in the *1001 Nights*," in *The 1001 Nights: Critical Essays and Annotated Bibliography*, special issue of *Mundus Arabicus* 3 (1983): 1–4.

[39] *Alf Layla*, ed. Mahdi, 1:71–72.

[40] Ibid., p. 62.

[41] Ibid., p. 64.

men are sex objects. Clearly, all women preceding Shahrazâd's entrance in the text are physical, if not overly physical, beings. Their exploitive use of desire is part of the problem that must be corrected by the vizier's daughter.

Earlier females are limited to the vagina, which means that their desire functions on an exclusively physical plane. Shahrazâd adds to this the word, permitting, as we shall see, a transposition and transformation of desire. There is a sense, however, in which Shahrazâd comes close to other members of her gender. The earlier women's behavior was defined in terms of its *kayd*: its guile, its trickery.[42] Shahrazâd also uses a ruse, that of narration, to achieve her ends. Her storytelling, after all, consists of structuring the stories so that the listener will be left in suspense at the break of dawn. Hers could be argued to be the ultimate in female trickery, since it represents a continual game of attraction (the storytelling) followed by denial of satisfaction (the end of the story, which must await yet another night).

This manipulation of narrative desire is far more than merely a means of gaining time, though, of course, in the beginning it is that. It is a key pedagogical tool. Rather than taking on directly the king's fractured pattern of physical lovemaking, Shahrazâd shifts the problem of desire from the area of sex, the realm of Shâhriyâr's trauma, to the superficially more distant and more malleable world of the text.[43] Her storytelling teaches a new type of desire, a desire that continues from night to night, a desire whose interest does not fall and which can, therefore, leap the intervening days. In sexual terms, this is a replacement of an immature male pattern of excitement, satisfaction, and termination with what can be called a more classically female pattern of extended and continuous desire and pleasure. Of course, it is this extension of desire through time that permits the forging of relationships, and with it the nonexploitive approach to sexuality. In effecting this transformation, Shahrazâd functions as a mistress of desire, not unlike the sexually wise women of the erotic manuals, one of whose duties is the initiation of males into a more sophisticated sexuality.[44]

Shahrazâd's mastery of the entire process can be most easily seen when

---

[42] Of course, the two kings also resorted to a ruse when they pretended to go hunting, but the text does not characterize them in these terms.

[43] Cf. the remark by Abdelkebir Khatibi, *La Blessure du nom propre* (Paris: Denoël, 1986), pp. 168–169: "If Chahrazâd escapes death by telling a story every night, it is because her discourse undoes the patriarchal frenzy, transcends it in a novelistic consciousness." Cf., also, Kattan, "Du récit," pp. 174–175; Susan Gubar, " 'The Blank Page' and the Issues of Female Creativity," in *Writing and Sexual Difference*, ed. Elizabeth Abel (Chicago: University of Chicago Press, 1982), pp. 73–93. On desire and writing, see, for example, Raymond Jean, *Lectures du désir* (Paris: Editions du Seuil, 1977), pp. 7–28.

[44] See chapter 2 below.

her story is compared with an ancient Egyptian ancestor, best known as *The Eloquent Peasant*. Like the frame of *The Thousand and One Nights*, the Pharaonic tale is concerned with the interrelationship among text creation, justice, and the whim of an all-powerful monarch.[45] The Old Kingdom peasant, however, is manipulated by his sovereign, rather than the other way around. Justice is apparently denied him by an aesthetically sophisticated ruler who wishes to stimulate the peasant's eloquent pleas for justice, in order that they may be written down and preserved for posterity. Of course, another difference, often overlooked by those who wish to make Shahrazâd a model of Arabic woman's authorship,[46] is that the vizier's daughter, unlike the peasant from the oasis, has not created her text. She has merely learned it and is transmitting it. Similarly, the parallel writing of the generated text at the end of each tale has a different function. It does not consecrate Shahrazâd's authorship but merely transfers oral to written transmission, a point to whose significance we shall return.

Shahrazâd's desire, couched in her wish to liberate the world from Shâhriyâr's tyranny, is to wed the monarch. This is by no means insignificant. She wishes to set in motion once again the heterosexual couple, which previously has only been contrasted with the homosocial male couple, in various explosive and unnatural situations. It is not coincidental that Shâhzamân, we are told, has been dispatched to his own kingdom. The danger of another male couple forming and threatening the Shahrazâd-Shâhriyâr heterosexual duo has been averted.

But this task is by no means a simple one. Shahrazâd must rectify the situation by restoring proper sexuality, proper rhythm, and proper desire. She, a woman, must undo the lessons that have been instilled by another woman, the ʿifrît's companion. Dunyâzâd and Shahrazâd act as a pair in the transition from sex to text, just as Shâhriyâr and Shâhzamân were jointly possessed by the ʿifrît's female prisoner.

Several lessons and intellectual constructs that have been learned by the monarch will simply have to be unlearned, if not completely dismantled. Male knowledge before Shahrazâd's arrival on the scene was aggressively visual. References to the act of seeing abound. Shâhzamân watches the scene of his sister-in-law's infidelity from beginning to end, and his act is,

---

[45] For the story of the Eloquent Peasant, see Gustave Lefebvre, *Romans et contes égyptiens de l'époque pharaonique* (Paris: Adrien-Maisonneuve, 1949), pp. 47–69; Miriam Lichteim, *Ancient Egyptian Literature*, vol. 1: *The Old and Middle Kingdoms* (Berkeley: University of California Press, 1975), pp. 170–182. For an analysis of the text, see Allen Douglas and Fedwa Malti-Douglas, "al-ʿAdl wal-Fann fî al-Fallâh al-Fasîh," in *Shâdî ʿAbd al-Salâm wal-Fallâh al-Fasîh*, ed. Salâh Marʿî et al. (Cairo: al-Hayʾa al-Misriyya al-ʿAmma lil-Kitâb, forthcoming).

[46] See, for example, Harlow, "The Middle East," p. 1165.

in effect, a voyeuristic one. As such, it parallels the earlier discovery of his own wife's infidelity. When Shâhzamân reveals to his brother the queen's infidelity, he speaks of "the misfortune he saw." Shâhriyâr does not believe the accusations and insists that he must see the events with his own eyes. Shâhzamân replies that "if you wish to see your misfortune with your own eyes" to believe it, then they should pretend to go out on a hunt, and instead enter the city secretly and go up to the palace, where Shâhriyâr can see the events with his own eyes. To quote Muhsin Mahdi, "The general frame does not cease emphasizing the central importance of seeing with one's own eyes and of direct experience."[47]

These repeated allusions, when combined with Shâhzamân's voyeuristic activity, call attention to a certain type of male active power, of the subject/looker on the object/looked upon. This is male scopic activity, to use Luce Irigaray's terminology.[48] The males would then be in the active position. Male visual dominance certainly rules. But, at the same time, male power is called into question, subverted. The women, the objects watched, are, in fact, the active members in another relationship, the sexual, since they are the ones whose activity (sexual) is of interest. Even the moral character of this voyeurism is ambiguous. As obsessional activity, it could be seen as "illicit sight" in Phyllis Trible's terms,[49] though the females' adultery is also clearly blameworthy. This visual/scopic emphasis is a commentary on desire as well. Shâhriyâr's insistence that he must "see" shows the force that is driving him. Again it is the fulfillment of this improper desire that sets in motion drastic narrative events.

Shahrazâd's path is clearly the opposite. She narrates a text. Hers is the oral approach, in which the male becomes the auditor, the passive partner. Sight and hearing are cast in the frame of the *Nights* as alternative ways of acquiring knowledge. We are firmly on the ground of a debate well entrenched in medieval Islamic mentalities, that of the relative value of the senses, specifically the oral versus the visual. Which was the better, hearing or vision? In his introduction to his biographical compendium of the blind, the Mamlûk polymath Khalîl ibn Aybak al-Safadî (d. 764/1363) adduces linguistic and philosophical arguments to conclude that hearing is superior to seeing.[50] Seen (if the use of that word be excused here) in this perspective, the frame of the *Nights* is certainly in the Islamic mainstream. Shâhriyâr's continued attempts to find the truth through his faculty of vision have only led him astray. It is rather through his faculty

---

[47] Mahdi, "Exemplary Tales," p. 8.

[48] Moi, *Sexual*, pp. 143–144.

[49] Phyllis Trible, *Texts of Terror: Literary-Feminist Readings of Biblical Narratives* (Philadelphia: Fortress Press, 1985), p. 43.

[50] Al-Safadî, *Nakt al-Himyân fî Nukat al-'Umyân*, ed. Ahmad Zakî Bâshâ (Cairo: al-Matba'a al-Jamâliyya, 1911), pp. 17–18.

of hearing, through listening to Shahrazâd's narratives, that all will be set aright.

Shahrazâd's stories lead to another dichotomy, that between "reality" and fiction. Shâhriyâr's search and desire for reality through what he can plainly see is illusory, since this is shown to be the wrong tactic. Rather, it is through fiction that the proper uses of desire can best be learned. The odyssey he has undertaken with Shâhzamân, his *rihla fî talab al-ʿilm* (the medieval Islamic journey in search of knowledge), is a physical voyage whose consequences must be corrected by Shahrazâd's narrative voyage. Her narrative "nights" become, then, journeys into desire and the unconscious. Again, literature must correct experience. But it is not a modern conception of literature that is at issue here. What the learned Shahrazâd provides in an entertaining form is the accumulated wisdom of her civilization, which, delivered in the right manner, can correct the mislearnings of a far more limited individual experience.

It is perhaps in the closure of the frame story that the consequences of Shahrazâd's lessons on desire come to fruition. Closure refers to the conclusion of the story, here, the happy resolution, following Marianna Torgovnick's distinction between closure and ending. The latter would be, according to her, "the last definable unit of work—section, scene, chapter, page, paragraph, sentence,"[51] while closure is the logical conclusion for a story. The closure of the frame occurs at the end of the *Nights*, in what some have called the epilogue. This may seem much too obvious a point. But when the work is compared with a similar text, *The One Hundred and One Nights*, which also operates around female infidelity and narration, a very important difference emerges. The closure of the story in that text is presented before the narration even begins.[52] In fact, closure in classical Arabic literature poses special critical problems, and *The Thousand and One Nights* from this perspective comes closest to a Western text.

Two versions for the closure of Shahrazâd's *Nights* exist, a shorter one and a longer one. In both versions, Shahrazâd has meanwhile given birth to three sons. She makes this fact known to the monarch and asks him to spare her life for the sake of his sons, who will otherwise have no mother. He replies that he had long ago decided not to kill her, having discovered

[51] Marianna Torgovnick, *Closure in the Novel* (Princeton: Princeton University Press, 1981), p. 6.

[52] *Les cent et une nuits*, presented and translated by M. Gaudefroy-Demombynes (Paris: Sindbad, 1982), pp. 21–30. A variant of the closure from another manuscript of the same text is provided on p. 271. This particular variant, however, does not concord with the opening of the frame: for example, the roles of Shahrazâd and Dunyâzâd are reversed in it. Gaudefroy-Demombynes makes it clear in his notes that this is the way one manuscript closes the story, p. 318.

that she was "virtuous, pure, free, and pious" ('*afîfa, naqiyya, hurra, taqiyya*). When the monarch extols her virtues to her father, he exchanges her piety for her intelligence (*hurra, naqiyya, 'afîfa, zakiyya*).[53] The king extends his generosity to the entire kingdom, the city is decorated, goods are distributed to the poor: beneficence reigns. Only death brings an end to this idyllic situation.

The longer version distinguishes itself by the presence of an elaborate marriage ceremony. Shâhriyâr declares that he will wed Shahrazâd and then summons Shâhzamân. The older king tells his younger brother all that has befallen him, including Shahrazâd's stories, at which point Shâhzamân reveals that he has also been bedding one woman every night and then killing her the next morning. Now, he wishes to marry Dunyâzâd. Shahrazâd agrees to this only if the couple remains with them. The two women are then paraded in an array of dresses before their respective spouses, for a total of seven dresses. The narrator describes first one woman, and then the other, with Arabic verses. The narrative and verse descriptions make it clear that an elaborate erotic game is being played out. The young women's costumes are associated with different erotic models and roles, some quite traditional and others more daring, even suggesting the erotic appeal of transvestism and gender ambiguity. Shahra-zâd smiles and sways seductively; and as Burton puts it, the performances of the two sisters leave their royal mates "bewitched," filled with "amorous longing."[54] At the end of the fashion show, each male retires with the appropriate female. The vizier is appointed ruler of Samarkand. As for the two brothers, they rule alternately for one day each. Shâhriyâr orders that all that has befallen him with Shahrazâd be inscribed by copyists and the books stored in his treasury. Again, only death disturbs this idyllic arrangement. Another ruler then follows who discovers the books, reads them, and has them copied and widely distributed.

The closure demonstrates, first and foremost, that Shahrazâd's desire, expressed in her wish to wed the king, was indeed the proper one. The sexual act has been transformed from one linked with death to one leading to creation. She has, after all, given birth to three sons. This change is a result of a shift in rhythm. It is the extension of desire into longer relationships that permits the begetting of sons. Shâhriyâr's (and, in the longer version, Shâhzamân's) earlier system, if it provided sexual pleasure, prevented the personally and politically vital creation of heirs. These men would have seen their lines come to an end.

In some respects, this closure stands in contrast with the somewhat

[53] *Alf Layla*, Bûlâq edition, 2:619.
[54] Richard F. Burton, *The Book of the Thousand Nights and a Night* (Burton Club Edition), 10:58–60.

feminist implications of the prologue of the frame story. After all, there we saw an independent, courageous Shahrazâd, risking her life to save those of her sisters, and in the process, despite appearances, controlling the situation and educating the monarch. Little wonder that the conclusion of the tale has angered some feminists, like Ethel Johnston Phelps. Such an ending must be the invention of male storytellers, she implies in her feminist rewriting of the classic. Why would a courageous, well-educated heroine like Shahrazâd marry an obvious lout like Shâhriyâr? Instead, Phelps has Shahrazâd continue telling stories until the king's early demise, upon which she herself handles the revision and publication of the text.[55]

Of course, the original tale is far more traditional in its morality, recuperating, even conjuring away, the feminist implications of the prologue in the epilogue. This recuperation is made even clearer in the longer version of the closing section. Shahrazâd is in both versions no longer a storyteller, since an anonymous narrator is talking about her. Of course, this situation obtained in the earlier sections of the frame story as well. But she has become in a much more real sense the object, rather than the producer or even the controller, of literary discourse. This is achieved through the poetic selections, given over completely to the physical description of Shahrazâd and Dunyâzâd in their erotic displays. And poetry, it should be remembered, has always had a far greater literary prestige in Arabo-Islamic society than prose. Nor is it a coincidence that the poetry describes, even magnifies, a situation in which Shahrazâd is the object of desire. Further, most of these verses are repeated from an earlier part of the *Nights*, where they were effectively part of Shahrazâd's narration. No longer their narrator, she becomes their object.

But the display is more than literary—it is also preeminently visual; and as admiring audience for this floor show, Shâhriyâr and Shâhzamân regain their scopic relationship to desire, now in a context of sexual mastery. As the women become objects of desire, the male has regained his active role and the female her passive one. In place of her intellect, it is now Shahrazâd's physicality that comes to the fore.

Even the male homosocial couple is recreated, since, at Shahrazâd's

[55] Ethel Johnston Phelps, *The Maid of the North: Feminist Folk Tales from Around the World* (New York: Henry Holt and Company, 1981), pp. 167–173. Samar al-'Attâr in "al-Rihla min al-Hamajiyya ilâ al-Hadâra wa-Darûrat Taqyîd Hurriyyat al-Mar'a al-Jinsiyya: Mithâlâ Imra'at al-Sundûq wa-Shahrazâd fî *Alf Layla wa-Layla*," in *al-Fikr al-'Arabî al-Mu'âsir wal-Mar'a* (Cairo: Dâr Tadâmun al-Mar'a al-'Arabiyya, 1988), pp. 53–54, examines some of the ways in which Shahrazâd might or might not be considered liberated in our terms. See, also, Fedwa Malti-Douglas, "Shahrazâd Feminist," in *The Thousand and One Nights in Arabic Literature and Society*, ed. Fedwa Malti-Douglas and Georges Sabagh (Cambridge: Cambridge University Press, forthcoming).

request, Shâhzamân and his bride will live with Shâhriyâr and Shahrazâd. The fusion of the royal brothers is also accomplished, since they will jointly rule the kingdom. With a solution like this, of course, one no longer risks dangerous voyages. The brother-brother (and the sister-sister) couples are no longer a threat to the heterosexual one, since this last is now established on solid foundations. Sibling and matrimonial relationships are harmonized. The presence of children shows how restoring the heterosexual couple saves patriarchy.

The longer version also clarifies Shahrazâd's relationship to literature. She may have narrated the stories, but it is Shâhriyâr who has them written down, to be eventually copied and distributed by his male successor. Her world is the evanescent one of oral performance. It is both measured by and linked to time: a thousand and one nights. To the males is reserved the authority and permanence of written literature.[56] Thus, the longer version of the closure makes explicit what was only implicit in its shorter form. Shahrazâd's extraordinary role is also a temporary one: necessitated by a crisis, it comes to an end with the end of that crisis. The frame story is a giant parenthesis whose closing is both the closure and the conclusion of the *Nights* as a whole. The "nights" are like dreams that end with the rise of the literary sun of vision, reality, and male preeminence.

In the process, body has been transmuted into word and back into body. Corporeality is the final word, as Shahrazâd relinquishes her role of narrator for that of perfect woman: mother and lover.

[56] Some may want to see in this assignment of orality to the woman a sign of power, especially given the increased emphasis on oral narratives in nondominant cultural expression. See, for example, Henry Louis Gates, Jr., *The Signifying Monkey: A Theory of African-American Literary Criticism* (Oxford: Oxford University Press, 1988), especially part 2. In the context of the *Nights*, however, it is the reference to the written, deliberately added in a situation where it is narratologically superfluous, that implicitly devalues the oral. In Arabo-Islamic culture generally, the oral is not divorced from high culture, where it is central, for example, in Qur'ân and poetry recital, *hadîth* and other scholarly tradition, etc. Hence, it is also, for the most part, a realm of male dominance. See, for example, Fedwa Malti-Douglas, "*Mentalités* and Marginality: Blindness and Mamlûk Civilization," in *The Islamic World from Classical to Modern Times: Essays in Honor of Bernard Lewis*, ed. C. E. Bosworth et al. (Princeton: Darwin Press, 1989), pp. 228–231.

CHAPTER 2

The Anecdotal Woman

IF SHAHRAZÂD was able to manipulate discourse, it was at a price. It is through her female copulative body that she is provided with the opportunity to narrate, and it is through this same but now procreative body that she will take on fully the role of monarch's wife. But Shahrazâd's narration is also a ruse, a trick she exploits to dupe Shâhriyâr and save her life. Three elements come together to make her narrative voyage an unforgettable one: woman's speech or eloquence, the problem of ruse or trickery, and woman's sexuality.

These same textual dynamics bring Shahrazâd close to her literary cousins, those female characters who populate the medieval Arabic anecdotal literary corpus, the ubiquitous adab works. An intertextual treasure trove, these works, designed to be at once entertaining and didactic, contain both religious and secular material, both prose and verse. Always the responsibility of male scriptors, adab works can be subject-oriented or designed to elucidate a social character type, such as a miser or a party crasher. Further, adab works could be either monographic in nature or encyclopedic. The latter, multisubject in nature with semiotically significant organizations, most often arrange their contents according to a social hierarchy, in which women invariably find themselves near the bottom of the ladder, toward the end of the work.[1] Syntagmatically, women's social neighbors in this male-conceived hierarchy are marginal character types, like the insane or beggars.[2] Woman, willy-nilly, becomes defined not only through her own essence but through that of her textual neighbors. Marginality unites the character types who populate the latter parts of the adab works. But the marginality of the women is exclusively

[1] For a definition of *adab* and the delimitation of an adab work, including subject arrangement, see Fedwa Malti-Douglas, *Structures of Avarice: The Bukhalâ' in Medieval Arabic Literature* (Leiden: E. J. Brill, 1985), pp. 7–16. This organization with women bringing up the rear is, incidentally, the one present in some biographical dictionaries in which women appear. There was certainly nothing to keep a biographer/compiler from simply inserting the women in their proper alphabetical or genealogical positions in the compendium. See, for example, Ibn al-Mu'tazz, *Tabaqât al-Shu'arâ'*, ed. 'Abd al-Sattâr Ahmad Farrâj (Cairo: Dâr al-Ma'ârif, 1968), pp. 421–427; al-Sakhâwî, *al-Daw' al-Lâmi' li-Ahl al-Qarn al-Tâsi'* (Beirut: Manshûrât Dâr Maktabat al-Hayât, n.d.), vol. 12.

[2] See, for example, al-Nuwayrî, *Nihâyat al-Arab fî Funûn al-Adab* (Cairo: Tab'at Dâr al-Kutub, n.d.), 4:16–23; al-Djawbarî, *Le voile arraché: L'autre visage de l'Islam*, trans. René R. Khawam (Paris: Editions Phébus, 1979–1980), 2:235–257.

social, whereas that of the mentally or physically unusual is first of all statistical.[3]

Woman, however, is not only a socially marginal entity. She represents physicality in its most rudimentary form. The prototypical multivolume encyclopedic adab work, Ibn Qutayba's (d. 276/889) *ʿUyûn al-Akhbâr* (The fountains of stories), closes with "The Book of Women" ("Kitâb al-Nisâʾ "). This multisectioned "book," contains, as the reader would expect, the types of material normally associated with women in the medieval scriptor's mind: e.g., looking at women, intercourse, dowry, marriage, childbirth, divorce, and the like. More important, it also incorporates sections on various parts of the body of both sexes (e.g., noses, eyes), physical characteristics (e.g., being tall, being short, being ugly), and, most provocative, physical handicaps and diseases (e.g., lameness, leprosy, having a scrotal hernia).[4] Physically deficient males are then, of course, included in the mix—indeed, in many cases exclusively. For the scrotal hernia, this is obvious. But the section on lameness, for example, also avoids women.

Amalgamating and embedding all these various physically circumscribed topics under the heading of "Women" redefines the nature of woman, as well obviously as the nature of the physical characteristics. The physically normal and healthy female subsumes in her essence the body, including the male body, especially as the latter becomes deficient or abnormal. Woman's physicality transcends mere sexuality.

This association of the physically deficient male with a healthy or normal female functions as a mental structure in the medieval Islamic conceptual world and is not simply a phantasm of the ninth-century Ibn Qutayba. To take but one example: Ibn Qutayba relates, in the section on women, an anecdote about a hunchback male who, upon falling into a well, trades his hump for a scrotal hernia.[5] Al-Husrî (d. 413/1022), in his adab compendium, places this anecdote alongside one on women,[6] whereas Ibn Qayyim al-Jawziyya (d. 751/1350) repeats it in his monographic adab work on women.[7]

---

[3] On different types of marginality, see Guy H. Allard et al., *Aspects de la marginalité au moyen âge* (Montreal: Les Editions de l'Aurore, 1975), pp. 15–22.

[4] Ibn Qutayba, *ʿUyûn al-Akhbâr* (Cairo: Dâr al-Kutub, 1963), 4:1–147.

[5] Ibid., 68.

[6] Al-Husrî, *Jamʿ al-Jawâhir fî al-Mulah wal-Nawâdir*, ed. ʿAlî Muhammad al-Bijâwî (Beirut: Dâr al-Jîl, 1987), p. 199.

[7] Ibn Qayyim al-Jawziyya, *Akhbâr al-Nisâʾ*, ed. Nizâr Ridâ (Beirut: Manshûrât Dâr Maktabat al-Hayât, 1982), p. 20. The book in question may really be the work of Ibn al-Jawzî. See Basim F. Musallam, *Sex and Society in Islam* (Cambridge: Cambridge University Press, 1983), p. 161. I will, however, retain the name of Ibn Qayyim, since that is how the book is published.

The social hierarchy so predominant in encyclopedic adab works also obtains in adab works that present one subject, but this time through the lens of different social types or categories. To take but one example: the *Akhbâr al-Adhkiyâ'* of Ibn al-Jawzî (d. 597/1200), spanning the intelligent, the witty, and the cunning, includes one chapter on women whose adventures or tricks fall into that category. The men, by contrast, are divided into different social groups, ranging from rulers and judges through physicians and poets to thieves and uninvited guests. Here, the women do appear but embedded between the intelligent madmen and animals.[8]

From a being whose gender happens to be female, woman, because of her gender, is transmuted in this overarching adab vision to a social category, a social character type. The specialized anecdotal works on women must be placed alongside the parallel literary corpora of the male character-type literature, like that on misers or uninvited guests, to take but two examples.[9] I know of no specialized anecdotal works on men, defined solely through their gender.

The implications of woman's integration into the pantheon of adab character types are far-ranging. Just as a character who happens to be male performs actions that define him as a character type, so can a woman, but this time defined by her womanhood, perform these actions. The male gender of the medieval Arabic character type is a philosophical accident, as it were, whereas the gender of the counter female character type is a philosophical essence. It is as a female that the woman in the adab work accedes to the rank of trickster figure.

What are the textual dynamics that permit this accession? To confine, to delimit the female adab character type to a narrowly conceived and uniform vision would be sheer madness. But the three elements that skyrocketed Shahrazâd to literary stardom reappear with her female cousins in the adab works: woman's eloquence, woman's ruse, and woman's sexuality. Woman's eloquence can span a continuum ranging from that of the pious women to that of the ubiquitous singing slave girls, those Islamic geishas of the classical period who livened up many a male gather-

[8] Ibn al-Jawzî, *Akhbâr al-Adhkiyâ'*, ed. Muhammad Mursî al-Khawlî (Cairo: Matâbi' al-Ahrâm al-Tijâriyya, 1970).

[9] Ibn Qayyim's *Akhbâr al-Nisâ'* is one such work. For the misers, see, for example, al-Jâhiz, *al-Bukhalâ'*, ed. Tâhâ al-Hâjirî (Cairo: Dâr al-Ma'ârif, 1971); al-Khatîb al-Baghdâdî, *al-Bukhalâ'*, ed. Ahmad Matlûb, Khadîja al-Hadîthî, and Ahmad al-Qaysî (Baghdad: Matba'at al-'Anî, 1964). For the uninvited guests, see al-Khatîb al-Baghdâdî, *al-Tatfîl wa-Hikâyât al-Tufayliyyîn wa-Akhbâruhum wa-Nawâdir Kalâmihim wa-Ash'âruhum*, ed. Kâzim al-Muzaffar (Najaf: al-Maktaba al-Haydariyya, 1966).

ing.[10] *Dhakâ'* (wit, intelligence) and kayd (cunning, guile) are the two key, at times overlapping, concepts whose parameters have important civilizational implications for woman's sexuality and her power over discourse.[11] Dhakâ', seemingly more positive, will guide our footsteps in this chapter, whereas kayd will more easily lead us to understanding the misogynist forces behind the male visions of Ibn al-Batanûnî and Ibn Tufayl.[12]

The privileged link of the female to ruses is well articulated in the thirteenth-century adab encyclopedia of al-Jawbarî. In introducing the chapter on women, the narrator assures himself of his reader's knowledge that women have recourse to ruses more often than men, if only because they lack the spirit of decision, as well as the notions of faith and honor.[13]

The multitextual (and heavily intertextual) nature of adab works means that adab texts are composed of independent literary units, most often anecdotes. Adab texts, from their inception in the second/eighth century and onward, remained a favorite literary form, thus spanning nearly the entirety of the medieval Arabic literary production. But this by no means implies that an adab work written in the eighth/fourteenth century contained completely new material. Rather, the literary tradition remained alive, and later writers freely adopted and adapted material from earlier ones, sometimes with a different focus and different implications. Thus it is that many an anecdote is repeated from one work to another and exists in multiple renditions. The nature of these literary texts might make the reader expect the only result of their analysis to be the delineation of an unchanging and static Islamic essence. Quite the contrary. The tradition itself was alive, and later authors dialectically interacted with earlier ones, as we shall ourselves be doing in this chapter.

Anecdotal units in these ubiquitous adab texts can range in length from a few lines to a few pages. Unlike the text of *The Thousand and One Nights* discussed in chapter 1, the medieval Arabic adab text is by no

[10] For the wide-ranging aspects of female eloquence, see Ibn Abî Tâhir [Tayfûr], *Balâghât al-Nisâ' wa-Tarâ'if Kalâmihinna wa-Mulah Nawâdirihinna wa-Akhbâr Dhawât al-Ra'y minhunna wa-Ash'âruhunna fî al-Jâhiliyya wal-Islâm*, ed. Ahmad al-Alfî (Tunis: al-Maktaba al-'Atîqa, 1985). In light of the comparison between a woman and a marginal male character type, it is worth comparing this title with that of al-Khatîb's *Kitâb al-Tatfîl*, cited above. The similar formulation of the two titles is an eloquent argument in and of itself. On the Islamic slave girl, see al-Jâhiz, *Risâlat al-Qiyân*, ed. and trans. A.F.L. Beeston as *The Epistle on Singing-Girls of Jâhiz* (Warminster, England: Aris & Phillips, 1980).

[11] On the central position of the concept of kayd, see, also, Fatna Aït Sabbah, *La femme dans l'inconscient musulman* (Paris: Albin Michel, 1986), pp. 70ff.; Ghassan Ascha, *Du statut inférieur de la femme en Islam* (Paris: L'Harmattan, 1989), pp. 29–31. For more on kayd, see chapter 3 below.

[12] See chapters 3 and 4 below.

[13] Al-Djawbarî, *Le voile*, 2:241.

means an extended narrative. It is thus that a seven-page chapter on slave
girls and women in the *Latâ'if al-Lutf* (The witticisms of courteousness)
of al-Tha'âlibî (d. 429/1038) contains twenty-three independent literary
units.[14]

Adab anecdotes by their nature are normally transmitted or introduced
by third-person narrators, who may or may not themselves be participants in the actions unfolding in the text. This type of discourse—"reported discourse," to use Abd El-Fattah Kilito's terminology[15]—is seemingly gender-neutral, in the sense that it applies to stories involving both
male and female protagonists. Stories involving women's ruses are dis-
course-controlled by male narrators. Rare is the anecdote in which the
female introduces the literary unit and speaks directly in the first person.

The sexual politics of any narrative choice are, of course, important,
and "reported discourse" with the male holding the key to the story does
play an important function in the context of woman's narrative voice and
her ability to control discourse. It is the literary equivalent of having a
woman speak from behind a curtain, something that was done with female transmitters of *hadîth*s, the sacred and normative traditions of the
Prophet.[16] That on the one hand. On the other hand, literary closure, as
The Thousand and One Nights so eloquently showed, is equally important.[17] Closure in an adab context is problematic, to say the least. Can
each anecdotal unit be analyzed as an entity, or must we only consider
the entire collection that forms the physical thing that is the book or the
manuscript? For the sake of analysis, I should like to argue that each anecdote can be viewed as an independent literary unit. Each unit will then
have its own closure, and similarly structured units the same closure.
Only in this way will it become clear how the woman, through her body,
seeks to reverse male narrative control.

A great number of female witticisms and ruses in adab works revolve
around female sexuality and women's bodies. The dynamics of woman's
control over her narrative voice can vary from the simple retort to the
more complex give-and-take.

An oft-repeated anecdote involves a man asking a slave girl whose purchase he was considering whether she could do something with her hands.
She replied: "No. But with my feet." And the texts then add that she

---

[14] Al-Tha'âlibî, *Latâ'if al-Lutf*, ed. 'Umar al-As'ad (Beirut: Dâr al-Masîra, 1980), pp.
97–104.

[15] Abd el-Fattah Kilito, "Le genre 'Séance': Une introduction," *Studia Islamica* 43
(1976): 34–35; Tzvetan Todorov, "Style," in Oswald Ducrot and Tzvetan Todorov, *Dictionnaire encyclopédique des sciences du langage* (Paris: Editions du Seuil, 1972), p. 386.

[16] Al-Safadi, *Nakt*, p. 62.

[17] See chapter 1 above.

meant she was a dancer.[18] A reasonably simple male question and female answer seem to need, nevertheless, a commentary from that intrusive third-person narrator of the adab anecdote. Perhaps it is because this witty female has shifted the register of the question from its seemingly neutral informational aspect to a more sexual focus.

The poet al-Bâhilî recounts that he said to a black slave girl, "Heat in you is greater," to which she replied, "He knows the heat of the bathhouse who has entered it."[19] Al-Jâhiz, the great ninth-century prose litterateur, relates: "I inspected a slave girl and said to her, 'Do you play the ʿûd well?' She replied, 'No, but I can sit on it well.' "[20] The Arabic word ʿûd not only refers to the famous stringed musical instrument but can also mean a stick, a rod, a pole: a clear allusion to the male sexual organ.

These two short texts are representative of an anecdotal type that is reasonably simple in structure and in which the two parties, one male and one female, treat the reader to a verbal duel. The male is attempting to delimit or define the woman, even putting her on the spot. She, however, faces the issue head-on and counteracts with a verbal display involving a pun or a play on words that calls attention to her body or her sexuality. The male is left speechless. - *How do we know?*

Note the onomastic interplay in the text. The male characters are identified; the females remain nameless. The personhood, to use Phyllis Trible's word,[21] of the woman is lacking. That on the one hand. On the other hand, occulting the identity of the female character transports her actions from the domain of the specific to that of the general. Some adab anecdotes do omit the names of their male protagonists, but the omission of women's names here is all the more conspicuous since the males are provided with an onomastic identity. Further, the juxtaposition of named male and unnamed female is more striking than that of named male and unnamed male. And since most anecdotal units identify their transmitter(s), invariably of the male gender, it means that most anecdotes show a male onomastic presence. Lest an objection be made that the namelessness in the above examples is not an anomaly but rather the norm because the anecdotes deal with slave girls: suffice it to say that this is a recurring phenomenon which will speak for itself. Prominent women, such as the Prophet's wife ʿAʾisha or other holy women, are, of course, named. It is

[18] Ibn al-Jawzî, *Akhbâr al-Zirâf wal-Mutamâjinîn*, ed. Muhammad Anîs Muharât (Damascus and Beirut: Dâr al-Hikma, 1987), p. 223. The same anecdote appears with minor variants in: Ibn al Jawzî, *Adhkiyâʾ*, p. 232; al-Nuwayrî, *Nihâyat al-Arab*, 4:19; al-Thaʿâlibî, *Latâʾif*, pp. 103–104.

[19] Al-Thaʿâlibî, *Latâʾif*, p. 103; Ibn Qutayba, *ʿUyûn*, 4:111.

[20] Al-Thaʿâlibî, *Latâʾif*, p. 103.

[21] See, for example, Trible, *Texts of Terror*, p. 15.

the relative absence of personhood of the everyday or common woman that must be signaled.

Woman's body, articulated through both male and female narrative voices, becomes in certain dimensions of the adab vision a pawn in the game of textual sexual politics.[22] The male endeavor to marginalize or criticize the female leads, through the woman's reply, to the textual subversion of this masculine attempt at what can only be interpreted as male physical dominance.

To take but one example: the same al-Jâhiz relates that while eating with some people in al-'Askar,[23] he once saw a very tall woman. Wanting to joke with her, he said, "Come down so that you can eat with us." But she replied, "And you, come up so you can see the world."[24]

The male is calling attention to what he perceives to be an abnormality in the female body, her height. She, however, by her reply negates this criticism. More important is the structure of the verbal game. The imperative "come down" followed by "so that" proposed by the male is countered by the female with the opposite imperative, "come up" followed by "so that." At stake as well is the entire visual activity itself. The male narrator relies on his sense of vision ("I saw") to ascertain that the female is overly tall. When she proposes that he come up, it is to "see" the world. Behind her response is an implied denunciation of male scopic activity. Male vision is not necessarily the true vision: thematic echoes of Shâhriyâr and Shâhzamân.[25]

From a literary character who begins the narrative in a defensive (might we add marginal?) position, the woman (once again unnamed) is able to reverse the narrative dynamics and call into question the male's superior status. Her anecdotal situation, involving the subversion of the dominant discourse, is very similar to that of the blind, a narrative category defined by the physicality of its protagonists. In the case of the visually handicapped, however, the dominant group whose verbal exercises in superiority are defeated is the sighted.[26] This close relationship between women and the blind will be further explored below.[27]

Verbal games and wit are part and parcel of the adab discourse on character types. And wit plays a pivotal role in an intricate system of exchange

[22] With apologies to Toril Moi for taking liberties with her book title.

[23] Al-'Askar is the name of a number of locations. See Yâqût, Mu'jam al-Buldân (Beirut: Dâr Sâdir, 1979), 4:122–124.

[24] Ibn al-Jawzî, Adhkiyâ', p. 228; Ibn al-Jawzî, Zirâf, p. 222. A sexual allusion may also be present.

[25] See chapter 1 above.

[26] See the anecdotes discussed in Malti-Douglas, "Mentalités and Marginality," pp. 231–233.

[27] See chapter 6 below.

that governs the anecdotes. What wit can be exchanged for obviously depends on the adab character in question. In the case of an uninvited guest, for example, it can buy him entry into a gathering that is otherwise off limits.[28] Wit can even avert punishment in the case of a criminal. A thief, for example, could buy off his punishment with his wit.[29] In the case of women, wit, sexuality, and the female body interact in an explosive literary mixture that leads to interesting exchanges indeed.

A slave girl was being shown to al-Mutawakkil,[30] so he said to her, "Are you a virgin or what?" She replied, "Or what, O Emir of the Believers." He laughed and bought her.[31] This is one of the most popular anecdotes in the adab anecdotal corpus on women, so popular that another male, the grammarian Ibn Khâlawayh (d. 370/980–981), attributed it to himself.[32] No matter what the identity of the male, however, the sexual problematic remains the same. As with the earlier stories, the structure is a question-and-answer one, with the identified male posing the question and the unidentified female replying. But the differences are as eloquent as the similarities. It is the male questioner who lays the groundwork for the response, avoiding any open reference to the loss of virginity. The clever female takes the opening, and her wit counteracts her physical deficiency, which might normally disqualify her from purchase. Wit neutralizes a lack in the female body, a lack related to a woman's sexual behavior.

Two slave girls were shown to a man, one a virgin and one who had been deflowered. He inclined to the virgin, so the deflowered one said, "Why do you desire her since there is only one day between her and me?" But the virgin replied, "And surely a day with thy Lord is as a thousand years of your counting."[33] The two pleased him, so he bought them.[34] In a variant ending, the man buys only the virgin.[35]

At issue once again is woman's body, defined through her sexual experiences. And wit again saves the day. In one variant, the interchange with the two females causes the male to buy both, thereby effectively obliterating the physical deficiency of having been deflowered. In the

---

[28] Fedwa Malti-Douglas, "Structure and Organization in a Monographic *Adab* Work: *Al-Tatfîl* of al-Khatîb al-Baghdâdî," *Journal of Near Eastern Studies* 40, no. 3 (1981): 234ff.

[29] Ibn al-Batanûnî, *Kitâb al-ʿUnwân fî Makâyid al-Niswân*, MS, Cairo Adâb 3568, 82ʳ.

[30] Al-Mutawakkil was an ʿAbbâsid caliph who ruled during the period 232–247/847–861.

[31] Ibn al-Jawzî, *Adhkiyâʾ*, p. 233. See, also, Ibn al-Jawzî, *Zirâf*, p. 224.

[32] Al-Husrî, *Jamʿ al-Jawâhir*, p. 199. On Ibn Khâlawayh, see A. Spitaler, "Ibn Khâlawayh," *EI².*

[33] *Al-Qurʾân*, Sûrat al-Hajj, verse 47. I have used Arberry's translation. A. J. Arberry, *The Koran Interpreted* (New York: Macmillan Publishing Co., 1974), 2:33.

[34] Ibn al-Jawzî, *Adhkiyâʾ*, p. 236.

[35] Ibn al-Jawzî, *Zirâf*, p. 224.

other, it is the virgin who is purchased, by implication because of her reply to her colleague's question. This response, taken from a Qur'ânic verse, is suggestive, to say the least. Woman's eloquence is shown in its spontaneity and in her ability to manipulate the tradition. The quotation is intertextually a reference to the afterlife and the punishment inflicted by the deity, whom the text mentions explicitly (*rabbika*, your Lord).[36] But *rabb* is ambiguous in the anecdotal context, since the word can also refer to a human master, here, the male proposing to purchase the slave girl(s). The virgin, by criticizing her colleague, is reinforcing the masculine values regarding woman's body and its need to be virginal, thus clearly playing into the male relations of power.

The manipulation by slave girls of that dynamic mixture of wit and sex was an essential part of their social role in the medieval Islamic world. Their purchase, however, was not simply dependent on their abilities. Their voices are at times completely occulted, and they become a commodity (like male slaves), to be bought and sold, as al-Jâhiz argues.[37] They were also quite commonly given as gifts, sometimes without any choice on their part.[38] Most professional women poets were slaves, whereas most professional men poets were free.

While the majority of slave girls do remain nameless in the adab anecdotes, a great number, nevertheless, had a status and a reputation in the medieval Islamic literary sphere. Aspects of their lives appear in the famous biographical and literary collections, like the *Kitâb al-Aghânî* (Book of songs) of Abû al-Faraj al-Isfahânî (d. 356/967) or the compendium of poets, the *Tabaqât al-Shuʿarâ'* of Ibn al-Muʿtazz (d. 296/908).[39] Their biographies are telling, however. Where a male subject is most often introduced by an onomastic chain that fully identifies him and places him genealogically and occupationally, the female slave girl in her biography is identified merely by a first name, followed by the name of her owner. The slave girl enters posterity through the male who possesses her.

The names of slave girls are also revealing. It might be tempting to link their appellations to their economic status, such as the famous Danânîr,

---

[36] For the commentaries on this verse, see, for example, al-Qurtubî, *al-Jâmiʿ li-Ahkâm al-Qur'ân* (Cairo: Dâr al-Kitâb al-ʿArabî lil-Tibâʿa wal-Nashr, 1967), 12:77–78; Fedwa Malti-Douglas, "Playing with the Sacred: Religious Intertext in *Adab* Discourse," in *Medieval and Renaissance Humanism*, ed. George Makdisi and Giles Constable, forthcoming.

[37] Al-Jâhiz, *Qiyân*, p. 12.

[38] See, for example, the anecdotes in Ibn Qayyim, *Akhbâr al-Nisâ'*, pp. 180–183, 185, 207–208, 210–211, 219; al-Jâhiz, *Qiyân*, p. 9. See, also, J. C. Bürgel, "Love, Lust, and Longing: Eroticism in Early Islam as Reflected in Literary Sources," in *Society and the Sexes in Medieval Islam*, ed. Afaf Lutfi al-Sayyid Marsot (Malibu: Undena Publications, 1979), pp. 102–103.

[39] Abû al-Faraj al-Isfahânî, *Kitâb al-Aghânî* (Beirut: Reprint of Bûlâq edition, 1970); Ibn al-Muʿtazz, *Tabaqât al-Shuʿarâ'*.

whose name is the grammatical plural of *dînâr*, a monetary unit.[40] But, in fact, many names have no economic or monetary connotation. What is certain, however, is that with some exceptions, the names of slave girls and those of free women derive conceptually from different realms.[41]

A woman's slave or free status is not always specified in the anecdotal corpus. This absence of information ties in with the namelessness to create simply a female voice, unidentified and nonspecific. Al-Jâhiz related that he once came across two women while riding a female donkey. When the donkey broke wind, one of the women said to the other: "Shame! The *shaykh*'s donkey is breaking wind." Al-Jâhiz, angered by her statement, reined in the donkey and said that no female had ever carried him without breaking wind. The woman then slapped her companion's shoulder and said, "The mother of this one was in great difficulty for nine months because of him."[42]

Gender politics are at play here, with the female donkey taking a major role. Her breaking wind instigates the woman's initial comment. The male's attempt to rein in the female animal is symbolic of his more significant attempt to rein in the human female with his verbal response. This endeavor, however, fails: the woman has the last word. Not only that, but her retort has effectively shown the absurdity of the male position by extending his comment to a most sensitive area, that of his biological mother. The female body (both animal and human) is exploited by both sexes, but it is the woman who exits the text victorious.

That important questions of gender and the female body are at issue is evident from the considerable play that this story receives in the anecdotal literature. For example, it is related with another male protagonist, the poet al-Farazdaq (d. 110–112/728–730).[43] In the variant, only one female counters the male, rather than the duo as with al-Jâhiz. The version with al-Farazdaq highlights the peculiarities of the Jâhizian story. There, both instances of female speech are directed to the other female, who remains speechless and acts the role of the seemingly neutral observer in the events. This female intermediary is missing in the variant, leaving the poet

[40] On Danânîr, actually the name for two different slave girls, see, for example, 'Umar Ridâ Kahhâla, *A'lâm al-Nisâ'* (Beirut: Mu'assasat al-Risâla, n.d.), 1:415–419. How similar this is to the names of Greek prostitutes! See Eva C. Keuls, *The Reign of the Phallus: Sexual Politics in Ancient Athens* (New York: Harper & Row, 1985), p. 192. We shall have occasion to hear more about one Danânîr in chapter 9 below.

[41] Even a cursory examination of the five-volume biographical compendium of women, the *A'lâm al-Nisâ'*, of Kahhâla will confirm this.

[42] Ibn al-Jawzî, *Zirâf*, p. 221. This anecdote has a variant in which the male protagonist is the poet al-Farazdaq. See Ibn 'Abd Rabbihi, *al-'Iqd al-Farîd*, ed. Ahmad Amîn et al. (Cairo: Matba'at Lajnat al-Ta'lîf, 1962), 4:52.

[43] See Ibn Abî Tâhir, *Balâghât al-Nisâ'*, p. 165.

to interact on a one-to-one basis with the female speaker. The body is debated directly.

Marital sexual politics also play a role in woman's struggle to control discourse and manipulate her body. Shuʿayb[44] wanted to marry a woman, so he said to her, "I am ill-natured." She replied, "More ill-natured than you is the person who makes it necessary for you to be ill-natured." So he said, "You are then my wife." Clearly, wit on the part of a woman can operate outside the constraints of sexuality and the female body. Hers is a manipulative technique that effectively deflects any negative aspects of the male's character, placing the responsibility for his deficiencies on someone other than himself. The subject in question, needless to say, appreciates this cleverness.

Note the dynamics of the anecdotal unit, however. The male is onomastically identified, the female not. More important, it is his assertion about his ill-nature that permits the woman to retort with her wit. Her narrative voice is subservient to his. And this is a subordination that ultimately reflects the general literary situation of the anecdote. Framing the story is the male's overt link to marriage: the beginning posits his wish to wed this woman, while the ending represents his words that this woman will indeed be his wife. The woman, despite her wit, is but a pawn in the literary mating game, a game in which the male has the superior narrative position.

Though this unidentified heroine does get her man, it is without any recourse to the body. A very interesting and opposite case is that of al-ʿUtbî, who relates the following story in his own words.[45] When he spots a woman whose aspect pleases him, he asks her if she has a husband. She answers in the negative, and al-ʿUtbî then asks if she would like one. "Yes," she retorts but warns him that she has a characteristic which she does not think will please him. He inquires what it is; it is, she tells him, whiteness in her head. He pulls away on his horse, but she calls him back and takes him to an empty spot where she proceeds to uncover hair like black clusters. Then she explains that she is not yet twenty years old, but that she has made him aware "that we hate in you what you hate in us." Al-ʿUtbî is embarrassed and goes away reciting a verse of poetry: He requested union with her while his gray hair beckoned her to not do it.[46]

The male's choice of the woman is based on external criteria: her aspect pleases him. She, however, is not impressed with his external appearance: he has gray hair. Clearly, the body, be it male or female, is important for the opposite sex. But the extremely clever woman does not overtly criti-

[44] Shuʿayb ibn Harb al-Madâʾinî was a hadîth authority who died in the last decades of the third century A.H. See Ibn al-Jawzî, Zirâf, p. 223.

[45] Al-ʿUtbî was a literary personality and poet, who died in 228 A.H. See ibid., p. 163.

[46] Ibn al-Jawzî, Adhkiyâʾ, p. 231.

cize the man or refuse his marriage proposal. She falsely attributes to herself a physical characteristic that he possesses without considering it crucial, and he in turn rejects her for it. By then baring her hair and unmasking the trick (it is a trick, after all), she shames him. The woman has covertly attacked the older man's body by falsely using her own. Her explanation, "I have made you aware that we hate in you what you hate in us," is central. It takes her action, expressed in the first person singular, and generalizes it to the entirety of her sex, through a change to the first person plural. It is woman speaking through a woman's body that can effectively put to shame the man's body and speak on behalf of all womankind.

By its placement in the section on women, this anecdote in Ibn al-Jawzî's work foregrounds the cleverness of the female protagonist and her ability to manipulate the discourse on the body. But the story was also used to stigmatize gray hair: witness its inclusion by al-Nuwayrî (d. 732/ 1332) in a variant rendition in the section on the blame of gray (or white) hair. In either form, it highlights male-female tensions expressed through the body—and the idea of older men marrying younger women.

Woman's body (and by extension, it could be argued, man's body as well) becomes a battlefield on which issues of sexuality and narration are debated. Mazîd asked his wife to let him have anal intercourse with her, to which she replied that she did not want to turn her anus into a second wife (*darra*) to her vagina, despite their closeness.[47] The wife's reply to her husband's desire to commit a seemingly unnatural sexual act with her[48] creates a link between the physical and the sociological. The exploitation of the female body through anal intercourse is made the equivalent of the sociological exploitation the first wife would be subjected to had the husband taken a second one. In Islam, the man has a right to wed up to four women concurrently, with the stipulation that he treat all four equally. By her reply, Mazîd's wife implicitly criticizes both the institu-

---

[47] Al-Râghib al-Isfahânî, *Muhâdarât al-Udabâ' wa-Muhâwarât al-Shuʿarâ' wal-Bulaghâ'* (Beirut: Dâr Maktabat al-Hayât, n.d.), 2:267. According to the editor of Ibn al-Jawzî's *Zirâf*, Mazîd can be a variant for Muzabbid, the name of Abû Ishâq Muzabbid al-Madanî, the hero of many an adab anecdote. See Ibn al-Jawzî, *Zirâf*, p. 151 n. 1.

[48] The question of whether anal heterosexual intercourse was permissible was debated in the context of medieval Islamic civilization. Al-Râghib himself, in this mini-section of his discussion of women, adduces arguments both in favor of the practice and against it. The anecdotes and debate around this issue make it clear that whether sanctioned or not, this form of penetration was practiced. See al-Râghib, *Muhâdarât*, 2:267–268. The chapter on women and anal intercourse in al-Tîfâchî's anecdotal erotic work includes examples of both women who request and who resist anal intercourse. See Ahmad al-Tîfâchî, *Les délices des coeurs*, trans. René R. Khawam (Paris: Editions Phébus, 1981), pp. 247–255. See, also, James A. Bellamy, "Sex and Society in Islamic Popular Literature," in Marsot, *Society and the Sexes*, pp. 36–37.

tions of anal intercourse and of polygamy. The anecdote, however, is still effective on a literal level because in either case, the woman's vulva receives less attention, since vaginal intercourse is reduced: in one case because of her anus, in the other, because of the second wife. Woman exercises her wit, in a situation in which her female body is exploited, to assume her body and overturn that exploitation.

In this context as well should be seen the numerous anecdotes in which wives are the initiators of discourse against their husbands, often bearing accusations before a judge of either improper penetration (anal) or insufficient sexual attention.[49] The female body is once again in these situations a pawn in the game of narration and wit.

That woman's speech along with its link to sexuality and the body are at stake can be seen in a ubiquitous anecdote. A male narrator relates the following: 'Imrân ibn Hittân,[50] who was extremely ugly and short, came in to his wife one day. She was beautiful and had adorned herself. When he looked at her, she increased in beauty in his eyes, and he kept looking at her. When she asked what the matter was with him, he answered that she had become beautiful. She replied, "Rejoice, for you and I are in Paradise." When he asked her how she knew this, she said: "Because you were given the likes of me and were grateful, and I was afflicted with the likes of you and was patient. And the patient and the grateful are in Paradise."[51]

Woman's eloquence and cleverness are clearly highlighted here. More than that, her verbal skills are linked to her beauty and to her husband's ugliness, both ultimately manifestations of the body. Significant is the fact that it is she who makes the declarations about Paradise. The story begins with the husband's physical ugliness and ends with the wife's intellectual cleverness.

That adab anecdotal material is never innocent but rather subject to manipulation and hence redefinition by different authors is clear with this particular story. Al-Husrî includes it in a section on lovers and names 'Imrân's wife: she is Humra. After the narrator's assertion of the husband's ugliness and the wife's beauty, she expresses a clear desire that they be in Paradise. This woman is less confident than her paradigmatic and unnamed counterparts. But at the same time the expression of desire makes her a better subject for inclusion in the section on lovers.[52]

This textual organization demonstrating the woman's verbal link to

[49] See, for example, the anecdotes in al-Râghib, *Muhâdarât*, 2:268–269.

[50] A famous Khârijî orator and poet who was learned in traditions of the Prophet. He died in 84 A.H. See his mini-biography in Ibn al-Jawzî, *Adhkiyâ'*, p. 221 n. 2. See, also, J. W. Fück, "'Imrân b. Hittân," *EI².*

[51] Ibn al-Jawzî, *Adhkiyâ'*, p. 221.

[52] See al-Husrî, *Jam' al-Jawâhir*, p. 198.

Paradise dominates most of the variants of this story.[53] But not always. Though this anecdote is obviously a favorite with the adab compilers, some authors used it to play narrative gender games. Al-Ibshîhî (d. after 850/1446) includes the text in a section on praiseworthy women. The unit begins not with the male's ugliness but with the woman's beauty, foregrounding her. It is not she, however, who makes the pronouncements on Paradise but the husband.[54] In al-Ibshîhî's compendium, the wife is limited to her beauty, her physicality. Her praiseworthiness, which in fact is more apparent in the other renditions, must by definition in al-Ibshîhî's vision be restricted to this physicality. The woman, labeled as a positive force, has been effectively silenced. A reverse organization obtains: the story begins with the wife's physical beauty and ends with the husband's intellectual prowess.

Control of discourse and eloquence as they intersect with the female body would seem to be a threatening formula, indeed. They can even be fatal, as in the following story. The famous pre-Islamic poet-king Imru' al-Qays[55] had had no male children and was extremely jealous. Whenever a girl was born to him, he would kill her. When his women saw this, they hid the female children among various bedouin tribes. Discovering this, the poet would ride to one or another of the tribes and, upon seeing a group of young girls playing, would offer his riding animal to whichever of them could match his verse with another verse on the same rhyme and meter. The girls would all be quiet, except for his daughter, who would take up the challenge. After she recited her verse, he would kill her. Three daughters are disposed of consecutively in this way.[56]

The opening section of this complex anecdote introduces the habitual actions of the poet that lead to the women's hiding his female children. This is but a backdrop against which the pattern of pursuit, discovery, and murder is played out and repeated three times:

1. The arrival of the poet at the tribe
2. The discovery of the young girls
3. The challenge thrown at them and the gift promised
4. The silence on the part of the girls

[53] An almost identical version of the *Adhkiyâ'* rendition can be found in Ibn al-Jawzî, *Zirâf*, p. 217. See also, for example, al-Râghib, *Muhâdarât*, 2:215.

[54] Al-Ibshîhî, *al-Mustatraf fî Kull Fann Mustazraf*, ed. Mufîd Muhammad Qumayha (Beirut: Dâr al-Kutub al-'Ilmiyya, 1986), 2:489.

[55] For a biography of this poet, see S. Boustany, "Imru' al-Kays," *EI²*.

[56] Ibn Qayyim, *Akhbâr al-Nisâ'*, pp. 108–110. Although this anecdote is related on the authority of Ibn Qutayba in Ibn Qayyim al-Jawziyya's text, Ibn Qutayba, in his biography of Imru' al-Qays in *al-Shi'r wal-Shu'arâ'*, presents a variant of this story in which the poet merely finds the girls and kills them without any verbal display either on his part or on theirs. Ibn Qutayba, *al-Shi'r wal-Shu'arâ'* (Beirut: Dâr al-Thaqâfa, 1969), 1:63.

5. The challenge taken up by the daughter
6. The recitation by the poet of his verse
7. The counterrecitation of a verse by the daughter
8. The daughter's murder
9. The departure of the poet

This recurrent narrative structure is extremely effective in highlighting the cold-blooded manner in which the father pursues the killing of his female offspring. Even the last action is significant: after the third murder, when the poet will no longer be searching for more daughters, his departure is still mentioned. He is able to kill and simply walk away with no remorse—a pre-Islamic king whose murderous actions foreshadow those of his later literary historical successor, the ruler Shâhriyâr. Both are involved in the repeated and premeditated destruction of the female. But unlike his literary descendant, Imru' al-Qays is not avenging a battered male ego; he is simply practicing his own brand of female infanticide. More important, the virgins whom Shâhriyâr deflowers and then murders are silent partners in the gynocidal serial murders.[57] The fall of Imru' al-Qays's daughters comes through their speech. It is only their verbal skills that permit their recognition and subsequent murder.

The eloquence of a female can bring about the destruction of her body. It is in a sense her (applied at once individually and collectively to all three daughters) hubris, her conviction that she can match the male poet at his own game, that leads to her physical downfall. When the young girl accepts the challenge, she simply retorts with "Let us have it," confident of her wit and her ability to counter the male.[58] This story suggests that women are as capable of composing poetry as men, and that Imru' al-Qays's daughters had inherited their father's poetic skills. But the road to survival is certainly surer, we also learn, if the female hides her verbal skills.[59]

The female body is problematic. Ability to manipulate discourse may or may not permit the woman to transcend that physicality with which she has been plagued, to control it in a conceptual universe where her body represents a threat, a source of fear. Fatima Mernissi has analyzed the Islamic idea of *fitna*, chaos provoked by woman's sexuality.[60] The Moroccan sociologist also calls attention to the eye's being "an erogenous zone in the Muslim structure of reality, as able to give pleasure as the

[57] See chapter 1 above.
[58] See Ibn Qayyim, *Akhbâr al-Nisâ'*, pp. 109, 110.
[59] Lesser sanctions are also possible. Showing off in front of his wife, a man invites her, in a line of poetry, to serve wine. When he subsequently farts, she asks if she should serve that also, upon which he divorces her. Ibid., pp. 80–81.
[60] Mernissi, *Beyond the Veil*, pp. 4, 10, 11, for example.

penis."[61] But the programmatic manuals used by Mernissi, such as *The Revivification of Religious Sciences* (*Ihyâ' 'Ulûm al-Dîn*) of al-Ghazâlî (d. 505/1111)[62] or the hadîth collections, only provide a partial view of the issue. The legitimacy of the scopic in Islam, complex as it is, is not within the purview of this book.[63] The intersection of the gaze, woman's body, and woman's narrative voice, however, is.

Since the principle that men's eyes should be averted from women (read: women's bodies) was not universally accepted by medieval Muslims,[64] it is no surprise that the debate on this controversy should find its way into the anecdotal corpora, sometimes with women expressing themselves on the issue. A eunuch walked in on a woman combing her hair. She shaved it off, explaining that no hair which had been seen by someone who should not see it would accompany her.[65] In a case like this, the woman, both by her actions and by her narrative explanation, is conforming to the male-generated system which dictates that the male gaze automatically defiles and dishonors.[66] Another woman, finding the male look extremely bothersome, accused those looking of not heeding the advice of the *Qur'ân*—"Say to the believers, that they cast down their eyes and guard their private parts"[67]—or of the poet. Embarrassed, the men ceased their gazing.[68] This nameless protagonist turns attention away from her body, both textually and literally, through her eloquence. To fight off the male gaze, she has recourse to two highly esteemed (one sacred) traditions, the *Qur'ân* and poetry. The religious and the secular are brought together by the woman to shame the gazers.[69] Woman turns from observed and passive object to active subject. It is only her ability to seize discourse that has effected this drastic change in her anecdotal status.

These cases of eloquent women clearly demonstrate a form of narrative male-female encounter: the woman may speak, but it is at the instigation of the man. The latter directs his words or his actions at a specific member

[61] Ibid., p. 83.

[62] Al-Ghazâlî, *Ihyâ' 'Ulûm al-Dîn* (Beirut: Dâr al-Qalam, n.d.).

[63] I am exploring the entire question of looking and vision in a study currently in preparation.

[64] See, for example, the discussion in al-Jâhiz, *Qiyân*, pp. 4ff. Looking at a beardless youth could also be problematic. See Ibn Qayyim, *Hukm al-Nazar*, pp. 17–18.

[65] Ibn Qayyim, *Akhbâr al-Nisâ'*, p. 175; Ibn Qutayba, *'Uyûn*, 4:87.

[66] Cf. J. C. Bürgel, who deals with lyrical poetry, which is outside the purview of this study. J. C. Bürgel, "The Lady Gazelle and Her Murderous Glances," *Journal of Arabic Literature* 20 (1989): 1–11.

[67] *Al-Qur'ân*, Sûrat al-Nûr, verse 30. Arberry, *Koran*, 2:49.

[68] Ibn Qayyim, *Akhbâr al-Nisâ'*, pp. 174–175; Ibn Qutayba, *'Uyûn*, 4:85, who only includes the first half of the Qur'ânic quotation, eliminating the reference to the "private parts."

[69] Malti-Douglas, "Playing with the Sacred."

of the opposite gender, rather than at women as a category. This cross-sexual verbal interaction often takes the form of a response on the woman's part, rather than a true dialogue between the male and female.

One woman stands out above these predominantly nameless female anecdotal protagonists and embodies in her essence the female adab character type: Hubbâ from Medina, who flourished in the first/seventh century. All adab character types have a prototypical personage, often historical, who carries the flag for the group. This prototypical character is not only the protagonist for many anecdotes but also normally advises other individuals on how to accede to the particular type. He/she embodies the combination of adab characteristics, usually wit, with the professional aspects of the character type in question. For uninvited guests, for example, Bunân is the subject of many stories and freely counsels his listeners on how to maximize their gains, be they food or goods.[70] Buhlûl plays the same role for the wise fools.[71] Hubbâ's literary existence is a witness that women, defined by their gender, are an adab social category. The best source for stories on Hubbâ is the *Balâghât al-Nisâ'*, an ostensibly approbatory collection of female eloquence.[72]

A woman who married frequently, Hubbâ seems to have derived part of her fame from her marriage to a young man. Her son, an older man himself, complained of this to the governor of Medina, who called the two of them in. She, however, was not at all disturbed and simply expressed, in no uncertain terms, her desire for sexual intercourse with the young man. This verbal assault earned her the privilege of immortality in the medieval Arabic proverb collections: "More lewd than Hubbâ."[73] As proverbs on that pattern do, this is meant to indicate that the named individual possesses the characteristic to such a degree that he/she becomes the model against which others are measured.

The women of Medina called Hubbâ "Eve, the Mother of Mankind" because she taught them different positions for sexual intercourse, on which she then bestowed names.[74] In the Qur'ânic system, Eve shares with Adam the blame for expulsion from Paradise.[75] Her position is,

---

[70] Malti-Douglas, "Structure and Organization." See, also, Fedwa Malti-Douglas, "The Classical Arabic Detective," *Arabica* 35 (1988): 72.

[71] Ulrich Marzolph, *Der Weise Narr Buhlûl* (Wiesbaden: Kommissionsverlag Franz Steiner GMBH, 1983).

[72] Ibn Abî Tâhir, *Balâghât al-Nisâ'*.

[73] Al-Maydânî, *Majma' al-Amthâl* (Beirut: Dâr Maktabat al-Hayât, n.d.), 1:537–538; al-Zamakhsharî, *al-Mustaqsâ fî Amthâl al-'Arab* (Beirut: Dâr al-Kutub al-'Ilmiyya, 1977), 1:185–187. Her curtailed biography, with the lewd story missing, can also be found in Kahhâla, *A'lâm al-Nisâ'*, 1:237.

[74] Al-Maydânî, *Majma' al-Amthâl*, 1:537–538; al-Zamakhsharî, *al-Mustaqsâ*, 1:186.

[75] For the Qur'ânic story, see *al-Qur'ân*, Sûrat al-A'râf, verses 19–23; Sûrat Tâhâ, verses 120–121. On the Islamic Eve, see J. Eisenberg and G. Vajda, "Hawwâ'," *EI²*. Cf. John A.

however, ambiguous, since in a later misogynist vision, she is accountable for the Fall.[76] The onomastically based metaphor provocatively links Eve, through Hubbâ, with sexuality.[77] Eve becomes Hubbâ: sexual knowledge is responsible for englobing all of mankind under her aegis. After all, procreation does not demand an intricate knowledge of sexual techniques. Through the metaphoric trope, Hubbâ also becomes Eve, the archetypal female. This vision is, in a certain sense, however, true to Hubbâ's name. Grammatically, *hubbâ* is the feminine elative form for "most beloved." While this is a female name, as the lexicographers note,[78] a name in the intricate Arabic onomastic system is never denuded of its primary signification. The connection is made: love carried to its furthest possible limit defines the individual called Hubbâ.

The appellation "mother of mankind" does signal something important. By calling attention to the procreative function, it highlights the physicality of woman. But Hubbâ as mother is not merely giver of life; she is also purveyor of knowledge. These two roles come together in the anecdotal material. Hubbâ's son, urged by other men eager for the information, inquired of his mother what women liked best in sexual intercourse. She explained to him how men should sexually possess older women (like herself), as well as younger women.[79] She herself asked her daughters how they preferred to be taken by their husbands, inserting at need her approval or disapproval.[80] Hubbâ as source of wisdom went beyond sexuality, for she was also asked how she defined honor and degradation.[81]

It is the relationship between Hubbâ's narrative voice and her female body that differentiates her as the prototypical woman. She is uncontrollable sexuality that expresses itself not only through actions but also through words. After her third daughter explained her favorite way of being possessed by her husband, Hubbâ replied: "Be quiet immediately. Your mother is urinating from desire." She hesitates neither at a sort of bestiality nor at aggression against the male body.[82] Her biological func-

---

Phillips, *Eve: The History of an Idea* (San Francisco: Harper & Row, 1984), pp. 148–155. The book as a whole is extremely interesting, but the section on the Islamic Eve, short as it may be, gets bogged down in the negative image of women in Muslim civilization and relies too heavily on Mernissi's *Beyond the Veil* and the sources she uses in that study.

[76] See chapter 3 below.

[77] Cf. Phillips, *Eve*, p. 150, who links the Islamic Eve with sexuality through eating from the tree and "the knowledge of why it is that the genitals are shameful."

[78] Al-Zabîdî, *Tâj al-'Arûs*, vol. 2, ed. 'Alî Hilâlî (Kuwait: Matba'at Hukûmat al-Kuwayt, 1966), p. 233.

[79] Ibn Abî Tâhir, *Balâghât al-Nisâ'*, p. 155.

[80] Ibid., pp. 155–156.

[81] Ibn Qutayba, *'Uyûn*, 3:139; Ibn Abî Tâhir, *Balâghât al-Nisâ'*, p. 142.

[82] See, for example, Ibn Abî Tâhir, *Balâghât al-Nisâ'*, pp. 155, 165–166.

tion is tied to her discursive function, more intimately than was the case with Shahrazâd, whose procreative abilities eradicate her narrative role.

The presence of Hubbâ, with her overtly (and overly) sexual nature, as a character in the adab literature brings this type of text close to the medieval Arabic sexual and erotic manuals. Works by the likes of al-Tîfâshî (d. 651/1253), Ibn Kamâl Bâshâ (d. 940/1534), and the Tunisian al-Nafzâwî rival the *Kama Sutra* in their appeal.[83] Some even found themselves incorporated in the Western corpus of erotica thanks to translations into European languages as early as the nineteenth century.[84] Extremely popular and reprinted numerous times,[85] these works are a literary combination of practical and medical how-to manuals with anecdotal material. Fatna Aït Sabbah, speaking of two of these manuals, notes that they are destined for male readers.[86] But since the primary reader for all of the medieval Arabic literary corpus was most likely male, the gender identification here seems superfluous.

The term *omnisexual*, proposed by Fatna Aït Sabbah to characterize a vision of the female heroine of the sexual manuals, is appealing. Its use for a being whose personality and behavior are determined by its sexual organs needs, however, to be nuanced.[87] Woman is not alone in this sexual category. The material on homosexuals in al-Tîfâshî's work, for example, paints an image of an overabundant sexuality on their part that certainly rivals that of women.[88]

In these works of erotica, the woman is without a doubt primarily a physico-sexual entity governed by her body, and not necessarily by her body as a vehicle for her wit, or vice versa. But exceptions do exist, such as Badr al-Budûr (Moon of Moons) in al-Nafzâwî's erotic manual, whose

[83] Al-Tîfâchî, *Les délices*; Ibn Kamâl Bâshâ, *Kitâb Rujû' al-Shaykh ilâ Sibâh* (Marrakech[?]: n.p., n.d.); al-Nafzâwî, *al-Rawd al-'Atir fî Nuzhat al-Khâtir* (Marrakech[?]: n.p., n.d.). For an English translation, see Nefzawi, *The Perfumed Garden of the Shaykh Nefzawi*, trans. Sir Richard F. Burton (Secaucus, N.J.: Castle Books, 1964). A more scholarly translation is the French one: Mouhammad al-Nafzâwî, *La prairie parfumée où s'ébattent les plaisirs*, trans. René R. Khawam (Paris: Editions Phébus, 1976).

[84] See, for example, René R. Khawam, "Introduction," in al-Nafzâwî, *La prairie*, pp. 9–38, who also presents a criticism of the earlier translations.

[85] On the popularity of this erotic literature, see, for example, Aït Sabbah, *La femme*, p. 47; Khatibi, *La blessure*, p. 139. See, also, Salâh al-Dîn al-Munajjid, *al-Hayât al-Jinsiyya 'ind al-'Arab* (Beirut: Dâr al-Kitâb al-Jadîd, 1958); Abdelwahab Bouhdiba, *La sexualité en Islam* (Paris: Presses Universitaires de France, 1979), pp. 171–193.

[86] Aït Sabbah, *La femme*, p. 51. Though Michel Foucault in his *Histoire de la sexualité* (Paris: Editions Gallimard, 1984–1988) nowhere discusses Arabic materials, he notes correctly that Islam is one of the civilizations possessing an *ars erotica*. The texts under discussion do fit his characterization of that erotic tradition. See vol. 1: *La volonté de savoir*, pp. 76–77.

[87] See Aït Sabbah, *La femme*, p. 51.

[88] See, for example, al-Tîfâchî, *Les délices*, pp. 131–135, 169–246, 275–352.

adventures sound like a veritable tale from *The Thousand and One Nights*. Hers is the case of the woman who uses her intellectual acumen to avert male aggression against her female body. Surrounded by omni-sexual women, she succeeds, thanks to her verbal and poetic skills, in delaying the forceful advances of a relentlessly sexual slave. She is the only virtuous woman in the story, the others giving in to their passion at the sight of the slave's sexual organ. Though this story appears in the chapter on praiseworthy women, the narrator concludes it by blaming women for their trickery.[89] The moral and the sexual come together in a vision that I shall analyze below.[90]

Hubbâ of the adab works champions the character type of women in anecdotal literature, but she is still an individual. It is when women, collectively and not individually, turn into the subject of debate that the verbal interaction becomes most lively. A poet, passing by a group of women and being pleased by their appearance, began to recite,

> Women are devils who were created for us.
> God save us from the evil of the devils.

But one of the women answered him and began reciting,

> Women are aromatic plants who were created for you.
> And all of you desire the most aromatic of aromatic plants.[91]

The male poet's aggressive condemnation of the female gender occurs as he comes into contact with a group of women, rather than one. But his pronouncement is effectively reversed by the eloquent woman, whose poetic retort matches the original verse in meter and rhyme. Yet to be truly efficacious, the woman carries the literary technique in her response even further: she follows the poet's verbal and syntactic structures to build her counterverse. She takes his poetic line, retains his grammatical constructions, and simply substitutes new words to effect the transformation. His word *shayâtîn* (devils) is paired with *rayâhîn* (aromatic plants). From supernatural frightening beings, women turn into something palpable and pleasurable. Divine protection is replaced with desire. The blame initially placed on the women is metamorphosed into blame on the men: it is they whose desire is in question.

With this, woman's narration and its intersection with her physical body enter a different realm. Expressing a judgment on the collectivity of the female gender elevates the antifemale discourse from the specific to the general. The humoristic and ludic elements so important in earlier

[89] See, for example, the extended anecdote in al-Nafzâwî, *al-Rawd*, pp. 12–19.
[90] See chapter 3 below.
[91] Ibn al-Jawzî, *Adhkiyâ'*, p. 231.

examples are reduced here. Seeking God's protection from women/devils is a far cry from the dialogue on breaking wind. This poet is, of course, not alone in his assessment: a close, when not intimate, relationship exists between woman and the devil in the medieval Islamic unconscious. The Prophet is quoted as saying: "Woman is something shameful and impure ('awra).[92] If she goes out, the devil gazes at her."[93] A proverb states, "Women are the snares of the devil."[94] Women are also said to make up the largest percentage of the inhabitants of Hell.[95] This latter assessment, based on a saying of the Prophet, is still a lively subject for debate in the contemporary Middle East.[96]

Ibn al-Jawzî cites this poetic match of woman as devil/aromatic plant in his collection of anecdotes on the intelligent and perspicacious, the *Akhbâr al-Adhkiyâ'*. As such, it testifies to the dhakâ' (intelligence, perspicacity, cleverness) of women. But in its latent message about the nature of females, the anecdote is more representative of a type of misogynist attitude better exemplified by the word *kayd* (craftiness, cunning, stratagem). *Dhakâ'*, obviously the more positive of the two terms, has a primary meaning of completion, especially when applied to age or understanding.[97] *Kayd*, on the other hand, embodies the characteristics of deception and malevolence. Behind it lurks as well the idea of ruse or stratagem. More provocative is the meaning of *kayd* used only for women: that of menstruation.[98] A menstruating woman in Islam is far from a positive force. The menses dictate the nonfulfillment of religious duties, as well as the male abstention from vaginal penetration.[99] The se-

---

[92] On this extremely important concept, see, also, chapter 6 below.

[93] Ibn al-Jawzî, *Ahkâm al-Nisâ'* (Beirut: Dâr al-Kutub al-'Ilmiyya, 1985), p. 33. See, also, al-Tirmidhî, *al-Jâmi' al-Sahîh—Sunan al-Tirmidhî*, vol. 3, ed. Muhammad Fu'âd 'Abd al-Bâqî (Beirut: Dâr al-Kutub al-'Ilmiyya, 1987), p. 476.

[94] Al-Maydânî, *Majma' al-Amthâl*, 2:390; al-Tha'âlibî, *al-Tamthîl wal-Muhâdara*, ed. 'Abd al-Fattâh Muhammad al-Hulw (Cairo: 'Isâ al-Bâbî al-Halabî, 1961), p. 215.

[95] Ibn al-Jawzî, *Ahkâm al-Nisâ'*, pp. 65–66.

[96] See the little pamphlet edited by Samîra 'Itânî, *Hal Sahîh anna Akthar Ahl al-Nâr Hum al-Nisâ'?* (Is it true that most of the people of Hell are women?) (Beirut: Dâr al-Fath lil-Tibâ'a wal-Nashr, 1979[?]).

[97] See, for example, al-Zabîdî, *Tâj al-'Arûs* (Beirut: Dâr Sâdir, n.d., reprint of Cairo edition), 10:137. Ibn al-Jawzî, *Adhkiyâ'*, as befits a solid adab writer, has a lexicographical introduction in which he presents substantially the same material.

[98] Al-Zabîdî, *Tâj al-'Arûs*, vol. 9, ed. 'Abd al-Sattâr Ahmad Farrâj (Kuwait: Matba'at Hukûmat al-Kuwayt, 1971), pp. 122–124.

[99] See, for example, Ibn al-Jawzî, *Ahkâm al-Nisâ'*, pp. 17–18; Ahmad ibn Hanbal, *Ahkâm al-Nisâ'*, ed. 'Abd al-Qâdir Ahmad 'Atâ (Beirut: Dâr al-Kutub al-'Ilmiyya, 1986), pp. 54–59, which also includes a general discussion of menstruation. Fatima Mernissi, in *Le harem politique: Le Prophète et les femmes* (Paris: Editions Albin Michel, 1987), pp. 94ff., argues that this attitude was not part of the original Prophetic message. Once again, of course, we are examining the expressed positions of a historically embodied civilization.

mantic field of the term *kayd* links the unclean female body to the notions of deception, or of stratagem conceived negatively.

The misogynist vision in Islam (and subsequently in the medieval Arabic literary subconscious) has its literary roots in the Joseph story in the *Qur'ân*. Similar to the biblical tale of Joseph, the Qur'ânic version stands out in the Muslim holy book as a narrative tour de force. Joseph, the paragon of beauty in Islam, has an entire *sûra* devoted to him. Present are the special relationship Joseph enjoyed with his father, the betrayal by the brothers, the adventures in Egypt, and the final resolution to this much-beloved story.[100] As the proverbial literature shows, many aspects of the Joseph saga have been eternalized in the Arabic tradition, such as "Joseph's dreams," applied to truthful dreams, or "Joseph's wolf," applied to someone falsely accused of a crime.[101]

But more than any other element, it is perhaps Joseph's adventures with the ruler's wife that have been etched most strongly in the Muslim (and hence Arabic) cultural imagination.[102] This female protagonist remains unnamed in the *Qur'ân* but later takes on the name of Zulaykhâ. Hers is the aggressive female role dictated by physical desire: she attempts to seduce the young man and, of course, fails. "Indeed your guile is great," declares the Egyptian ruler when he discovers that Joseph is innocent, since his shirt is torn from behind. "Your guile" here is in the feminine plural, a form of address that transposes the seductive act of a single woman and exploits it to pass judgment on the totality of womankind. In an attempt to disculpate herself when faced with the gossip of other Egyptian women, the royal wife invites them all to a feast, hands them knives, and asks Joseph to serve them. Overtaken by his beauty, they cut themselves. In a sense, this act confirms the male assessment already directed at all women. They have merely proved the ruler correct. It is women's absence of self-control in the face of physical beauty that causes them to wound themselves.

The intensity of the gender dynamics in the Joseph text is such that the story carries forward a host of antifemale ideas, principal among which is the notion of kayd, and acts as a terrain on which the male-female sexual dialogue is played out.[103] A man said to a group of women, "You

[100] *Al-Qur'ân*, Sûrat Yûsuf. For Joseph as the paragon of beauty in Islamic culture, see, for example, al-Tha'âlibî, *Thimâr al-Qulûb fî al-Mudâf wal-Mansûb*, ed. Muhammad Abû al-Fadl Ibrâhîm (Cairo: Dâr al-Mʿârif, 1985), p. 49.

[101] For these and other proverbial expressions emanating from the Joseph story, see, for example, al-Tha'âlibî, *Thimâr*, pp. 45–50. See, also, al-Tha'âlibî, *al-Tamthîl*, pp. 19–20.

[102] For this story in a broader cultural context, see John D. Yohannan, *Joseph and Potiphar's Wife in World Literature* (New York: New Directions Books, 1968).

[103] I cannot agree with Bouhdiba who, in a sophisticated and provocative reading, sees the apparent misogyny of the story as effectively palliated: Bouhdiba, *La sexualité*, pp. 33–41. Cf. Ascha, *Du statut*, pp. 29–31, who criticizes Bouhdiba on this point. Leila Ahmed

are the companions of Joseph." So they replied: "And who threw him in the well? We or you?"[104] Once again, the female voice rises up in response to a male comment. Both attacks are general, directed to the entirety of the opposite gender. Rather than defending herself or justifying female acts, the woman responds by placing the responsibility for Joseph's fate in the male camp.

Why the companions of Joseph? According to al-Thaʿâlibî, this phrase, *sawâhib Yûsuf*, is used when one wishes to complain of women and to censure their character or morals. The polyhistor then explains that the Prophet said to one of his wives, scolding her, "You are the companions of Joseph (*sawâhibât Yûsuf*)," and al-Thaʿâlibî closes the discussion with a verse from the neoclassical poet Abû Tammâm (d. 231–232/845–846): "They are the enemies of Joseph and his companions."[105]

The Prophet did, according to Muslim tradition, direct this phrase to his wife ʿAʾisha, who is responsible for transmitting the hadîth in question. When Muhammad was ill with the sickness that would eventually bring about his death, he asked that Abû Bakr be summoned to lead the prayer. ʿAʾisha, Abû Bakr's daughter, suggested that since her father was sensitive and would cry, ʿUmar should be asked to lead the prayer. The Prophet repeated his command and retorted to ʿAʾisha, "You are the companions of Joseph." The commentators on this hadîth agree that the phrase refers to women's overpestering.[106]

Despite the fact that it is the Prophet's wife alone who is directly addressed in this interchange, the phrase is nevertheless in the feminine plural, englobing the totality of the feminine gender in its condemnation. ʿAʾisha has clearly put herself forward, questioning and usurping her

("Arab Culture," p. 48) has, in a way, gone further in this line of argument than Bouhdiba. For her, the incident with the women of Memphis shows that "while Zuleikha's conduct was wrong, it is portrayed as understandable." For Bouhdiba, however, this latter incident "gives to temptation its true dimension which is collective," Bouhdiba, *La sexualité*, p. 37.

[104] Ibn al-Jawzî, *Zirâf*, p. 229.

[105] Al-Thaʿâlibî, *Thimâr*, p. 304.

[106] For the hadîth and the commentary, see al-Nisâʾî, *Sunan al-Nisâʾî*, with commentary by Jâlal al-Dîn al-Suyûtî (Beirut: al-Maktaba al-ʿIlmiyya, n.d.), 1:88–100; Ibn Mâja, *Sunan Ibn Mâja*, ed. and commentated by Muhammad Fuʾâd ʿAbd al-Bâqî (Beirut: al-Maktaba al-ʿIlmiyya, n.d.), 1:389–390; Ahmad ibn Hanbal, *Musnad al-Imâm Ahmad ibn Hanbal* (Beirut: al-Maktab al-Islâmî lil-Tibâʿa wal-Nashr, n.d.), 4:412–413. For the political use of this hadîth, see Denise Spellberg, "Nizâm al-Mulk's Manipulation of Tradition, ʿAʾisha and the Role of Women in the Islamic Government," *The Muslim World* 78 (1988): 111–117. Cf. the version in Mernissi, *Le harem*, pp. 143–144, where she adds, concerning this expression, "My literature teacher in high school did not cease to repeat it to us each time one of us deformed a poem or mixed up dates." Unlike Mernissi, I do not consider the phrase in its original hadîth to be "anodine, at the limit tinted with tenderness." On women in hadîth, see, also, Barbara Freyer Stowasser, "The Status of Women in Early Islam," in *Muslim Women*, ed. Freda Hussain (New York: St. Martin's Press, 1984), pp. 29–43.

husband's authority. Her suggestion that because of his overly emotional nature, her father should be replaced by 'Umar might seem at the outset to be quite innocent. But in the context of later fights over who should succeed the Prophet (who did not arrange for this matter before his death), it becomes evident that she is interfering in something much bigger, men's political affairs.

With the raising of Joseph's specter, the crucial link is effected between woman's verbal meddling and the crime of sexual aggressiveness, so essential to the relationship of the Islamic Joseph with women. 'A'isha's overstepping of political bounds is assimilated to Zulaykhâ's overstepping of sexual bounds. All of woman's incorrect or aggressive behavior becomes subsumed into the Joseph story and unbounded sexuality. With a simple phrase, the shift has been effected: initially a story about power, the incident becomes redirected into one about sexuality. Woman's speech and her body seem to be inextricably intertwined.

That the subtext behind the Joseph connection is inherently sexual is evident in another anecdotal hadîth in which women are "companions"—but this time of Job, David, Joseph, and a certain Kursuf. The Prophet questioned 'Ukâf ibn Bishr al-Tamîmî about his marital status. The man being unmarried, the Prophet then inquired if he had a slave girl. Muhammad, spurred again by a negative answer, asked if the individual was well off. Since this was the case, the Prophet retorted that he was a brother of devils, and if he were a Christian would surely be one of their monks. The tradition of Islam is marriage, continues the Prophet. The Devil has no more effective weapon against holy men than women. Only married males are freed from fornication. This eloquent admonition against monkery closes with a warning about women: they are the companions of Job, David, Joseph, and Kursuf. Incited by 'Ukâf's curiosity, the Prophet recounts the story of Kursuf: he is someone who after centuries (three hundred years, to be exact) of worshiping God was led astray by a woman whom he loved. Though he abandoned worship of the Holy, he was eventually forgiven. There is also a happy ending for 'Ukâf: at the Prophet's urging that he wed, he asks the Prophet to marry him off, which is done.[107]

This is an intriguing and complex hadîth, indeed. Its two parts concern male interaction with women, in one case the unmarried 'Ukâf, whose dialogue with the Prophet provides a frame for the story of the holy man Kursuf. But the message about sexuality in the two stories is not necessarily without contradiction. Women's sexuality is a danger, but marital union with them is nevertheless advocated. The intrusive and destructive role that the female can play when it comes to man's devotion to the deity

---

[107] Ahmad ibn Hanbal, *Musnad*, 5:163–164.

is clearly outlined. Its magnitude, however, transcends this example. It leads to a misogynist worldview that will find expression in the philosophical allegory of *Hayy ibn Yaqzân*.[108]

The "companions of Joseph" phrase joins that pervasive notion of kayd (deceit or trickery) in crystallizing the misogynist vision and localizing it in the Joseph story. When the Egyptian ruler, addressing his spouse, declares, "Indeed your guile is great," he has immortalized not only his lustful wife but all of womankind in the role of uncontrollable sexuality. Once again, as with the Prophet and his wife ʿAʾisha ("You are the companions of Joseph"), we see a phrase directed to a single woman but employing the grammatical feminine plural. Through one woman, judgment is passed on the entirety of the female gender.

Thus, the idea of women's trickery (*kayd al-nisâ*ʾ), with all of its sexual overtones, enters into the Muslim unconscious. That compiler so pivotal for the history of Islamic mentalities, al-Thaʿâlibî, once again provides undeniably crucial observations. *Kayd al-nisâ*ʾ, he writes, can be used proverbially for all times and all places. He then proceeds to quote from one of his predecessors who argued that women's guile was greater than that of the Devil, because God after all said that the guile of the Devil was weak whereas that of women was great.[109] Lest someone counterargue, al-Thaʿâlibî continues, that this is not the deity's speech, since He only transmitted it from someone else who uttered it, we read that if this were to be denied, the deity would have denied it, and if it were blameworthy, He would have denounced it. Instead, God related it and did not find it blameworthy.[110]

Henceforward, the formula "Indeed your guile is great," and its variants (including "women's guile") will suffice to encode what is perceived as the negative and pervasive aspects of woman's sexuality. It is no surprise, then, that Shâhriyâr should have employed this phrase after his pivotal run-in with the ʿifrît's woman.[111] He is, after all, only drawing upon the male discourse on woman: a notion beginning in the holy book and maintained by the male scriptoral establishment of the medieval Islamic literary world.

[108] See chapter 4 below.
[109] *Al-Qurʾân*, Sûrat al-Nisâ*ʾ, verse 76; and Sûrat Yûsuf, verse 28.
[110] Al-Thaʿâlibî, *Thimâr*, p. 305.
[111] See chapter 1 above.

CHAPTER 3

Sacred History as Misogyny

THE NOTION of women's guile finds its fullest flowering in an adab collection on the tricks of women, the *Kitâb al-ʿUnwân fî Makâyid al-Niswân*, by the ninth/fifteenth-century Ibn al-Batanûnî.[1] The *Makâyid* redefines woman's trickery by combining it with sacred history.

Though this work is as yet unedited, it seems to have been quite popular in the medieval period, as evidenced by the extensive number of manuscript copies available.[2] In a brief introduction, the author informs his reader that he has entitled his work *al-ʿUnwân fî al-Ihtirâz min al-Niswân*, loosely, being on guard against women, in effect adding a second title to the one present on the title page.[3] From one point of view, one might want to give the authorial statement precedence over the coversheet formulation, which could be the work of a scribe. As a literary artifact, however, the text effectively comes down to us with two titles, one external and one internal. The tricks, ruses, or stratagems (*makâyid*) of women referred to in the title have been transformed into an attitude of caution (*al-ihtirâz min*) in the introduction. Ibn al-Batanûnî, it seems, was answering a request from a "brother" who asked him to compile a book that would comprise exhortations about women "ignorant" of legal precepts and religious matters and who concern themselves with their base desires and waste their efforts on things that bring about their destruction. The appeal to a brother expresses a need for male bonding and solidarity, essential before the male narrator can proceed to speak about women.[4] The clear link to the legal aspect makes of woman a being outside the control of the law. The problematic of the female as negative force has been posited.

Whether the title be imbued with the idea of women's tricks (the word *makâyid* is derived from the same grammatical root as the word *kayd*) or

[1] Ibn al-Batanûnî, *Niswân*. Carl Brockelmann, in his *Geschichte der Arabischen Litteratur* (Leiden: E. J. Brill, 1937–1949), 2:123 and Supplement, 2:152, calls him al-Batanûnî, but Ibn al-Batanûnî is on the manuscript.

[2] See Brockelmann, *Geschichte*, 2:123 and Supplement, 2:152.

[3] Ibn al-Batanûnî, *Niswân*, fol. 2ʳ.

[4] This answering of a request supposedly posed by a "brother" is a reasonably formulaic structure in medieval Arabic works and operates as a literary topos in a variety of texts, not all of which need be strictly literary. Its deeper civilizational implications will be analyzed in chapter 4 below.

with that of guarding oneself against women does not alter the antifemale nature of Ibn al-Batanûnî's compilation. The *Makâyid al-Niswân* is a collection of stories, some drawn from the rich Islamic corpus of tales of prophets, some from Islamic history, and some from general literary sources.[5] In the middle of his introduction, the author quotes the Egyptian ruler whose fame in Islam is tied to his words in the chapter on Joseph: "Indeed your guile is great."[6] This phrase uttered, the stage has been effectively set for Ibn al-Batanûnî's special misogynist perspective.

The author's agenda is clear. His is not a programmatic manual but rather an illustrative one. The text does not begin with a section of negative normative material cataloging women's vices. The adab vision, of which Ibn al-Batanûnî clearly forms part, is more complicated. An Ibn al-Jawzî, for example, when writing of the legal precepts of women, is quite comfortable presenting devastatingly negative data, such as women's having small intellects, populating Hell, and the like. But none of this finds its way into the same author's anecdotal collection on the *Adhkiyâ'* (the witty, the intelligent, the sagacious), to cite but one work, where woman enters the pantheon of the clever adab character type.[7] Other adab authors, like al-Râghib al-Isfahânî, can alter the outlook in their work by the inclusion of anecdotes whose ambiguous function hangs somewhere between generalized statement and mere anecdote. Such is the case of the man who said that no evil had ever entered his house, to which a wise man replied, "And how did your wife enter?"[8] The simple structure of this anecdote, consisting of a statement and a retort, combined with its anonymous nature, brings it closer to a normative unit.

When compared with other adab texts, that of Ibn al-Batanûnî appears more directed and singularly univocal. Story follows story as Adam leads a parade of prophets, rulers, and various other dignitaries of Islamic sacred and secular history who have all been somehow or other the subject of woman's trickery and guile. As we shall see momentarily, Ibn al-Batanûnî has a knack for construing events in such a way that the female turns into the source of all evil. Interspersed between the reinterpreted events or anecdotes is the ubiquitous refrain, "Indeed their guile is great," organizing and guiding the text. The narrator prefaces this semimagical formula with an invocation to the deity for protection from women's guile. This appeal is expressed grammatically in the first person plural (*we* seek protection from God, or may God protect *us*). There is no linguistic ne-

---

[5] It is not my task here to trace the sources of these stories. What is important is the way Ibn al-Batanûnî has brought them together in a misogynist perspective.

[6] Ibn al-Batanûnî, *Niswân*, fols. 1ᵛ and 2ʳ.

[7] See Ibn al-Jawzî, *Ahkâm al-Nisâ'*, which is replete with this material. The section on women in the same author's *Adhkiyâ'* is not.

[8] Al-Râghib, *Muhâdarât*, 2:217.

cessity for this grammatical game, however, it being quite possible for the narrator to speak in the first person singular. But this would restrict the referent of the narrator's speech to himself. Instead, by employing the first person plural, he is able to englobe other speakers, who would naturally be of the male gender since it is from the guile of the female gender that the deity's protection is sought. It is as though the entirety of the male gender had to be safeguarded from the entirety of the female one. More interesting, an opposition is created between God and men, on the one hand, and women, on the other. The male bonding that launched the text is maintained throughout the narrative.

This persistent hammering by the Batanûnian narrator constantly reminds the reader of the thrust of his argument. It also redefines all the female actions in the work through the lens of the Qur'ânic aborted seduction. On a larger literary level, the refrain gives unity and force to *Makâyid al-Niswân*. The text then functions as a recasting of Islamic sacred and semisacred history as misogyny, the entirety framed within the context of the Joseph story and its concept of kayd, both acting as a dominant subtext for the Batanûnian vision.

The terms *kayd* and *makâyid* bring more clearly into focus the nature of woman: she is a trickster motivated and manipulated by sexual desire. What is highly unusual in the case of these Batanûnian sexually defined adab characters is their undisputed connection and link to Islamic sacred history: they effectively recast it. Normally, adab character types are much less consequential and their role-defining actions do not affect the larger mythic constructs of the civilization. Women are different. Their uncontrolled sexuality, expressed through their kayd, is capable of altering the course of events. And all this is thanks to Zulaykhâ's powers.

How it is that one woman can have this enormous influence, albeit negative, is not for us to resolve. Suffice it to say that she does and that her impact on Islamic mental structures is enormous, both through the attempted seduction and through her existence as a member of a possible couple with Joseph. Her unfruitful adventures are there as a subtext in other narrative seduction attempts. Other ineffective seductresses do not fare nearly as well as Zulaykhâ, however. 'Umar ibn 'Abd al-'Azîz's wife, for example, failed in her attempt to lure a guest. The end of her story (and her end as well) comes in the form of her husband's hanging her.[9] Another wife who tries unsuccessfully to seduce a beautiful nephew is divorced by her husband.[10] Ironically, though Zulaykhâ's act earns condemnation for her gender, it does not bring direct physical or social harm to her. Her last words in the Qur'ânic story involve an admission

---

[9] Ibn Qayyim, *Akhbâr al-Nisâ'*, pp. 120–121.
[10] Ibid., pp. 177–178.

of her guilt in instigating the seduction and address God's mercy and forgiveness.[11]

In a sense, Zulaykhâ has bigger parts to play, and her escape facilitates this. Her fascination with the beautiful Joseph and her love for him will eventually pay off, at least in one continuation of the story provided by Ibn al-Batanûnî. Zulaykhâ, now old, blind, and poor, is brought before Joseph, who discovers her identity. She has three wishes, that her sight be restored, that she become beautiful again, and that she marry Joseph. As in a fairy tale, the three wishes are granted, and Zulaykhâ and Joseph live happily ever after.[12]

In order for this happy ending to come about and include the consummation that will eventually permit the couple to bring forth eleven sons (to equal in number Joseph's brothers), the initial seduction scene with Zulaykhâ as culprit has to be recuperated. On the wedding night, Zulaykhâ rebuffs Joseph's advances, something that increases his desire. He grabs her shirt; she pulls away, and her shirt is torn. The angel Gabriel appears and tells Joseph, "A tearing of a shirt for a tearing of a shirt and an escape for an escape."[13] Reconciliation can only come about through the exorcism of Zulaykhâ's original sin. This couple is not cast out of Paradise; rather they live in it eternally.

This absolution of Zulaykhâ, cited by Ibn al-Batanûnî, does not extend to her sisters, who are still inextricably tied to the notion of kayd. And the beauty of this kayd is that it is not anchored chronologically. It operates as a synchronic force that orders events and characters extending from Eve in the Garden of Eden to the sister of an ʿAbbâsid caliph.

There were two brothers, one of whom traveled a great deal and absented himself from home. The wife of this absent brother tried to seduce the other brother, but he would have nothing to do with her. When her husband returned, she accused his brother of trying to seduce her. The husband swore that he would not speak to this brother ever again. While on the pilgrimage route one year, the accused brother fell ill, died, and was buried. The couple had occasion to cross this very route on their own return from the pilgrimage. Some lines of poetry caused the wife to reveal the truth to her husband. He told her that if it were legally sanctioned, he would kill her. But he divorced her instead and spent the rest of his days crying and mourning at the grave of his brother. He died and was buried next to him, and the spot became known as "the grave of the two brothers."[14]

This story is clearly cited to illustrate women's perfidy. But more is at

---

[11] *Al-Qurʾân*, Sûrat Yûsuf, verses 51–53.
[12] Ibn al-Batanûnî, *Niswân*, fols. 32ᵛ–33ᵛ.
[13] Ibid., fol. 33ᵛ.
[14] Ibid., fols. 54ʳ–54ᵛ.

issue here. The wronged brother is a silent partner in the anecdote, serving as a foil first for the woman and then for the husband. Seen in this
light, the woman's seductive powers and the brother's homosocial ten-
dencies act as poles, pulling the text in one and then another direction.
The relationship of the two brothers, especially after the woman's revelation of her own guilt, is similar to that in the frame of *The Thousand
and One Nights*. A male finds solace in another male, and the homosocial
couple is instituted again, but this time with a truly dramatic ending. It is
significant that the burial spot is nameless when it serves only for the
silent brother but takes identity when it becomes a locus for the two.

Seduction is very much part of what makes the world go around for
Ibn al-Batanûnî. It almost becomes an obsession: the text even provides a
lexicographical explanation for the word borrowed from a work of
Qur'ânic exegesis.[15] Normally, adab works provide a philological and
lexicographical discussion of the key terminology illustrating the specific
adab text. Thus, to take but one example, in the case of the collection on
Adhkiyâ' the compiler provides a discussion of the linguistic parameters
of the terms involved.[16] If one were to set up a parallel with Ibn al-Batanûnî's *Makâyid*, then the work would be more about seduction than anything else.

Fortunately, however, for the much-sought-after males in the Batanûnian textual universe, Joseph seems always to be lurking in the back-
ground as guiding angel or general cheerleader. Sulaymân ibn Yasâr had
a strikingly beautiful face. A woman entered his house and tried to seduce
him, but he refused. When she asked him to come close to her, he ran
away from his own house, leaving her in it. After this, he saw Joseph in a
dream and asked him if he were Joseph, to which the apparition answered: "Yes, I am Joseph who was tempted, and you are Sulaymân who
was not."[17] Sulaymân had been identified earlier as one of the mystic
saints and had already rebuffed one particularly insistent woman on his
way to perform the pilgrimage. Taken with his beauty, she had entered
his tent and uncovered her face before him. After that incident too Joseph
appeared to him in a dream; when Sulaymân expressed his wonder at
what had happened with him and Zulaykhâ, Joseph retorted that what
had happened with Sulaymân and this particular woman was even more
wondrous.[18]

There is something almost uncanny in the fact that, according to these
accounts, the women will stop at nothing. They will violate spatial and

[15] Ibid., fol. 28ᵛ.

[16] Ibn al-Jawzî, *Adhkiyâ'*, pp. 10–11.

[17] Ibn al-Batanûnî, *Niswân*, fol. 59ʳ. This anecdote is also in Ibn al-Jawzî, *Dhamm al-
Hawâ* (Beirut: Dâr al-Kutub al-ʿIlmiyya, 1987), p. 203.

[18] Ibn al-Batanûnî, *Niswân*, fols. 57ʳ–57ᵛ.

other boundaries to satisfy their desires. In one case, the seductress enters the male victim's house; in another, his tent. In the first case, the male is forced to abandon his home; in the second, the female culprit appears to take a hint and goes back to her own tent, leaving the male victim in his. In the last example, the seduction attempt is made on the way to the pilgrimage, a most sacrilegious endeavor. Women seem to have no respect for religious duties, conveniently proving Ibn al-Batanûnî's point in the introduction to his book.

But then again, perhaps we should not be overly surprised at this turn of events. In the Batanûnian protracted account of Zulaykhâ's temptation of Joseph, there is a consistent and underlying binary opposition operating between woman and the deity. In a dialogue that smacks of that between Little Red Riding Hood and the wolf dressed as her grandmother, the pharaoh's wife tells Joseph, "How beautiful are your eyes," to which he answers, "With them I see my Lord." When she then asks him to look at her, he replies that he is afraid of blindness in his old age if he looks at her.[19] Gazing at the deity is set against looking at woman. More eloquent is the following interchange:

ZULAYKHÂ: Why do you keep away from me?
JOSEPH: I want to get close to my Lord.[20]

A sort of oppositional paradigmatic relationship exists between woman and God, as though closeness to one precluded closeness to the other. When the royal wife closes the doors of the room on the young man, the heavens open to him the doors of virtuousness and assistance.[21] Ibn al-Batanûnî borrows this image from al-Qushayrî's (d. 465/1072) mystical commentary on the Qur'ân, the Latâ'if al-Ishârât. The editor of the latter points to "the beauty of al-Qushayrî's expression emanating from the opposition between the 'closing' and the 'opening.' "[22] More is at stake than a beautiful image, however. By her antithetical relationship to the deity, woman is indirectly assimilated to the Devil. And this is an alliance that should not come as a surprise: it was operative in anecdotal material discussed above.[23]

The Batanûnian male-female interaction is fueled by seduction. And since what is at stake is man's (in the gender-specific sense) most important relationship, that with God, how much more dramatic can a temptation be than that of a woman trying to lure or mislead a pious man

[19] Ibid., fol. 29[r].
[20] Ibid.
[21] Ibid., fol. 29[v].
[22] Al-Qushayrî, Latâ'if al-Ishârât, ed. Ibrâhîm Basyûnî (Cairo: al-Hay'a al-Misriyya al-'Amma lil-Kitâb, 1981), 2:177, and n. 2 on that same page.
[23] See chapter 2 above.

away from his God? Alas, we discover that the case of Sulaymân ibn Ya-sâr is the rule rather than the exception.

The attempted seduction of a holy man becomes a veritable topos in the *Makâyid al-Niswân*. The example of Fadlûn is one such complicated and protracted case. So momentous was his ordeal that the angel Gabriel announced it to the prophet Muhammad even before its occurrence. This ordeal was to take place during the reign of 'Umar ibn al-Khattâb, and only 'Alî ibn Abî Tâlib, the Prophet's cousin and son-in-law, could save Fadlûn. A great worshiper of God who was also endowed with great beauty, the ascetic was enjoined by the Prophet to veil himself in order to avert the female gaze and its ensuing chaos. Fadlûn had the misfortune of having a woman fall in love with him. He rebuffed her advances but she was particularly creative, accusing him of various unsavory acts. She turned his nightlong worship at the cemetery into grave robbing. 'Umar, to solve the mystery, followed Fadlûn and discovered that he spent his night praying and beating himself. Not to be daunted, the woman contin-ued her vile acts during the pilgrimage. First, she attempted unsuccess-fully to have the saint give her money to the poor in the holy city as re-demption for her sin-to-be with him. Then, with the help of her slave girl, she set up the holy man for theft. When the judgment of this act was delayed until the return from the pilgrimage, she murdered her own slave girl and accused Fadlûn not only of the murder but of raping her as well. Fadlûn performed the pilgrimage in chains. After the pilgrimage, the holy man was brought before the ruler, who ordered that he be beaten.

It is only when the legal punishment is about to be inflicted that 'Alî makes an appearance, first in a dream and then in reality. 'Alî's arrival is truly miraculous: he crosses the distance between Kûfa and Medina, which should normally take twenty days, in a few steps. He tells 'Umar that he believes in Fadlûn and will show the ruler a judgment that will surprise even the angels in Heaven. He has the woman brought in and asks her about her accusations and her witnesses. Her witnesses are nu-merous, but 'Alî asks if she will go by the testimony of her fetus. She agrees; 'Alî has a rod that belonged to the Prophet brought in, places it on her belly, and asks the fetus to reveal the culprits of the various crimes. This the fetus does: his father is the woman's black slave; his mother is the murderess and the one responsible for staging the theft. 'Umar is very pleased, and 'Alî requests that the woman's punishment be delayed until she has delivered the baby and nursed it. 'Alî is given permission to return to Kûfa, and 'Umar waits until the woman has given birth. Her newborn is black and dies on the spot. She is killed, and Fadlûn spends the rest of his days worshiping the Most Holy.[24]

---

[24] Ibn al-Batanûnî, *Niswân*, fols. 61ᵛ–69ʳ.

What a complex and almost *Thousand-and-One-Nights*-like story! It contains the sex, the violence, and the magic of many a tale from that fabled work. The repeated attempts at seduction; the murder of the slave girl; the supernatural arrival of ʿAlî, down to the description of how the ground looked while he and his companion were speeding over it; the fetus who speaks out of his mother's womb: what more could a reader hope for? The crowning touch, without a doubt, is the woman's sexual adventure with her black slave Rayhân. This act is particularly reprehensible since we know, from her own admission to Fadlûn, that she comes from a good family and has rejected marriage proposals from the most important and wealthiest of men.[25] This is very much a topos from the *Nights*. Is it not the behavior that set that text in motion?[26] Even the slave's name, Rayhân, smacks of that classic.[27] The Prophet's "rod" used by ʿAlî to magically cause the fetus to speak is a sexual allusion: the word means at once a rod and the male sexual organ. Placing this instrument on the woman's belly is but a metaphorical reenactment of the sexual act.

But one is not in the literary domain of the *Nights* here. There are fictions operative in that text that help to create and account for its fanciful nature. This story about Fadlûn is predicated on historical verisimilitude. After all, its occurrence is forecast and announced by the angel Gabriel directly to the Prophet, it is sanctioned by the latter, and its message is, hence, all that much more powerful.

This Batanûnian female goes further than her sisters in the frame of *The Thousand and One Nights*: she is more complex. They were motivated by mere sexual appetite. We can only surmise her motives for the sexual adventure with the slave: is it revenge, since she will accuse the ascetic of rape? or is it some combination of desire and revenge? She also has a knack for exploiting religion, and religious duties in particular, to try to attain her lustful goals. In a sense, she is only doing what Ibn al-Batanûnî has set her up for in the introduction to his *Makâyid*: ignoring religious precepts and performing actions that will lead to her destruction. These are self-fulfilling prophecies.

Other elements come into play in the saga of Fadlûn. The duo of ʿUmar and ʿAlî is one that the Batanûnian narrator had already introduced in an earlier anecdote, to be discussed below. ʿUmar is the ruler, but ʿAlî effects the correct judgment. In fact, had the situation been left to ʿUmar's discretion, Fadlûn would surely have been unfairly punished. But thanks to ʿAlî, he is saved. A less than flattering portrayal is given of that supposed paragon of justice, ʿUmar. Never mind that the Prophet,

---

[25] Ibid., fol. 62ᵛ.
[26] See chapter 1 above.
[27] Burton, *Thousand Nights*, 1:186–254.

after receiving the information from the angel Gabriel, calls in ʿAlî and informs him in advance of the holy man's ordeal. ʿUmar is kept in the dark. The story could just as easily be interpreted as part of the complex pro-ʿAlid propaganda of medieval Islam. The evidence is all there: from the angel Gabriel to the use of the Prophet's "rod." But whatever the political implications of the story, they are largely occulted in favor of the gender politics. The dominance of the sexual over the political is reminiscent of the hadîth with ʿAʾisha discussed earlier, in which her meddling with the same rather fiery political issue (that of the succession to the Prophet) is redirected into the sexual domain.

Ibn al-Batanûnî's agenda is clear. He is not daunted either by political questions, counterarguments, or historical or chronological verisimilitude. His missionary zeal is so strong that he plays his own devil's advocate, always returning to his belief in the greatness of "their guile." A young man came to the caliph ʿUmar ibn al-Khattâb and asked him to judge between him and his mother. The youth claimed that she had abandoned him, to which the woman adduced four of her brothers and forty other witnesses to support her contention that she did not know the young man, that he was attempting to ruin her reputation, and that she was a virgin who had never married. After the arguments were repeated on both sides, ʿUmar ordered that the young man be thrown in prison. On the way to jail, the convoy passed by ʿAlî ibn Abî Tâlib. The young man screamed out for ʿAlî's help, and the entire group went once again before the ruler. The arguments were presented to ʿAlî, who proceeded to ask whether the two parties would be satisfied with his judgment. Receiving an answer in the affirmative, he then asked ʿUmar whether the latter would permit him to pass judgment. ʿUmar did, and ʿAlî, with the power vested in him and with his own money, married the woman to the young man. The latter took the money, grabbed the woman's hand, and told her to get up, at which she screamed out at ʿAlî, asking him if he would marry her to her own son.

It turns out that the young man is her son after all. She was married off by her brothers, who subsequently forced her to abandon her son. She takes the young man by the hand and goes home. The Batanûnian narrator then delves into a protracted explanation and justification for why it is that the woman is really to blame, although there might be some evidence to argue the contrary. She went along with her brothers in their wicked ways, and that suffices for him. After all, he continues, is not ʿUmar known for his justice? Why did she not go to him for help? All this simply supports her guile.[28]

This is an interesting story that demonstrates to perfection the ways in

---

[28] Ibn al-Batanûnî, *Niswân*, fols. 52ᵛ–54ʳ.

which the narrator of *Makâyid al-Niswân* manipulates material. He recognizes only too well that the guilt of the woman is questionable, but he does not let that stand in the way of his argumentation. The anecdote could, once again, be an example of pro-ʿAlid propaganda. As with the earlier story of Fadlûn, it turns the ruler into a less than effective justice giver: he orders the imprisonment of an innocent individual. It is only ʿAlî, in a Solomonic judgment, who brings the truth to light. Whatever political messages may be latent in this story, they are once again subordinated to the sexual, a pattern that should not overly surprise the reader of *Makâyid al-Niswân*.

There are other forces, both psychological and literary, operating in this anecdote and expanding its appeal. A mother abandoning her son and subsequently raising the specter of possible incest is a powerful motif. The dictatorial role of the brothers is one that will manifest itself differently in the analysis of the male utopian vision of Ibn Tufayl.[29] The structure of the story is not without literary sophistication. A change in roles occurs for almost all the protagonists in the story. The woman begins as seemingly innocent and ends up being a culprit. The brothers who were supporting her innocence turn out to have been the major perpetrators of the sordid actions. The son who, with his appeal to the ruler, is a major instigator of the events becomes almost a child as the mother takes him home by the hand. For her, this action also reverses the son's attempt to take her by the hand after the marriage ceremony.

This woman enters the pantheon of Ibn al-Batanûnî's evil heroines because she did not resist her brothers. She did not attempt to seduce anyone. She has, however, expanded the borders of the notion of kayd.

Can a woman possibly be a guileless individual? Ibn al-Batanûnî indicates to his reader in the introduction to the *Makâyid al-Niswân* that he has appended a chapter, albeit a short one, on pious women. Such a chapter does not exist. Is it an oversight? Or did the narrator get so carried away with his arguments and counterarguments that he convinced himself only too well of the perfidy of women? The work does come to a close with a tantalizing and ambiguous story, which forms a nice bit of closure for this misogynist but nevertheless important work.

At the time of the Israelites, the narrator tells us, there were six worshipers (of the male gender, of course) who had rejected the world and wanted to seclude themselves in the worship of the Almighty.[30] Their elder suggested that they go off in isolation. They settled close to a city and maintained their prayers, while managing to keep themselves alive by

---

[29] See chapter 4 below.

[30] The description would fit the Qumrân community. Cf. Peter Brown, *The Body and Society: Men, Women, and Sexual Renunciation in Early Christianity* (New York: Columbia University Press, 1988), p. 37.

making and selling mats. News of them reached the king of Israel, who had a young daughter whose mother had died. He started crying, and when the young woman asked why, he replied that he wished to join the seven worshipers, realizing that this world was worthless. His daughter, at hearing this, began crying and asked him how she would fare without him. He retorted that women had no business sitting with men either by day or by night. The girl answered that she was young and had nothing to do with men, so why did not her father get her some men's clothing, and she would accompany him. The king did this, and the two went to join the seven worshipers. The daughter was taken for a male, and she joined the men in their various activities. The king then fell ill and on his deathbed enjoined upon the others the care of his "son."

One day, while this young "man" was on the way to the city to sell some mats, he was seen by the daughter of that city's ruler. Taken by his beauty, she got her wet nurse to lure him to her house, on the pretense that the wet nurse had a sick son who needed the youth's religious intercession. Alone with the king's daughter, the young man, invoking the deity, resisted her advances. He was let out and continued on his way to the market.

The young woman's physical desire got the better of her, however, and with her wet nurse's help, she had sexual intercourse with a man who impregnated her. The mother discovered the pregnancy, and the king called his daughter in. She claimed to him that the one who had committed the act was the young man with the seven worshipers. He had his police beat up and bring in the entire group. The worshipers insisted on the young man's innocence, and the king decided on their advice to send this young man off alone to an isolated part of his kingdom. The daughter's newborn was sent there as well. When the young man/woman prayed to God that He should take care of this child, the deity asked Gabriel to commission a gazelle to take care of the infant, which was done. The young man/woman then asked God to take this child so it would not distract her from her prayers, which was also done. News of this worshiper reached the world, and the seven original worshipers asked the king to return their young companion to them. This was done.

In time, this individual became sick, and his[31] companions asked him for his testament. This completed, and at their insistence that he had to have the ritual washing of the dead, he requested that their eldest take a knife and open the armor he was wearing, and after that they could do with her what they wished. When death came, her request was followed: the elder opened the breastplate and found himself looking at a young

[31] These are the pronouns used in the text; the significance of their shift will be discussed below.

woman's chest. He dropped the knife and told the others of what he had seen. They told him to look again, but he insisted that they call in the women of the city to handle the case. This was done, and it was discovered that she was indeed a woman. The king realized his crime and had her properly buried. Her grave gave off a smell of musk. He also had his daughter killed and her head paraded around the city with words of warning. People listened and, according to the narrator, this was a great day, the likes of which had never been seen.

The narrator closes this anecdote with his usual warnings about women. "Look, my brother, at the actions of women," he admonishes his reader, and what they will do to fulfill their desires and direct their guile against men. "So we seek protection from God from their guile. Indeed their guile is great."[32]

If it were not for the warning appended to this, the closing story in *Makâyid al-Niswân*, it might be possible for the reader to imagine that this protracted narrative presents an ambiguous attitude to women. But no doubt is cast on the issue, and the narrator has maintained one, negative and unswerving, position throughout the work. He has also evoked that homosocial relationship which instigated the work.

This is a story that rivals Fadlûn's in complexity. Two kings with two daughters play their fortunes across the text. One ruler, in search of the deity, will provoke the transvestism and cross-sexual role in his daughter. The other ruler, still in control of the city and his worldly kingdom, has a sinful daughter. The issue is not as clear as it would initially appear. The sexual ambiguity of the first king's daughter maintains much of the tension in the story. How the narrator shifts from the masculine to the feminine gender when discussing her/his activities tells us as much about the ultimate gender issues as the development of the story itself. For example, when the second king has the child delivered to this supposed parent, the narrator refers to the latter with the masculine pronoun. A shift in grammatical gender to the feminine occurs as soon as the child is left with the young worshiper. "He" becomes a "she." It is then as a woman that she calls for the deity to take care of the child. The gazelle as mother substitute is an element that foreshadows the male utopian perspective in Ibn Tufayl.[33] Our "she" does not become a "he" until news of his/her religious activities spreads around the world.[34] Clearly, there are activities that are the domain of the female, and others that are the prerogative of the male. The exclusive religious experience belongs to men. It is, there-

[32] Ibn al-Batanûnî, *Niswân*, fols. 102ᵛ–107ʳ.

[33] See chapter 4 below.

[34] This play with pronouns to express gender ambiguity finds echoes in the case of the hermaphrodite Herculine Barbin. See Michel Foucault, ed., *Herculine Barbin dite Alexina B.* (Paris: Editions Gallimard, 1978), p. 68.

fore, only through her transvestism that the young woman can form part of this male group of worshipers.

Once again, we see the false accusation, familiar from Fadlûn's ordeal, of sexual impropriety on the part of a holy individual. But there are no miraculous appearances here, no magical rods or wands. Nothing comes to save the woman/man in this story. Yet the tales cross one another in areas that are important for woman's body and woman's word. In the case of Fadlûn, the disculpation of the wrongly accused man is through the medium of the woman's body. And this is the same body that attempted to lead him on the wrong path in the first place. With the transvestite worshiper, the situation is not as clear-cut. Woman's body (and hence woman's sexuality) must be conquered for its owner to join the ranks of the holy. But it is also this woman's body that will be its most eloquent defense at the end, since it is the breasts that establish beyond the shadow of a doubt that this holy transvestite could not possibly have been guilty of having illegitimately fathered the child of the second king's daughter.

Woman's body is indeed powerful, and dangerous, Ibn al-Batanûnî teaches us. Is it a wonder that there should be an attempt to create a male utopia that will be free from this uncontrolled body? The vision of Ibn al-Batanûnî prefigures for us that of Ibn Tufayl.

CHAPTER 4

Flight from the Female Body: Ibn Tufayl's Male Utopia

THE PROBLEMATIC NATURE of woman, her voice, her body, is not only shown positively in the Arabic textual tradition. Woman can be something other than a presence. She can also be an absence. This role she plays most clearly in medieval Arabo-Islamic philosophy.

What would a world be without woman? Would it not be an ideal world? But could such a world even be possible? This audacious dream, its justifications, and its possibilities are most clearly articulated in the twelfth-century Arabic philosophical classic and masterpiece of medieval Arabic prose, *Hayy ibn Yaqzân.*[1] Its author, the Andalusian philosopher-physician Ibn Tufayl (d. 581/1185–1186), has done so by constructing a male utopia.

Though the title *Hayy ibn Yaqzân* (Alive son of Awake) is taken from that of an earlier work by Ibn Sînâ (d. 428/1037), the text of Ibn Tufayl represents a clearly distinct, essentially original, narrative.[2] Scholars have long recognized and debated the philosophical aspect of Ibn Tufayl's tale and its place in the history of medieval Islamic philosophical and religious thought.[3] But the Tufaylian *Hayy ibn Yaqzân* is also alive and well in the

---

[1] The extended continuous narrative, so common to modern Western literature, was in fact reasonably rare in medieval Arabic letters, where preference went to anecdotal, repetitive, or enframed groupings of shorter narratives, like those discussed in chapters 2 and 3 above.

[2] See the three *Hayy ibn Yaqzân* texts by Ibn Sînâ, Ibn Tufayl, and al-Suhrawardî, ed. Ahmad Amîn (Cairo: Dâr al-Maʿârif, 1952). For an important examination of Ibn Tufayl in the context of the "literary character of Arabic philosophic writing," see Muhsin Mahdi, "Philosophy," in *The Cambridge History of Arabic Literature* (Cambridge: Cambridge University Press, forthcoming). For an extended analysis of the *Hayy ibn Yaqzân* of Ibn Sînâ and al-Suhrawardî, see chapter 5 below. My thanks to Muhsin Mahdi for a prepublication copy.

[3] See, for example, George F. Hourani's reevaluations of Léon Gauthier's thesis in "The Principal Subject of Ibn Tufayl's *Hayy ibn Yaqzân,*" *Journal of Near Eastern Studies* 15 (1956): 40–46. Léon Gauthier's ideas can be found in *Ibn Thofail, sa vie, ses oeuvres* (Paris: E. Leroux, 1909). I would like to thank Laurence Michalak, who provided me with a copy of this book on very short notice. For an examination of these and similar positions on Ibn Tufayl's text, see Lawrence I. Conrad, "Through the Thin Veil: On the Question of Communication and the Socialization of Knowledge in *Hayy ibn Yaqzân,*" in *The World of Ibn Tufayl: Interdisciplinary Perspectives on Hayy ibn Yaqzân*, ed. Lawrence I. Conrad (Oxford: Oxford University Press, forthcoming).

modern Arabic consciousness. Not only has it been reprinted on numerous occasions, but its hero and his adventures have become the subject of
paintings, films, television specials, and even children's comic strips.[4]

Ibn Tufayl unquestionably intended a religio-philosophical message to
his work. But casting his treatise into narrative form—and, further, into
the form of a story about the adventures and relationships of an individual—created other levels of meaning. Willy-nilly, once one is talking
about individuals and their relationships, one is obliged to take positions
on basic issues of human society. By adopting the literary form of a myth,
the Andalusian philosopher-physician automatically generated a
mythico-psychological discourse. This can be seen more clearly if one
compares Ibn Tufayl's work with the *Tadbîr al-Mutawahhid* of his predecessor and fellow Andalusian, Ibn Bâjja (d. 533/1139). Despite similar
arguments and conclusions, the latter's work is organized as a philosophical treatise, eschewing narrative and allegory.[5]

Allegory does not empty mythic discourse; it enriches it. Like any text
worthy of its name, Ibn Tufayl's classic is a nexus of complementary,
mutually defining meanings. Indeed, from the point of view of literary
structure, it is the mythic aspect that supports the philosophical. In *Hayy
ibn Yaqzân*, the two come together in the conception of a male utopia.

On one level, the Tufaylian narrative is an adventure story: an abandoned infant, Hayy ibn Yaqzân, grows up on an uninhabited island where
he is nurtured by a gazelle. He learns physical survival and discovers the
laws of the universe, eventually achieving a mystical state. His meeting
with Asâl, an inhabitant of another island, civilized this time, leads to his
contact with society. This contact is not fruitful, and both men return to
the original island to live happily ever after.

It is undoubtedly this adventurous aspect and the meeting with the
other (as well, obviously, as the availability of Popock's and Ockley's
translations of Ibn Tufayl's classic) that have led many critics to make a
connection between the twelfth-century Arabic text and Daniel Defoe's
Robinson Crusoe.[6] A few basic differences (some also noted by the Arab

---

[4] Fârûq Saʿd, "Introduction," to Ibn Tufayl, *Hayy ibn Yaqzân*, ed. Fârûq Saʿd (Tripoli,
Libya: al-Dâr al-ʿArabiyya lil-Kitâb, 1983), pp. 7, 13. See, also, Allen Douglas and Fedwa
Malti-Douglas, "Femmes, tradition, et bandes dessinées," *Revue tunisienne de sciences so-
ciales*, forthcoming.

[5] Ibn Bâjja, *Kitâb Tadbîr al-Mutawahhid*, ed. Maʿn Ziyâda (Beirut: Dâr al-Fikr al-Islâmî,
1978).

[6] On the comparison, see, for example, A.-M. Goichon, "Hayy b. Yakzân," *EI²*; Aly Ma-
zaheri, *La vie quotidienne des musulmans au moyen âge, Xᵉ au XIIIᵉ siècle* (Paris: Librairie
Hachette, 1951), pp. 142–143; Riad Kocache, "Introduction," in *The Journey of the Soul:
The Story of Hai bin Yaqzân as Told by Abu Bakr Muhammad bin Tufail*, trans. Riad
Kocache (London: The Octagon Press, 1982), pp. viii–x. The latter does recognize some
differences between the two texts but still opts for the borrowing. Fârûq Saʿd, in his "Intro-

critic Madanî Sâlih) should, however, lay to rest any exaggerated comparisons: (1) Crusoe's arrival on his island takes place when he is already an adult, as opposed to Hayy, who arrives there as an infant; (2) Crusoe arrives with all the accoutrements and knowledge of civilization, whereas Hayy acquires all this on his own; (3) Crusoe's relationship with Friday is an altogether different one from that between Hayy and Asâl. The Western text sets up a clear "imperialist" relationship between the shipwrecked adventurer and his "man Friday."[7] The very different Hayy and Asâl relationship, as we shall see, is crucial to an understanding of Ibn Tufayl's narrative.

To characterize *Hayy ibn Yaqzân* as a male utopia is to call attention to the problem of gender, to the play of male and female, in Ibn Tufayl's text. What do we mean, however, by a utopia, and are we justified in interpreting *Hayy ibn Yaqzân* as one? A utopia (based on a pun from two Greek words meaning "no place" and "good place") is a text that sets up an ideal society, ordinarily a total one. M. H. Abrams notes that "most utopias . . . represent their ideal place under the fiction of a distant country reached by some venturesome adventurer."[8] In the words of Kathryn Hume: "We see people who exemplify the virtues of the system. We see children being educated to fit and fulfill the ideals of the society. We usually follow the adventures of an outsider, surrogate for ourselves, who ultimately wishes to convert to this new way of life." The critic continues by noting the two key themes in utopian fiction: reason and conditioning. Hume recognizes that utopias possess a "static plot structure" and then proceeds to discuss those which diverge from this.[9]

At first view, *Hayy ibn Yaqzân* seems to fulfill some, but by no means all, of these textual demands. There are voyages, though strictly speaking no adventurers. First one character and then a second embrace the mystical way of life. There are no children, and if there is an outsider, it would have to be Asâl, who only appears toward the end of the text. These differences are important ones, but they contribute in their own way to giv-

---

duction," pp. 41–44, cites still more authorities to buttress this linkage and his own belief in it. The most sensible critic by far who deals with this question is Madanî Sâlih in *Ibn Tufayl: Qadâyâ wa-Mawâqif* (Baghdad: Dâr al-Rashîd lil-Nashr, 1980), pp. 167–178. It is worth noting in this connection that other literary progenitors, popular accounts of the survival of shipwrecked sailors, were also available to Defoe at the time. See the appendix to Daniel Defoe, *Robinson Crusoe*, ed. Angus Ross (New York: Penguin Books, 1983), pp. 301–310.

[7] Defoe, *Robinson Crusoe*.

[8] M. H. Abrams, *A Glossary of Literary Terms*, 3d ed. (New York: Holt, Rinehart and Winston, 1971), p. 177.

[9] Kathryn Hume, *Fantasy and Mimesis: Responses to Reality in Western Literature* (New York: Methuen, 1984), pp. 106–111, which includes a discussion of dystopias, and for the quotation, p. 106.

ing *Hayy ibn Yaqzân* many of the aspects of what, after Hume, we can call a utopia of reason.[10]

Hayy's story begins with his birth. The reader encounters two variants for this all-important event. Variants, of course, form part and parcel of classical Arabic narrative literature. This is the case in the secular schol-arly corpus, be it in the *adab* works, the biographical dictionaries, or the historical accounts, as well as in religious works, like the hadîth texts where variants are the rule rather than the exception.

But in the Tufaylian work, variants are not the norm. In fact, the two accounts of Hayy's birth are the only variants in the text. This should alert us immediately that something unusual is taking place. Michael Rif-faterre has called attention to what he calls the "ungrammaticality" of a text, signaled by elements that seem "less acceptable than their context," relating the entire notion to the presence of the intertext.[11] We can extend Riffaterre's notion to include any actions in a story, or significant ele-ments in its narration, that break clearly with the generically recognizable basic principles of the text's composition.

In its composition and narration, *Hayy ibn Yaqzân* follows the mode of classical Arabic fictional texts. Its facts, unlike those, for example, in an adab anecdotal collection, are not presented as historically true. Fur-ther, most classical Arabic fictional texts (and this is probably what dis-tinguishes them most from nonfictional narratives, no matter how enter-taining) avoid variants, presenting a direct, uninterrupted narrative.[12]

It is partly also this aspect of Ibn Tufayl's text that provoked the judg-ment of Gauthier: "I do not believe that one can find in all of Arabic literature a work more admirably composed than *Hayy ben Yaqdhân*: not a superfluous detail, no faults in organization, no digressions. Every-thing in it flows with an impeccable logic, following a continuous pro-gression."[13] If there is a digression, a discontinuity, it is the intrusion of the variant, itself introduced in the conventional nonfictional style: some believe this, some believe that. It is not at all coincidental that in this

[10] Ibid., p. 106. All of this also distinguishes Ibn Tufayl's narrative from works like the *Kitâb Arâ' Ahl al-Madîna al-Fâdila* of al-Fârâbî (d. 339/950), ed. Albîr Nasrî Nâdir (Bei-rut: Dâr al-Mashriq, 1973), a discussion of the ideal city, whose nonnarrative, nonallegor-ical discourse highlights no significant gender issues.

[11] Michael Riffaterre, "Intertextual Scrambling," *Romanic Review* 68 (1977): 197.

[12] The categories of fiction and nonfiction have not been used habitually in discussions of classical Arabic prose. Nevertheless, one can distinguish between texts like *The Thousand and One Nights*, *Kalîla wa-Dimna*, or the *Maqâmât*, which are not meant to recount his-torically true events (whatever their moral truth) and the more common adab, biographical, geographical, or other narratives, which are presented as true and accompanied by appro-priate attributive apparatus. (Fictional attributions are another problem, of course.)

[13] Gauthier, *Ibn Thofaïl*, p. 65.

narrative, ungrammaticality highlights an episode crucial to a gender-conscious understanding of the text.

I shall first present the two accounts in summary form and then analyze them.

The island of al-Waqwâq on which Hayy flourishes, the narrator tells us, is one on which people are born "without mother or father."[14] Some claimed that Hayy ibn Yaqzân was one of these individuals, but there were others who denied this. The narrator then presents the first version of Hayy's birth.

The island facing this island was ruled by a jealous man who had a beautiful sister. Though he prevented her from getting married, she did so secretly to a relative of his named Yaqzân. She then became pregnant and had a male child. Fearing that her secret would be discovered, she placed him in a wooden case/casket (*tâbût*) and went out at night with a group of her trusted servants to the seashore. Though "her heart burned with ardent love and out of fear for him," she recited a prayer and cast him on the water (*fî al-yamm*). The child was carried by the water to the other island, and washed up on an especially verdant and well-protected part of it. The casket stayed in that location and the sands provided a barrier, blocking the water from entering the area. Hence, the tides never reached that particular spot. The nails and boards of the casket had loosened when it was tossed by the water.

When the child became hungry, he began to cry. A gazelle (*zabya*) heard him and followed the sound, thinking it was her lost young, until she reached the casket. She managed to open it by removing a board from the top and proceeded to care for the child. This, then, according to the narrator, is the beginning of Hayy's state as far as those who deny spontaneous generation are concerned.

This account is followed by that of "those who claim that he was generated from the earth/ground." On a part of the island, mud had fermented, eventually mixing with "the hot and the cold, the humid and the dry," in such a way that equilibrium was achieved. This piece of fermented mud was very large, and some parts of it were better for the formation of tissue. Its middle was the most temperate and the closest to the physical constitution of man. The narrator provides a detailed description of the natural conditions and changes that eventually permitted a human embryo to take shape in such a setting. When the infant became hungry, the gazelle who had lost her young reenters the narrative to take care of the child. And this is the point at which the two accounts merge.[15]

[14] The importance of the island of al-Waqwâq and other locations as zones of socio-sexual abnormality will be discussed in chapter 5 below.

[15] Ibn Tufayl, *Hayy*, pp. 117–128. I will be using the Fârûq Saʿd edition, cited earlier.

The first extended account of the genesis of the hero is essentially a natural one, since it involves a father and a mother, as distinguished from the second, representing some sort of spontaneous generation.

The first, or natural, version has important resonances in the Islamic tradition, the clearest being the similarity of certain elements with the Moses story as related in the *Qur'ân*.[16] The baby Moses is cast afloat on the water (fî al-yamm) in a casket/coffin (tâbût) by his mother.[17] Aside from the similarities in the events, the same phrases are employed in the Tufaylian narrative, creating a clear parallel between its birth account and that in the most sacred of Islamic texts. The word *tâbût*, meaning at once a case and a coffin, signals the rebirth that occurs in both narratives, though in a more forceful way in that of Ibn Tufayl, where even the name of the young child, Hayy (Alive), stresses this idea.

In his *The Great Code: The Bible and Literature*, Northrop Frye notes: "Like that of many gods and heroes, the birth of Jesus is a threatened birth: Herod orders a massacre of infants in Bethlehem from which Jesus alone escapes. Moses similarly escapes from an attempt to destroy Hebrew children."[18] Hayy's birth is in these terms, of course, also a threatened birth. He escaped whatever fate was due him when he was cast on the water. But it is the implications of this that become significant for our perspective. By the circumstances of his birth, Hayy joins his two distinguished predecessors, Jesus and Moses, to become most certainly a mythic figure, if not a prophetic one.[19]

Though the similarities appear at first glance to dominate these threatened birth narratives, there are crucial differences. In the Jesus and Moses stories, the infant children are saved from some threatening outside political force. Their mothers are completely innocent and play totally positive roles.[20] In the Tufaylian narrative, this is not the case. Hayy's mother, after her clandestine marriage to her brother's relative, her pregnancy, and her delivery of the baby, sets the young protagonist afloat out of fear lest "she be exposed and her secret be revealed."[21] As a character, she is far from completely positive. First, she marries against her brother's will.

[16] Cf. Antonio Pastor, *The Idea of Robinson Crusoe* (Watford: The Gongora Press, 1930), p. 90.

[17] *Al-Qur'ân*, Sûrat Tâhâ, verse 39; Sûrat al-Qasas, verse 7.

[18] Northrop Frye, *The Great Code: The Bible and Literature* (New York: Harcourt Brace Jovanovich, 1983), p. 172.

[19] On such accounts, cf. Otto Rank, *The Myth of the Birth of the Hero: A Psychological Interpretation of Mythology*, trans. Dr. F. Robbins and Dr. Smith Ely Jelliffe (New York: Robert Brunner, 1957).

[20] *Al-Qur'ân*, Sûrat al-Qasas, verses 7–13; Sûrat Tâhâ, verses 36–40. The pious and important character of Mary can be seen in the fact that, among other references, she has a sûra named after her in the *Qur'ân*, Sûrat Maryam.

[21] Ibn Tufayl, *Hayy*, p. 121.

But even more serious, unlike the other two mothers, her motivations for casting her child on the water are not instigated by political circumstances beyond her control. Instead, it is her own fear that provokes her action. And that fear is related to her transgression. The word used in the text to express exposure or discovery, *yaftadih*, carries implications of dishonor and shame. Al-Zabîdî, in his *Tâj al-ʿArûs*, illustrates this aspect of yafta-dih with a hadîth about Bilâl's tardiness in calling the prayer, explaining that he missed the appropriate time and linking the discovery (yaftadih) of the act to shame (*ʿayb*).[22] The narrator does explain that just before Hayy's mother casts him onto the water, she feared for him. But this fear for the child comes in almost as an afterthought, the earlier fear for her-self superseding it.

Also unlike Moses' mother, Hayy's does not nurture him after his safe arrival on the new island.[23] Rather, that role is fulfilled by a gazelle who becomes the mother substitute, obviating the biological mother.

E. García Gómez has identified an earlier Arabic text with a plot very similar to this, biological, variant of the birth of Hayy. In the earlier work, however, the image of the mother is less negative. She even survives to greet her son at the end of the story.[24] The relatively antimaternal as-pects of Ibn Tufayl's far more famous version stand out all the more clearly.

The second Tufaylian birth account involves no biological mother or father, dealing as it does with spontaneous generation. But here again, the gazelle makes an appearance, linking the two variants.

The gazelle was textually a good choice for that function, having a dis-tinctively positive image in the Arabic literary tradition. Not only is it one of the animals that will enter Paradise, but it was considered a friendly creature that mixed easily with people. Furthermore, it was the best ani-mal for suckling and it had the reputation for efficient weaning.[25]

But it is not only in the Arabic tradition that an abandoned child is taken care of by a graceful animal. In folklore, a doe's caring for an aban-doned child is a common element.[26] And the Hayy story does, indeed,

[22] Al-Zabîdî, *Tâj al-ʿArûs*, vol. 7, ed. ʿAbd al-Salâm Muhammad Hârûn (Kuwait: Matbaʿat Hukûmat al-Kuwayt, 1970), pp. 21–22.

[23] Cf. *al-Qurʾân*, Sûrat al-Qasas, verses 12–13.

[24] Emilio García Gómez, "Un cuento árabe, fuente común de Abentofáil y de Gracián," *Revista de archivos, bibliotecas y museos* 30 (1926): 1–67, and for the Arabic text, pp. 261–269.

[25] Al-Jâhiz, *al-Hayawân*, ed. ʿAbd al-Salâm Muhammad Hârûn (Cairo: Matbaʿat Mus-tafâ al-Bâbî al-Halabî), vol. 2 (1965), p. 155; vol. 3 (1965), pp. 161, 395; vol. 4 (1966), pp. 421, 423.

[26] See Stith Thompson, *Motif-Index of Folk-Literature* (Bloomington: Indiana University Press, 1958), 6:5, 218, where he cites the same tale. See, also, Pastor, *The Idea*, pp. 146–

contain folkloric elements: the abandonment on an island, the child floated in a casket, and so forth.[27] This should not be overly surprising, since as Edmund Leach, among others, has noted, "many Bible stories have their close parallels in folklore."[28]

The accounts of Hayy's birth, taken separately or together, reflect manifest ambivalence and barely concealed anxiety/hostility to the idea of motherhood. In the natural version, the abandonment results from the effective transgression of a less-than-perfect mother. Indeed, a careful examination of the story shows that Hayy's birth and separation from society result from the tensions of concealed sexuality and brother-sister sexual jealousy. It is the sexual possessiveness of the brother, his incestuous desire, that blocks his sister's normal sexual expression through a socially recognized marriage. The noted expert on Arabic folklore Hasan el-Shamy has argued that brother-sister sexual attraction and consequent jealousy is so powerful in Arab culture that it replaces in its psychological centrality the Oedipus conflict of Western society.[29] Whether or not one wishes to accept such a daring hypothesis, this attraction/jealousy is certainly ubiquitous in the Arabic tradition. More important, it is certainly no coincidence that the most famous examples of rithâ', that classical poetic genre reserved for women, should be laments of sisters over their dead brothers.[30] In *Hayy ibn Yaqzân*, this brother-sister relationship clearly defines sexuality and its resultant motherhood as a problem.

Indeed, in this account, considerable narrative development is given to the relationship between the king and his sister, as well as to that between mother and son. The life of the licit heterosexual couple—that is, Yaqzân and the king's sister—is almost completely occulted. Just as in the frame of *The Thousand and One Nights* the crucial rupture is created by the

---

148, where he discusses the exposure of a child and its being suckled by an animal in the context of the Western classical and a variety of religious traditions.

[27] See, for example, Thompson, *Motif-Index*, 6:5, 134, 427.

[28] Edmund Leach and D. Alan Aycock, *Structural Interpretations of Biblical Myth* (Cambridge: Cambridge University Press, 1983), p. 35.

[29] See, for example, Hasan el-Shamy, *Brother and Sister Type 872*: A Cognitive Behavioristic Analysis of a Middle Eastern Oikotype*, Folklore Monographs Series, vol. 8 (Bloomington, Indiana: Folklore Publications Group, 1979), and for the jealous brother, p. 36; Hasan el-Shamy, "The Brother-Sister Syndrome in Arab Family Life, Socio-Cultural Factors in Arab Psychiatry: A Critical Review," *International Journal of Sociology of the Family* 11 (1981): 313–323, especially p. 320.

[30] R. A. Nicholson, *A Literary History of the Arabs* (Cambridge: Cambridge University Press, 1969), pp. 126–127. Echoes of such relationships exist in modern literature as well, even Francophone. See, for example, Andrée Chedid, *Le sommeil délivré* (Paris: Flammarion, 1976); Tahar Ben Jelloun, *La nuit sacrée* (Paris: Editions du Seuil, 1987). Malek Chebel in *L'esprit de sérail: Perversions et marginalités sexuelles au Maghreb* (Paris: Lieu Commun, 1988), p. 127, recounts a popular song whose hero succeeds only in seducing his own sister. See, also, chapter 9 below.

juxtaposition of a male homosocial sibling couple with a weak heterosexual couple, in *Hayy ibn Yaqzân*, the rupture flows from the confrontation of a problematic heterosexual sibling couple (brother-sister) with a licit heterosexual one.

The casting of Hayy onto the water, while clearly a type of rebirth, also stresses his growth outside the normal familial and social structure, that *enfant sauvage* aspect of his story.[31] After all, he is left with no mother (and, of course, no father).[32] And the island on which he "lands" is uninhabited.

The birth account involving spontaneous generation is an even more radical rendering. Hayy develops not just outside society, as he does in the threatened birth account, but outside the biological chain of humanity, since no human agents are responsible for his conception. He is, indeed, "of no woman born."[33]

More interesting, however, is what the two birth accounts imply for the problem of biological maternity and the role of the mother. The threatened birth posits sex as a problem and a threat, in which the biological mother is a dangerous and negative force. The spontaneous generation account handles the problem in a much neater way: the mother figure is eliminated altogether. The net result of both accounts, however, is to dispense with the female of the species, to preclude her further appearance in the text.[34]

Why should the Hayy story, however, present the reader with two variants of the hero's birth? First and foremost, the presence of two accounts

[31] See Roger Shattuck, *The Forbidden Experiment: The Story of the Wild Boy of Aveyron* (New York: Farrar Straus Giroux, 1980).

[32] Hayy is, of course, completely fatherless. But, unlike the mother, the father never appears except as an element of Hayy's name. His absence is, therefore, nonproblematic. That is, for example, his behavior is not called into question, and no replacements are created for him. Hence, the elimination of fatherhood is not a problem in the text, as the elimination of motherhood is. For the father as a generally positive figure in the medieval Arabo-Islamic philosophico-mystical universe, see chapter 5 below.

[33] It is also possible to see the nonbiological birth as a chthonic origin, and the two variants as reflecting Lévi-Strauss's interpretation of the Oedipus myth, that is, the problem of human versus nonhuman origin, birth from one/birth from two. We are, however, dealing with two variants and not a single myth exploring this relationship (whose contours are, therefore, not fully present in the Hayy story). Nonetheless, such levels of meaning may be attached to earlier mythical sequences which thus appear in fragmentary form in Ibn Tufayl's work. Such elements of signification, however, in no way obviate the gender reading that fits the work as a whole. See Claude Lévi-Strauss, *Anthropologie structurale* (Paris: Librairie Plon, 1974), pp. 235–240.

[34] In all fairness, it should be noted that there are a few negative male figures as well in the text of *Hayy*, such as the brother who does not permit his sister to marry. But the negative males pale in the presence of the positive ones. By contrast, there are no positive human female characters. There was, after all, nothing to keep the narrator from including pious female figures, who certainly exist in the Arabic tradition.

introduces the principle of unresolved duality. The narrator seems reluctant to express openly a preference for one or the other of the two accounts. After explaining the conditions on the island where man can be born without father or mother, the text alerts the reader to the fact that he has only been told this because it is one of the things that "testifies to the correctness of what was mentioned concerning the possibility of man's being born in that spot without mother or father." The narrator continues by stating that some argue that Hayy was one of these individuals and others deny it.[35] It is at this point that the two birth accounts are presented. Some might want to see in this discussion a preference on the part of the narrator for spontaneous generation and an implicit rejection of one of the variants in favor of the other. After all, from a strictly logical point of view, the narrator has found in favor of the possibility of spontaneous generation and then labeled one variant as being the version of those who do not believe in spontaneous generation. But in a mythic account like *Hayy ibn Yaqzân*, much more than strict logic is involved. Given the work's fictional structure, the writer could easily have suppressed the biological variant had he so wished. Or he could have clearly expressed his preference for the nonbiological birth of the hero. Even the ordering of the arguments carefully maintains the full presence of the two variants, since the discussion of the possibility of spontaneous generation is followed not by this variant but by the biological one. In effect, by maintaining both variants, and refusing to draw the literary narrative conclusions of a carefully laid philosophical implication, the work shows its fundamental ambivalence and refusal to choose between the two birth accounts. Duality is a central, organizing force in the narrative of Ibn Tufayl.

And this original duality is one that the text never allows us to forget. When introducing the island from which Asâl comes, the text begins by mentioning that the island is "close to the island on which Hayy ibn Yaqzân was born according to one of the two different accounts" of his beginning.[36] Given that the reader is well acquainted with the two accounts, the invocation of their existence seems superfluous, serving only as a reminder that this is indeed a significant issue for the narrative.

Another echo occurs in the encounter between Hayy and Asâl. When Asâl asks Hayy how he came to the island, the latter informs him that he was not aware of "a beginning, nor a father or mother, other than the gazelle who brought him up."[37] This, of course, is an absolutely true statement of Hayy's knowledge of his own origin and by no means im-

---

[35] Ibn Tufayl, *Hayy*, p. 121.
[36] Ibid., p. 218.
[37] Ibid., p. 226.

plies a preference on the part of the narrator for spontaneous generation. Seen from Hayy's perspective, even the threatened birth would leave him with no awareness of "father or mother," since his own consciousness begins on the island after the abandonment.

The unresolved duality casts a shadow on the entire Tufaylian account. Its narrative ambivalence reflects psychological ambivalence. The mother is guilty or she is nonexistent. Sex is problematic or perhaps not necessary at all. As I shall have occasion to show, this unresolved duality forms a striking contrast with the tendency toward the resolution or concordance of opposing forces so characteristic of *Hayy ibn Yaqzân*.

The absent biological mother is replaced by the gazelle. The animal fulfills a maternal function, feeding and protecting the child. Later, the child and the gazelle take care of each other. When the gazelle dies, the young boy is greatly saddened. Nevertheless, the precocious Hayy proceeds to dissect her to discover the cause of her demise, and we understand this act as a furthering of his own scientific knowledge. But the decline, death, and dissection of the gazelle represent an important break in the narrator's description of the relationship between human child and animal nurturer. Hitherto, the gazelle was merely that, a gazelle. After these events, the animal becomes textually Hayy's "mother." Before her death, she was never so labeled. After her death, she is repeatedly referred to as "my mother," "his mother."[38]

An important key in deciphering this episode is clearly the gazelle's change of status. The text links the dissection to the establishment of motherhood, since this is the first time the word *mother* is used.[39] But there is more to this than meets the eye. The dissection on the part of the young boy expresses a mastery over the object being dissected, a female animal. In this sense, it is the opposite of motherhood, which normally implies dependence on the part of the child. It is as if the narrator could not acknowledge the gazelle as mother until she was clearly eliminated. And this elimination involves not only her death but her physical destruction by her metaphorical son.

That this physical parting with the gazelle is an extremely significant episode can be further documented by an examination of narrative voices in the text. The text of *Hayy ibn Yaqzân* comprises a prologue and an epilogue, with the story of Hayy embedded between the two. Hence, Hayy does not relate his own adventures, unlike protagonists of other

[38] See, for example, ibid., pp. 138–139, with their numerous instances of this phrasing.

[39] A causal connection is not given, however, since the text indicates that Hayy became aware that his mother was this physical body, not the other way around. Ibn Tufayl, *Hayy*, p. 138.

utopias, who generally recount their escapades in the first person.[40] The issue of Hayy's ability to speak is, indeed, a central one in the hero's encounter with Asâl. The narrator explains in detail the inability of Hayy to understand Asâl, a difficulty heightened by Asâl's being somewhat of a linguist. In fact, Asâl proves an excellent language teacher to the talented Hayy.[41]

How significant it then becomes to have Hayy himself speak in the first person, and this for the first time, when he is in the process of dissecting his mother. Twice he comments in the first person on the heart, as "what I am searching for."[42] Given that Hayy does not have the faculty of speech until later, his ability to express himself directly (rather than through the indirect speech of a third-person narrator) becomes that much more crucial. The faculty of speech, even that of an unarticulated internal monologue, represents an advanced stage in the development of individual consciousness. This deepening of individual consciousness seems purchased at the price of the death of the gazelle/mother. Clearly, the death and dissection are not mere learning experiences in the young man's path to eventual maturity. At the same time, the dissection of the mother/gazelle, prefigured by an earlier dismemberment of an eagle,[43] places it firmly within an animal world dominated by the human (dissection of humans was frowned upon in medieval Islam).[44]

After the dissection, the corpse begins to emit quite a stench, and Hayy is revulsed by it "and wished to not see it." Then he happens to observe two ravens fighting until one kills the other, at which point the winner proceeds to bury the dead loser. Hayy admires this action on the part of the raven, though he does say to himself that the raven was wrong to have killed its opponent. The burial serves as an example of what he should do for his "mother." Hayy then does as the winner did and buries his mother's corpse.[45]

One could argue that the fight between the ravens was placed in the text to introduce the subject of burial. This is certainly true on one level. But the burial could have been dealt with differently. For example, an animal could have died accidentally (by falling from a tree) and been buried by a solicitous mate or parent. In our text, the killing of one raven by

[40] See, for example, Defoe, *Robinson Crusoe*; Thomas More, *Utopia*, ed. and trans. H.V.S. Ogden (Arlington Heights, Ill.: Harlan Davidson, 1949).

[41] Ibn Tufayl, *Hayy*, pp. 223–226.

[42] Ibid., pp. 136–137.

[43] Ibid., p. 132.

[44] See, for example, Manfred Ullmann, *Islamic Medicine* (Edinburgh: Edinburgh University Press, 1978), p. 67.

[45] Ibn Tufayl, *Hayy*, p. 139.

another is effectively juxtaposed with the dissection of the gazelle by Hayy, since Hayy's mother must be buried like the dead raven.

It is certainly also no accident that the narrator refers to the victorious raven as *al-hayy*. It could be argued that he utilizes this formulation in opposition to *mayyit* (dead) in the preceding sentence, and since the episode is to illustrate a point about death and burial, what else is the reader to expect? But in the context of the Tufaylian narrative, in which *Hayy* is in the title of the work as well as being the name of the central character, such an appellation is heavily loaded. Had the narrator wished to eliminate the presence of any ambiguity in the juxtaposition of *Hayy* and *al-hayy*, he could have resorted to speaking of the two ravens as the winner and the loser, or the killer (*al-qâtil*) and the killed (*al-maqtûl*), to take but two examples. More important, the formula *al-hayy*, without linkage to a noun, as in *al-ghurâb al-hayy*, becomes a quasi-title, bringing *al-hayy* even closer to Hayy himself. Reading the text intertextually strengthens this image. This incident is clearly based on the Qur'ânic version of the Cain-and-Abel story. There, the victorious brother learns burial from the sight of a single raven.[46] The Andalusian text places Hayy in parallel with the Qur'ânic murderer. The episode with the ravens, like the gazelle's change of title, expresses a problematical relationship between mother and son. Of course, the two ravens are also a manifestation of the principle of duality. But theirs is an aggressive duality, in which one party triumphs over the other.

Duality is introduced again with the appearance of Asâl. Asâl was one of two young men, Salâmân being the other, who had grown up on an island close to that of Hayy. The two young men were in basic disagreement, Salâmân being attached to *zâhirî* (exoteric) interpretation and Asâl to *bâtinî* (esoteric). Salâmân liked society, whereas Asâl preferred solitude. Their essential differences led to their separation and to Asâl's departure for Hayy's island. The duality is one of unresolvable opposition.

But Asâl plays a much more important role in another duality, indeed the ultimate one in the narrative: that created by his relationship with Hayy. When the two accidentally encounter one another on the island, each looks at the other. Asâl is certain that Hayy had arrived (*wasala*) on the island to seek isolation from people, "as he himself had arrived (wasala) on it."[47] Asâl, thus, identifies his own desires with those of Hayy, setting up a type of identity with the other personage.

Hayy, on the other hand, does not initially recognize what Asâl represents, even fearing him at first, having never encountered the likes of him. Hayy even interprets Asâl's clothing as part of his skin. It is only after

[46] *Al-Qur'ân*, Sûrat al-Mâ'ida, verse 31.
[47] Ibn Tufayl, *Hayy*, p. 221.

observing Asâl that Hayy, according to the narrator, "saw him in his image." He then comprehends Asâl's clothing as "like his own clothing."[48] In effect, identity is balanced with complementarity. Hayy initially thinks Asâl is different and quickly discovers he is the same. Asâl initially thinks that Hayy is the same and then discovers his difference.

This identification process presages their later involvement. Each is the alter ego of the other. After an abortive attempt to change the ways of the inhabitants on Salâmân's island, Hayy and Asâl return to their own island, to continue their isolated way of life.

Another crucial parallel in the Tufaylian narrative brings Hayy and Asâl together: the idea of the voyage. The voyage is an important structural component of a utopia, normally permitting a clear break with what comes before. It may serve to isolate the ideal society from the one implicitly under attack. For similar reasons, the voyage also often proves an important part of dystopias as well.[49]

Both Hayy and Asâl have voyages of departure as they do of return. In one version, Hayy's arrival on the island was provoked by his being cast on the water by his mother. And this represents his first voyage of sorts, permitting him to arrive on the uninhabited island, with a clear break from his past and the society that gave him birth. Asâl arrives at the island on a ship, whose sailors drop him off on the shore. Hence, each arrives on this island, which but for the two of them, remains unsullied by other humans. The narrator makes a point of informing the reader that the sailors on Asâl's ship left him onshore, implying that they themselves did not set foot on the land.[50]

The second voyage is effected by Asâl and Hayy together to the island of Asâl's birth. When the two decide to go to this island, they hang about the shore, hoping for some way to cross the water. It is only when a ship loses its way and is driven by chance to the shore of their island that Hayy and Asâl are able to get passage to the latter's original home.[51] After their abortive attempt to lead Salâmân and his people, the two return to Hayy's island. The narrator in this instance does not elaborate on how this took place, stating simply that God enabled them to make the crossing.[52] Hayy's island is not a place that one enters or leaves by normal means but is cut off from the world, like other utopias.

On none of the voyages or contacts with ships or sailors do other individuals set foot within the utopian territory. It remains a sacred space,

[48] Ibid., pp. 221–222.

[49] See, for example, the medical dystopia by Léon Daudet, *Les morticoles* (Paris: Bernard Grasset, 1956).

[50] Ibn Tufayl, *Hayy*, p. 220.

[51] Ibid., p. 230.

[52] Ibid., p. 234.

reserved for Hayy and Asâl. And the sea voyages represent clear breaks from one way of life into another, the water acting as both physical and spiritual boundary.

The absence of any specific description in the last return to the island highlights, in its own way, the isolative and asocial nature of Hayy's and Asâl's way of life. It is as if their seclusion from society and individual humans began with the decision to return to Hayy's island. And this return is not only a reentry into the utopian territory but also a commentary on prophecy. When Asâl first arrives on Hayy's island and describes the religion of his own island, he is called "a prophet."[53] But it is in fact Hayy whose path is closer to that of the prophets whose unsuccessful missions the *Qur'ân* repeatedly recounts. Traditionally, these prophets attempt to transmit their message of salvation, but they are ignored and their words go unheeded. This is closer to Hayy's misadventures on Salâmân's island. He is the one who wishes to guide its inhabitants on the right path but is, of course, unsuccessful. And thus it is that he and Asâl return to their isolated environment.

The asocial character of the Tufaylian utopia stands out even more sharply when compared with *al-Risâla al-Kâmiliyya fî al-Sîra al-Naba-wiyya* of Ibn al-Nafîs (d. 687/1288). The thirteenth-century Egyptian physician, like Ibn Tufayl, organized his argument around the life of a solitary autodidact. But unlike his Andalusian colleague, Ibn al-Nafîs integrates his hero into Islamic society, making the defense of existing Islamic institutions one of his principal aims.[54]

On a structural level, Ibn Tufayl's *Hayy ibn Yaqzân* portrays the resolution, but not the elimination or fusion, of potentially conflictual dualities. The text moves from opposite and irreconcilable duality to complementary and harmonious duality. Clearly, Ibn Tufayl's principal philosophical burden is the reconciliation of apparently contrary positions: natural reason versus revelation, philosophical knowledge versus mysticism. This process is personified, though not directly paralleled, in the relationship of Hayy and Asâl, who combine identity and complementarity. Their personal, essentially utopian harmony reflects ultimate intellectual compatibility, the resolution of duality on both the religio-philosophical and the personal levels.

But this harmony was not arrived at either easily or, and what is more important, without cost. Hayy's life, and hence the story as a whole, began doubly under the sign of unresolved duality. On a narrative level, it

---

[53] Ibid., p. 227.

[54] Ibn al-Nafîs, *The Theologus Autodidactus of Ibn al-Nafîs*, edited with an introduction, partial translation, and notes by Max Meyerhof and Joseph Schacht (Oxford: The Clarendon Press, 1968); Muhsin Mahdi, "Remarks on the *Theologus Autodidactus* of Ibn al-Nafîs," *Studia Islamica* 31 (1970): 197–209.

is marked by the uncertainty of incompatible variants. Socially, one of the two birth accounts is triggered by the unhappy pair of brother and sister, who cannot resolve their identity and opposition of being at once siblings and of opposite sexes. Hayy's infant existence is threatened by the problematic couple. As we have seen, neither of the two mother-child relations is free of problems; and the end of the second leads directly into the episode of the two ravens, an aggressive opposition that produces the death of one of the parties. Hayy's idealized duality with Asâl is preceded textually by the unresolved duality of Asâl and Salâmân, which provides an excellent contrast to the bliss that will follow.

The story begins, thus, with a problematic male-female sibling relationship and ends with a male pair, free of problems. Along the way, the narrator presents other possible dualities, but none except the male pair provides the ideal solution.

The text of *Hayy* is framed within a prologue and an epilogue in which the narrator addresses a metaphorical "brother."[55] Need it be noted that the relationship between narrator and reader is a nonconflictual one (from a literary point of view, there is nothing inevitable about this), and that it embraces the entire text? This is certainly not unheard of in Islamic literature. Al-Ghazâlî's spiritual autobiography, *al-Munqidh min al-Dalâl*, for example, begins with the narrator addressing his "brother in religion."[56] But there is certainly nothing obligatory about such a procedure either.

In Ibn Tufayl, this two-brother relationship is no accident. One can argue that it (as in al-Ghazâlî, we might add) represents an ideal Islamic social relationship, but here expressed in essentially religious terms. Clearly, the male couple is one of the ways of conceiving the ideal society in an Islamic context. Islamic society favors homosocial (distinct from homosexual) relations.[57] And this is where Ibn Tufayl's male utopia comes in. Though limited, it is a society of men and hence, by implication, of fellowship. If absolute solitude had been deemed necessary to the contemplative life, the narrator could easily have left Hayy and Asâl separately content on different islands.

For such an ideal world to be a world without women is certainly not unusual in literature, as Judith Fetterley has shown in her studies of Amer-

[55] Ibn Tufayl, *Hayy*, pp. 106, 236.

[56] Al-Ghazâlî, *al-Munqidh min al-Dalâl*, ed. ʿAbd al-Halîm Mahmûd (Cairo: Dâr al-Kutub al-Hadîtha, 1965), p. 62. For the translation of this text, see W. Montgomery Watt, *The Faith and Practice of al-Ghazâlî* (Chicago: Kazi Publications, 1982), pp. 19–85. As is clear from many of the studies in Conrad's volume, *The World*, a close relationship on more than this level exists between *al-Munqidh* of al-Ghazâlî and Ibn Tufayl's allegory.

[57] See chapter 1 above. See, also, Sedgwick, *Between Men*.

ican fiction.[58] But a utopia without women is more difficult to imagine. Women there are aplenty in Thomas More's text.[59] Even more interesting in this context is that a militant feminist utopia like *Les guerillères* of Monique Wittig includes men.[60] Nevertheless, many feminist utopias exclude men. But this is obviously less of a problem than its converse. Parthenogenesis, as in Charlotte Perkins Gilman's *Herland*,[61] is biologically plausible and male insemination is far briefer than pregnancy.[62] Such ideas were not foreign to the medieval Arab imagination either, as we shall see in the following chapter. In some versions, Ibn Tufayl himself notes the presence on the island of al-Waqwâq of trees that bear women as fruit.[63] In either case, this suggestion is never developed and Hayy never meets up with these vegetatively propagated females. Once again, Ibn Tufayl has eliminated the female with sexuality.

The reasonably positive image of the gazelle, when contrasted with the negative image of the biological mother, might make us think that the issue here is not so much procreation as it is nurturing. But the two birth accounts clearly dispel this. Both biological processes—procreation and nurturing—normally associated with the female, are problematic in Ibn Tufayl's text, and both create dilemmas that must be resolved.[64]

It is perhaps the radical elimination of sexuality and of the female of the species that is so distinctive in Ibn Tufayl's vision. The absence of the female is essential to the utopian, harmonious elements of Hayy's and Asâl's perfect society. Theirs is a world without sexuality, like a monastery in the desert. Sexuality is quite problematic. Hayy, as part of his

[58] Judith Fetterley, *The Resisting Reader: A Feminist Approach to American Fiction* (Bloomington: Indiana University Press, 1978), p. 19.

[59] See, for example, More, *Utopia*, pp. 33, 34, 40, 46, 59, 75, 78. On the role of women in men's utopias, see Elaine Hoffman Baruch, "Women in Men's Utopias," in *Women in Search of Utopia: Mavericks and Mythmakers*, ed. Ruby Rohrlich and Elaine Hoffman Baruch (New York: Schocken Books, 1984), pp. 209–218.

[60] See, for example, Monique Wittig, *Les guerillères* (Paris: Les Editions de Minuit, 1969), pp. 178, 197, 203, 204. See, also, Katharine Burdekin, *The End of This Day's Business* (New York: The Feminist Press, 1989).

[61] Charlotte Perkins Gilman, *Herland* (New York: Pantheon Books, 1979), especially p. 45.

[62] For the problem of fatherhood versus motherhood in feminist utopias, see Susan H. Lees, "Motherhood in Feminist Utopias," in Rohrlich and Baruch, *Women in Search*, pp. 219–232.

[63] Ibn Tufayl, *Hayy*, p. 117. Gauthier chose not to include these phrases, missing from some of the manuscripts. See Ibn Tufayl, *Hayy ibn Yaqzân*, ed. Léon Gauthier (Beirut: Imprimerie Catholique, 1936). Published as Léon Gauthier, *Hayy ben Yaqdhân, roman philosophique d'Ibn Thofaïl*, texte arabe et traduction française, p. 20.

[64] For an interesting comparison of the maternal as the nurturing versus the procreative, see Bynum, *Jesus as Mother*, pp. 110–169. The chapter is quite important and raises many questions that would be worth investigating in an Islamic context.

learning experience, becomes aware of the sexual needs of the human animal, which are placed in the same category as the other physical needs, such as shelter, food, or drink.[65] But the ascetic life-style precludes sexuality, and Lutz Richter-Bernburg may be correct in his assertion that the ascetic "regimen is also meant to subdue his [Hayy's] sexuality."[66] Sexuality and motherhood are presented in negative terms. The two birth accounts make this abundantly clear: the first, positively, through the problem couple; the second, through spontaneous generation, which is nothing more than the dream of life without sexuality and without motherhood. Imagery in this matter is consistent: when the narrator speaks of the conflict between this world and the next, he likens it to the dilemma of a man with two wives. He who pleases one angers the other.[67] Such a metaphorical use of marriage is, of course, a far cry from certain Christian images like that of the Church as the bride of Christ.[68] Nor does Ibn Tufayl base his mystical explanations on the familiar, erotically inspired vocabulary of Lover and Beloved.

Ibn Tufayl's utopia is one of reason (as opposed to one of conditioning), in that its members accede to it through the development of their own reason, not through their conditioning or education. By the same token, his perfect world demands separation from society and the female. It is a one-time male utopia, an ideal world that cannot be re-created.

The unusually strict, virtually monastic character of Ibn Tufayl's utopia is startling in an Islamic setting. Unlike Christianity, Islam never enjoined celibacy (as we saw with Kursuf).[69] The Andalusian physician's positions apparently reflect some of that Greek, especially Platonic, influence so important in many branches of medieval Islamic philosophy. But if Ibn Tufayl's *Hayy ibn Yaqzân* functions as a kind of extreme case, it nevertheless casts into sharper relief values shared by other medieval writers in the Arabic language.

[65] Ibn Tufayl, *Hayy*, pp. 184, 190.

[66] See Lutz Richter-Bernburg, "Towards an Anatomy of Ibn Tufayl's Medicine," in Conrad, *The World*. Franz Rosenthal has also noted the tendency of *Hayy ibn Yaqzân* to create a world without sexuality. Franz Rosenthal, "Sources for the Role of Sex in Medieval Muslim Society," in Marsot, *Society and the Sexes*, p. 8.

[67] Ibn Tufayl, *Hayy*, p. 215.

[68] See, for example, Brown, *The Body*, p. 57.

[69] See chapter 2 above.

CHAPTER 5

Sexual Geography, Asexual Philosophy

IBN TUFAYL'S idealized male couple spent their days in asexual mystical contemplation on the island of al-Waqwâq, an island that could conceivably create an individual without biological intervention. But this was also the island whose trees bore women as fruit.[1] Thus, though the Andalusian philosopher was able through his male utopian vision to cast aside the female, it would seem that woman's body was a permanent fixture of the world in which he set his tale. But why select al-Waqwâq at all? The choice manifests a tension between a philosophical ideal of a society devoid of sexuality and a geographical locus imbued with that very sexuality the philosophical ideal is fleeing. Sexual geography and asexual philosophy are two poles that Ibn Tufayl brings together. Nevertheless, the asexual philosophical and the sexual geographical visions have a point in common: they both create alternative societies in which gender plays a crucial role. Philosophical texts that are literary cousins of Ibn Tufayl's *Hayy ibn Yaqzân* present a male world in which the female is occulted or eliminated. Descriptions of islands whose trees bear women, islands of women, and even cities of women fuse the fantastic and the sexual.

The island of al-Waqwâq takes pride of place in the medieval Muslim geographical imagination. Although Ibn Tufayl's text identifies it as one of the Indian islands under the equator,[2] the only real certainty about its location is precisely its uncertainty. References to islands of al-Waqwâq seem to denote Japan as easily as Madagascar and have been used as evidence for the proposition that East Asia and South Africa are connected in the medieval Islamic geographical imagination.[3] Even the name is subject to change, appearing variously as al-Waqwâq, Wâq al-Wâq, al-Wâq Wâq, or Wâq Wâq. In order to avoid confusion, I will use the version of Ibn Tufayl, al-Waqwâq, whatever the spelling of the source in question.

---

[1] Ibn Tufayl, *Hayy*, p. 117.

[2] Ibid.

[3] See, for example, R. Hartmann and D. M. Dunlop, "Bahr al-Hind," *EI²*. See, also, André Miquel, *La géographie humaine du monde musulman jusqu'au milieu du 11ᵉ siècle* (Paris: Mouton, 1967–1975), 1:119 n. 2; 2:20–21, 80; and 2:79 for an excellent map showing the geographical span of al-Waqwâq; Marina Tolmacheva, "The African Wâq-Wâq: Some Questions Regarding the Evidence," *Fontes Historiae Africanae: Bulletin d'information*, Nos. 11/12 (1987/1988): 9–15.

Whatever the precise location of these islands, it is evident that they partake of fantasy and, more important, of sexual fantasy. A serious compiler, Yâqût (d. 626/1229), in his famous geographical dictionary, the *Mu'jam al-Buldân*, considers al-Waqwâq part of the world of fables or superstitions (*khurâfât*).[4] The islands appear in sailors' accounts, and, as André Miquel points out in his masterful and unparalleled work on the human geography of the medieval Muslim world, these stories are part of the realm of the fabulous as it touches on the sea and of the dreams this latter evokes.[5] Miquel also wisely recognizes that it is futile to try to pinpoint a precise al-Waqwâq; rather, one should simply understand it for what it is: "gigantic, far off, and half fabulous."[6] A tenth-century Arabic work on the wonders of India, in which al-Waqwâq plays a significant role, is littered with various sexual couplings, of which men and fish is perhaps the most fascinating, since it creates a sort of alternative creature (and society).[7] Places where humans perform the sexual act like beasts lie side by side with places of sexual abstinence.[8] Al-Waqwâq was also a locus of ambivalent sexuality containing an animal like a rabbit whose sex changed back and forth from male to female.[9]

Al-Waqwâq tickled the fancy of almost every medieval author whose work touched on the geographical or on that area of fantasy and marvel, the *'ajâ'ib*, normally rendered as "wonders."[10] The category of al-waqwâq even entered the medieval bestiaries and other works on animals. Al-Jâhiz, in his *Book of Animals*, describes it as a "wondrous creature," and al-waqwâq is mentioned in al-Damîrî's (d. 808/1405) book on animals as the equivalent of the *sa'lât*, a cross between a plant and an animal.[11] This is certainly a good beginning for the trees that bring forth women.

---

[4] Yâqût, *Mu'jam*, 5:381.

[5] Miquel, *Géographie humaine*, 1:127.

[6] Ibid., 2:511. In a contemporary short story, Daisy al-Amîr uses Wâq Wâq as a fictional locus without assigning it any other content. Daisy al-Amîr, "Matâr Wâq Wâq," in Daisy al-Amîr, *'Alâ Lâ'ihat al-Intizâr* (Baghdad: Bayt Sîn lil-Kutub, 1990), pp. 64–71.

[7] *'Ajâ'ib al-Hind*, attributed to Buzurk ibn Shahriyâr, ed. Yûsuf al-Shârûnî (London: Riyâd al-Rayyis lil-Kutub wal-Nashr, 1990), p. 64. This work has been translated by L. Marcel Devic as *Les merveilles de l'Inde* (Paris: Alphonse Lemerre, 1878).

[8] Al-Maqdisî, *al-Bad' wal-Ta'rîkh* (Beirut: Maktabat Khayyât, n.d.), 4:96; al-Qazwînî, *Mufîd al-'Ulûm wa-Mubîd al-Humûm*, ed. Muhammad 'Abd al-Qâdir 'Atâ (Beirut: Dâr al-Kutub al-'Ilmiyya, 1985), p. 414.

[9] *'Ajâ'ib al-Hind*, p. 140.

[10] See Mohamed Arkoun, Jacques Le Goff, Tawfiq Fahd, and Maxime Rodinson, *L'étrange et le merveilleux dans l'Islam médiéval* (Paris: Editions J.A., 1978). Roy Mottahedeh is presently completing a work on *'ajâ'ib* tentatively entitled *The Strange and the Marvelous in Medieval Islamic Thought*.

[11] Al-Jâhiz, *Hayawân*, 7:390 (in index); al-Damîrî, *Hayât al-Hayawân al-Kubrâ* (Beirut: Dâr Ihyâ' al-Turâth al-'Arabî, n.d.), 1:20–23, 2:390. Cf. al-Qazwînî, *'Ajâ'ib al-Makh-*

Whether the name of a "wondrous creature," a tree, an island, a complex of islands, or even a country, al-Waqwâq always insists on that aspect of its referent which is the corporal, ultimately leading to the sexual. When discussing India, al-Maqdisî (fl. 375/985) mentions the waqwâq tree whose fruit has the form of human faces.[12] Al-Qazwînî (d. 582/1283), that great collector of wonders, also notes the existence of this tree in India and adds that one can hear human voices emanating from it. He, however, leaves it unnamed.[13]

The medieval authors emphasize that the locus of al-Waqwâq is quite literally a gold mine and that its inhabitants use this metal for the chains of their dogs and the collars of their monkeys. People even sell shirts woven with gold.[14] Ebony also flourishes in that location.[15] Al-Waqwâq is a land of riches.

It is rich also in femaleness. Let us not forget that, as with virtually all the medieval texts, the narrators, the generators of the discourse, are male. And it is as males that they project their fantasies on places like al-Waqwâq, and on the exclusively female societies, like the islands and cities of women.

Al-Waqwâq as a complex of islands numbering more than a thousand receives one of its fullest treatments in the book of wonders by Ibn al-Wardî (d. 861/1457). The queen of these islands is a woman named Damhara who wears clothing woven with gold. She also has sandals of gold. No one walks on these islands with sandals other than herself, and if someone should presume to wear sandals, she cuts off his feet. This queen rides among her servants and armies on an elephant, with flags, drums, trumpets, and beautiful slave girls. Her abode is an island named Unbûba, whose inhabitants are clever in various crafts: weaving shirts in one piece, manufacturing large ships from small pieces of wood, and making houses of wood that can move on water.

'Isâ ibn al-Mubârak al-Sîrâfî, Ibn al-Wardî's narrator, recounts that he came to see this queen and found her naked on a bed of gold and with a crown of gold on her head. In front of her were four thousand ladies-in-waiting, virginal and beautiful. They were Zoroastrians and left their

---

lûqât wa-Gharâ'ib al-Mawjûdât, ed. Fârûq Sa'd (Beirut: Dâr al-Afâq al-Jadîda, 1981), p. 392.

[12] Al-Maqdisî, al-Bad', 4:94.

[13] Al-Qazwînî, Mufîd, p. 415.

[14] Ibn Khurradâdhbih, al-Masâlik wal-Mamâlik, ed. M. J. De Goeje, Bibliotheca Geographorum Arabicorum (Leiden: E. J. Brill, 1889), pp. 69, 70; al-Qazwînî, Athâr al-Bilâd wa-Akhbâr al-'Ibâd (Beirut: Dâr Sâdir, 1960), p. 33; al-Idrîsî, Nuzhat al-Mushtâq fî Ikhtirâq al-Afâq (Beirut: 'Alam al-Kutub, 1989), 1:92; al-Qazwînî, 'Ajâ'ib, pp. 154–155; Ibn al-Wardî, Kharîdat al-'Ajâ'ib wa-Farîdat al-Gharâ'ib (Cairo: Mustafâ al-Bâbî al-Halabî, n.d.), p. 104.

[15] Ibn Khurradâdhbih, al-Masâlik, p. 70.

heads uncovered. The ladies had combs of ivory and pearl. He concludes his account with some comments on the economic policies of this queen.

Ibn al-Wardî's narrative continues with a description of the women-bearing trees. On this island, he says, there are trees that bear "fruit like women, with shapes, bodies, eyes, hands, feet, hair, breasts, and vulvas like the vulvas of women. They are the most beautiful of face and hang by their hair. They come out of cases like big swords and when they feel the wind and sun, they yell, 'Wâq Wâq,' until their hair tears apart." When their hair tears, they die. The people of this island understand this sound and see it as an ill omen.[16]

The reader is told that he who goes beyond these women-trees will fall on women that also come out of trees but are greater than the earlier women in build, with longer hair and more perfect qualities. Their posteriors and vulvas are more beautiful, and the women have a good perfumed smell. When one of these women's hair gets torn, she falls from the tree and lives a day or part of a day. He who has cut her or has attended her cutting can have sexual intercourse with her. He will find a great pleasure in her, not to be found in normal women. The land of these women is the best of lands, with most of it scented. It also has rivers whose water is sweeter than honey and melted sugar. There are no inhabitants (other than the women) save for the elephants, with an elephant sometimes reaching eleven cubits. Many birds are there as well. No one knows what is beyond this island but God. A great torrential stream flows like tar from some of these islands to the sea, burning the fish, which then float on the water.[17]

Ibn al-Wardî's presentation of the island complex of al-Waqwâq is fascinating indeed: unusually rich in a detail suggesting precise knowledge. It highlights not only the fabulous aspects of the locality but also its phantasmagoric facets, centering on sexuality, woman's body, and woman's voice.

In this account, the queen of the locale is named: Damhara. The fact

---

[16] In a note to his translation of the *Nights* (8:60), Burton provides a naturalistic explanation linking the women-fruit to the calabash. There is obviously more to this fantasy than vegetable misidentification. The *'Ajâ'ib al-Hind* (pp. 80–81) cites a story that functions as a "reasonable" analogue of Ibn al-Wardî's. In al-Waqwâq, one finds trees whose fruit resemble squash, but also the human form. When the wind blows, the fruit make a noise. A sailor, the narrator adds, fell in love with one such form and cut it off the tree. However, the air was expelled from it, leaving him with something resembling "a dead crow" (*kalghurâb al-mayyit*)—strikingly enough, the same words used in Ibn Tufayl. In a chapter of al-Muwaylihî's *Hadîth 'Isâ ibn Hishâm*, later removed from the text, there is a slightly transformed citation of this passage as part of an attack on traditional Arab geography. See Muhammad al-Muwaylihî, *Hadîth 'Isâ ibn Hishâm* (Cairo: Matba'at al-Ma'ârif, 1907), p. 157. I am grateful to Roger Allen for this information.

[17] Ibn al-Wardî, *Kharîda*, pp. 104–105.

that she is the only one who wears sandals creates a type of personality cult around her.[18] Her amputation of transgressors' feet functions as a symbolic castration. Even the name of her island abode is significant: Unbûba, meaning "tube" or "pipe." The tension between the male/phallic and the female has been posited.

More interesting is the male narrator and authority for the description of this female ruler. 'Isâ ibn al-Mubârak al-Sîrâfî in Ibn al-Wardî is Mûsâ ibn al-Mubârak al-Sîrâfî in variants of this same story: a seemingly historical individual and a male.[19] What could be more provocative for a Muslim male narrator than a naked female ruler? As though this were not enough, this naked queen is surrounded by four thousand virginal ladies-in-waiting. In one version, they are naked as well; in another, simply bareheaded, a milder form of immodesty and erotic provocation.[20] How does 'Isâ/Mûsâ discover that he is in virginal company? On what basis does he make this judgment? Does he have a conversation with the queen? The reader is privy only to the information, not to how it was received by the narrator. Woman's voice is occulted; her body is not.

Body and voice have different dynamics in the portrayal of the women-fruit, which directly follows the description of the queen. One might initially wish to interpret this story as being about some kind of genesis—let us call it dendrogenesis. After all, the women emerge out of cases, or pods, like swords, as the text puts it—phallic imagery indeed. Add this to the idea of the tree, and one comes again under the sign of the phallus. An ambivalent sexuality is created.

But once the propagation is complete, once the women have emanated from the trees, more important issues come to the fore. The description of the women-fruit emphasizes their sexuality: their vulvas are "like the vulvas of women." None of the other body parts, not even the hair and breasts, are explicitly linked to the equivalent body parts of women. The narrator needs to reaffirm the female sexuality of these beings.

The imagery of the women-fruit is not innocent: women hanging by their hair, who, when they feel the wind and sun, yell, "Wâq Wâq," until their hair tears, bringing about their death. The link is made: woman's voice causes her demise. There is no biological or physiological reason for the hair to break when the sound is made. What permits the fantastic construction to function is its access to deeper civilizational mental structures. Woman's hair (that should not be uncovered) and woman's voice

---

[18] Cf. H. M. Zaki, "Utopia and Ideology in *Daughters of a Coral Dawn* and Contemporary Feminist Utopias," special issue on "Feminism Faces the Fantastic," *Women's Studies* 14, no. 2 (1987): 126, who discusses the fact that in one particular feminist utopia, the leader alone is permitted to wear certain colors.

[19] See, for example, al-Qazwînî, *Athâr*, p. 33; al-Qazwînî, *'Ajâ'ib*, p. 154.

[20] Ibn al-Wardî, *Kharîda*, pp. 104–105; al-Qazwînî, *Athâr*, p. 33.

(that should not be heard) come together under the heading of ʿawra, a notion embodying shame and imperfection, whose perimeters ultimately encompass the entirety of woman's body.[21] The hair, a point of erotic fascination in a society where modesty entails head covering, becomes the link between the human and the vegetal.

That woman's voice has negative reverberations is reinforced by its being considered an ill omen by the inhabitants of the island. This pessimistic interpretation of the sound uttered by these women-fruit prior to their destruction is not unique to Ibn al-Wardî but is to be found in, for example, al-Qazwînî.[22] A third author, Shaykh al-Rabwa al-Dimashqî (d. 727/1327), in his depiction of the islands of al-Waqwâq, describes the tree that bears a fruit in the image of a "human," leaving it non–gender specific. The sound emanating from this fruit is also subject to interpretation, but this time in a much more ambivalent fashion. On the one hand it is a good omen, but on the other it functions as a reprimand.[23] It would seem that gender neutralizing the human fruit alters the negative nature of its sound.

Ibn al-Wardî divides his women-fruit into two groups, the second of which far surpasses the first in sexuality and physicality. Only the vulvas of the first group were singled out. This differentiated body part is overshadowed in the second by bigger posteriors as well as larger vulvas. Both vaginal and anal intercourse are being alluded to here.[24] The hair, a pivotal element for both species of women-fruit, is longer in the case of the second group.

That it is the sexuality of the woman-fruit which is under scrutiny becomes clearer if the actual text is examined more closely. The narrator, in his depiction of the second variety, plays games with the pronouns in extremely suggestive ways. The description begins with the feminine plural, a generalized and global portrayal of the women-fruit. But as soon as the shift is made to the torn hair and the fall from the tree, the pronoun shifts as well, to the feminine singular. The return to the plural comes about with the description of "their land" and its qualities. The torn hair, the fall from the tree, the brief survival, the sexual intercourse and its unique pleasure: all these elements are grammatically in the feminine singular. The account has been personalized at a critical moment: when the woman-fruit is transformed into the object of the sexual act. The carnal

---

[21] For a more in-depth discussion of this term, see chapter 6 below.

[22] Al-Qazwînî, Athâr, p. 33; al-Qazwînî, ʿAjâʾib, pp. 154–155.

[23] Shaykh al-Rabwa al-Dimashqî, Nukhbat al-Dahr fî ʿAjâʾib al-Barr wal-Bahr, ed. A. Mehren (Leipzig: Otto Harrassowitz, 1923), p. 149.

[24] It is true that the buttocks were an element of female beauty, but other celebrated parts of woman's anatomy are not similarly highlighted. Cf. Salâh al-Dîn al-Munajjid, Jamâl al-Marʾa ʿind al-Arab (Beirut: Dâr al-Kitâb al-Jadîd, 1969).

act with this woman-fruit is further singularized when it is opposed to that with "normal" women.

The woman-fruit, the catalyst of this brief sexual interlude, is the ultimate disposable woman. Fresh from the tree, she lives but a short time, during which the male can achieve with her a pleasure unlike the one he experiences with the female of his own species. A self-destructing female, this object of male desire does not even need to be eliminated as were the former virgins in Shâhriyâr's literary world. But the dynamics of the male-female sexual experience in the two instances are similar: both the Waqwâqian creature and her literary cousin, the virgin of *The Thousand and One Nights*, come to a physical end after their one-time fling with the male.

It might be tempting to interpret the women-fruit that fall from the tree and die as an unconscious and indirect commentary on the Adam-and-Eve story. Eve, the woman who plucks the forbidden fruit and partakes of it with Adam, becomes, in this version, a fruit that dies, but not before it can be partaken of by the male. In a Christian setting, a notion of punishment would be plausible. But the dynamics of the Islamic Adam-and-Eve story differ, and, as we saw earlier, Eve is not generally held solely responsible for that fatal transgression.[25]

There is a sense, however, in which the entire Waqwâqian environment has resonances that make of it an earthly counterpart to the Muslim Paradise. The sexual and the liquid aspects of the Qur'ânic Garden are echoed in the description of the islands. The rivers whose water is sweeter than honey and melted sugar suggest the rivers of honey in the Qur'ânic Paradise, just as the women-fruit whose sexual enjoyment surpasses that with normal women irresistibly evoke the ever-virginal black-eyed *hûrîs*, or maidens. The language of the famous Qur'ânic commentary of al-Tabarî confirms this parallel.[26]

But this locus is far from completely positive. Its rivers may be suggestive, but the salutary aspects of their waters are opposed to a much more powerful liquid. This is the tarlike torrent that kills the fish in the ocean. Whatever sexual phantasms al-Waqwâq may have elicited, its description ends on a negative, destructive note.

This island complex is also, literally, a no-man's-land. But the women-fruit, the ultimate self-destructing females, who populate al-Waqwâq are

---

[25] See chapter 3 above. For the Adam-and-Eve story, see, for example, al-Thaʿâlibî, *Qisas al-Anbiyâ'* (Beirut: Dâr al-Qalam, n.d.), pp. 24–49.

[26] Al-Tabarî, *Jâmiʿ al-Bayân ʿan Ta'wîl al-Qur'ân* (Cairo: Mustafâ al-Bâbî al-Halabî, 1968), 30:320–325. For a different way in which these Qur'ânic images can be exploited, see Suzanne Pinckney Stetkevych, "Intoxication and Immortality: Wine and Associated Imagery in al-Maʿarrî's Garden," in *Critical Pilgrimages: Studies in the Arabic Literary Tradition*, ed. Fedwa Malti-Douglas, *Literature East and West 25* (1989): 29–48.

but one pole in the medieval Muslim sexual geographical imagination. They show the male in control. What happens if woman is in control? The Island of Women described in the work on the wonders of India encapsules such a vision. Sailors land on this island and are surrounded by innumerable women. The females proceed to fall on the men, a thousand or more to each male. They drag the men to the mountains and take physical advantage of them. The women then fight among themselves for the men, who end up with the strongest females. One by one, the men die of exhaustion, a turn of events that does not appease the women's sexual appetites—on the contrary. The lone survivor is a man carried off by a woman who takes care of him. The two of them eventually leave the island together, the woman converting to Islam. It is she who then explains the peculiar circumstances of this island. This convert is, thus, the only female narrator in this whole literature.

The women originally hailed from a country of fire worshipers. There, the females would give birth alternately first to one male and then to two females. This led to the women's outnumbering the men and wishing to dominate them. So the men threw the women on this island, declaring to the fire deity that they belonged to him and that they, that is, the men, no longer had any power over them. The women, having been left on this island, began to die off. The arrival of the sailors was the first they had seen of men since their enforced isolation began.[27]

This society of women is, in a sense, artificial, its members having been cast off by the men of the original land. Nevertheless, its existence is telling. Men are chased and physically exploited by women whose carnal appetite seems to know no bounds. The power of this sexual act is such that it kills the male partners. The petite mort has become a true death. Women's body is a locus of danger, if not an instrument of death.

But the Island of Women does not merely exploit the idea of woman as insatiable sex machine. The Muslim imagination here focuses also on woman as procreative tool. The perceived imbalance in alternately bringing forth one male and two females leads to the biological depletion of the masculine. It would seem at the outset that woman's desire for power (over the male) is a natural corollary.

This particular Island of Women, despite the sexual violence of its inhabitants, operates on the notion that biology is central and that copulation between the two sexes is what propagates the species. After all, the woman who escapes with the sailor of her choice notes that prior to the arrival of his colleagues and the sexual orgy, the women were dying off one after another. One could easily assume that were it not for the sailors,

[27] 'Ajā'ib al-Hind, pp. 57–62.

the female species on that island would have become extinct.[28] This is biological poetic justice, since it was women's initial numerical force that led to their desire for domination. But what happens to the males who effected this drastic change? They must have sealed their own extinction.

Perhaps the ideal state is embodied in what Shaykh al-Rabwa al-Dimashqî describes, the Armiyânûs Island for Men and the Armiyânûs Island for Women. Only men live on the first, and only women on the second. Every year in the spring the two groups gather for two months and have sexual intercourse. Then they leave one another. These two islands are, according to this text, very difficult of access: abundant clouds, a dark sea, and big waves get in the traveler's way. Besides, our authority is quick to add, these wonders, dispersed in remote regions, are only to be seen accidentally.[29]

These two parallel locations are at once independent and interrelated. The two sexes live in isolation one from the other, but the physical need for sexual intercourse is ever present. Although the sexuality here is far from the violent one operating in the Island of Women, the gender dynamics are not all that dissimilar. Physical union is important for the upkeep of the sexual and social order. It would seem that true gender equality can be achieved, but only with the maintenance of two distinct societies.

Similar, but more provocative, heterosexual dynamics operate in the City of Women. According to al-Qazwînî, this is a big, wide city on an island in the Sea of the Maghrib. It owes its description to a certain al-Tartûshî. The inhabitants of this city are women, over whom no men rule. They ride horses and make war by themselves, displaying great strength and fortitude when they meet. They have male slaves, each of whom visits his lady at night and spends the entire night with her. He awakens at dawn and leaves under cover when the sun appears. If one of the women gives birth to a male, she kills him on the spot; whereas if she gives birth to a female, she lets the baby live. According to al-Tartûshî, "The City of Women is a certainty, in which there is no doubt."[30] A City of Women with similar features is located in the "countries of the North."[31]

[28] Cf. Miquel, *Géographie humaine*, 2:494. Miquel does not carry this point to its logical end, the extinction of the female. He does, however, posit the physical need of the women for the men and, hence, the fate that awaits the sailors.

[29] Shaykh al-Rabwa, *Nukhba*, p. 135; Miquel, *Géographie humaine*, 2:487 also notes the existence of two islands, one for men and one for women. His source is the *Hudûd al-'Alam*, which does contain some variants and some additions, such as the fate of the children born of this copulation: the boys join the men at age three.

[30] Al-Qazwînî, *Athâr*, p. 607.

[31] Miquel, *Géographie humaine*, 2:494–495, who, based on another Arabic source, places the city "in the countries of the North." This locus also finds its way into later travel

As with al-Waqwâq, what is problematic about this city concerns more the fantastic aspect of its society than the exactitude of its geography. The sexual arrangement with the slaves smacks of *The Thousand and One Nights*. It is intriguing, to say the least, and raises more questions than it answers. If the sexual relationships are the same for all the women, why the clandestine behavior of the slave, his leaving at dawn, under cover? The concern here is clearly not exclusively procreation, since the sexual act does not necessitate spending the night. The slaves' sneaking away suggests illicit behavior. The fact that no men rule over the women is the first indication that something is wrong. Uncontrollable, they ride horses and wage war, both questionable activities for a female. The sexual act with the slaves is perhaps the worst sort of ignominy and operates as a literary topos that suggests a deeper civilizational attitude toward woman and her sexual depravity.[32] And these women practice male infanticide. Everything in their life-style is a violation of Islamic norms.

Despite differences, these various communities of women operate within the same matrix: that of biological heterosexual propagation. Fortunately, however, other female groups are more sexually self-sufficient. Al-Qazwînî tells of an Island of Women in the Sea of China on which there are only women; there has never been a man among them. They impregnate themselves from the wind and give birth to women like themselves. It is said, our source adds, that the women inseminate themselves by eating the fruit of a tree they have. One merchant related that the wind threw him to that island, where he saw women without men. Gold on this island was like dust. The women intended to kill him, but one of them protected him, placing him on a board and leaving him on the ocean. The winds carried him to China, where he told the ruler about the island and its gold. The ruler sent emissaries to bring him news of it. But they went for three years without finding it, so they returned.[33]

The eyewitness account presented in the first person attests to a need for the personal experience: a literary ruse to substantiate the veracity of the tale. More than that, however, it tells us a great deal about gender dynamics. The account by the male witness forms part of a male-generated literature. His venture on that island is accidental but dangerous: he was blown there by the wind, and the women want to kill him. His is the passive role, as he is first the object of the wind, then of the fury of the women, and last of the winds (in al-Qazwînî) and of the waves (in Ibn al-

accounts of Europe: Bernard Lewis, *The Muslim Discovery of Europe* (New York: W. W. Norton & Co., 1982), p. 286.

[32] Similar dynamics, of course, operate in *The Thousand and One Nights*. See chapter 1 above.

[33] Al-Qazwînî, *Athâr*, p. 33. Ibn al-Wardî, *Kharîda*, p. 107, has much the same account of this island.

Wardî). Were it not for the one woman who carries him on a plank and leaves him on the ocean, in an action that clearly echoes the Moses story, he would have been destroyed. A purely female society, the message says, can be hazardous to the life of a male. And that danger is associated with his passivity.

This all-women island is more radical in its structuring than the other women's groups, which need males for their physical continuity. A self-sustaining female society, this community propagates itself without need of heterosexuality. The insistence in the account on the fact that there has never been a man among these women calls attention to this seeming oddity. This is highlighted further when the narrator notes that the inhabitants of this island give birth only to "women like them." Let us stop a moment at this locution, "women like them," employed in the accounts of both al-Qazwînî and Ibn al-Wardî. The word for women is nisâ', the plural of imra'a, a fully grown woman and not an infant of the female gender. The addition of "like them" increases the alterity of this procreative act: the women give birth to fully grown women. Priority is placed not so much on the gender of the newborn as on her being identical to her "mother."[34] This is an eternal female essence, in no way altered through the reproductive process.

The eloquent strangeness of these female societies taken as a whole resides at once in their sexuality and in their danger. Geographical alterity is almost de rigueur here, serving as a backdrop against which this combination of sexuality and danger plays itself out. An island is the ideal locus: at once protected and isolated. In addition, that most of the locations should be very difficult of access or quite remote only enhances their titillating effect on the reader or listener: it is highly unlikely that he would ever reach them in reality. But there would seem to be no harm in nurturing his fantasy. Or is there? The unusual, he learns, is linked to the dangerous. Copulation takes place either with men during a limited period, or with slaves under illicit conditions; or the men may enjoy the pleasures of a woman-fruit just as she dies. It would appear that these places of fantasy initially encourage behavior that is sanctioned by neither the religion nor the society. Hence, it should come as no surprise that the male is at great physical risk in a number of these societies: in one, the males die of too much sexual activity; in another, the women wish to kill the merchant; in the City of Women, the male offspring are disposed of on the spot. The only island where the male can be assured of safety is al-Waqwâq, where it is the women-fruit who die.

Is it a wonder, then, that Hayy and Asâl should have been made to live

---

[34] Miquel, *Géographie humaine*, 2:490, discusses this Island of Women and notes the impregnation by the wind and the giving birth to "girls" (*filles*).

their life of serene mystical contemplation on the island of al-Waqwâq? How much more potent and powerful their seclusion then becomes and how strong their drive for union with the deity, when set in the physical context of the women-fruit. The danger of woman is a constant: be it as a physical presence in sexual geography or as an element that lurks in the background in asexual philosophy. Ibn Tufayl certainly chose his location well.

But the civilizational and philosophical encoding in Ibn Tufayl's asexual allegory transcends al-Waqwâq, radiating outward and redefining other classics of Islamic philosophy. Not only is Hayy ibn Yaqzân himself a character worthy of investigation, but so is the problematic duo of Salâmân and Asâl, whose breakup gave birth to the homosocial couple of Hayy and Asâl. Like al-Waqwâq, Hayy, on the one hand, and Salâmân and Asâl, on the other, create resonances and reverberations in the Arabo-Islamic world of gender, sexuality, and woman's body.

Asâl, the more inward-looking member of the couple he forms with Salâmân, appears as Absâl in certain versions of Ibn Tufayl's *Hayy ibn Yaqzân*. Henry Corbin in fact chastises Léon Gauthier, who, in his scholarly edition of Ibn Tufayl's classic, renders the name as Asâl. Corbin calls this a "deformation" of the name, noting that Ibn Tufayl himself admitted taking it from Ibn Sînâ and that the Absâl form is equally extensive in manuscripts of the Andalusian text.[35] Salâmân and Asâl, Salâmân and Absâl: in its Absâl form, the couple has a long history in Arabo-Islamic thought, a history whose commentary on gender questions is almost as eloquent as that of Joseph. It is perhaps no accident, then, that Ibn Sînâ, the master of Islamic philosophy, should bring the two together in one of his epistles, that on fate. Not everyone, we are told, has the chastity/virtuousness (*'isma*) of Joseph when he saw God's proof or of Absâl when he saw her face.[36] (We will get to this mystery lady momentarily.) *'Isma*, a word whose semantic range extends from chastity and virtuousness through infallibility, is a particular characteristic of prophets.[37] Absâl, it is clear from this reference, has, like Joseph, resisted physical temptation. Through the concept of 'isma, Absâl's rank has been elevated to that of Joseph, whose adventure with Zulaykhâ was so important in defining women's perfidy.[38]

---

[35] Henry Corbin, *Avicenne et le récit visionnaire* (Paris: Adrien-Maisonneuve, 1954), 1:261 n. 364. Ibn Sînâ uses the form Absâl. See, for example, Ibn Sînâ, *al-Ishârât wal-Tanbîhât*, commentary by Nasîr al-Dîn al-Tûsî, ed. Sulaymân Dunyâ, vol. 4 (Cairo: Dâr al-Ma'ârif, 1968), p. 50.

[36] Ibn Sînâ, "Risâlat al-Qadr," in Ibn Sînâ, *Rasâ'il (Traités Mystiques)*, ed. M.A.F. Mehren (Leiden: E. J. Brill, 1899), pp. 5–6, and for French translation, p. 2.

[37] See, for example, al-Râzî, *'Ismat al-Anbiyâ'*, ed. Muhammad Hijâzî (Cairo: Maktabat al-Thaqâfa al-Dîniyya, 1986).

[38] See chapter 3 above.

Nasîr al-Dîn al-Tûsî (d. 672/1274), in a commentary on a work by Ibn Sînâ, notes the importance of the Salâmân-Absâl duo in medieval Arabo-Islamic mentalities. He then presents two stories, clearly important for their gender dynamics, the first of which he attributes to an Arabic translation from the Greek by the Christian Hunayn ibn Ishâq (d. 260/873).[39] A. J. Arberry, in his study *FitzGerald's Salâmân and Absâl*, discusses the Persian Jâmî's (d. 898/1492)[40] rendition of the Salâmân-and-Absâl story and notes al-Tûsî's assertion, concluding that "no such Greek original has so far been discovered; and the tale may not have been Hellenistic at all, but the invention of some austere Christian monastic moralist, or even conceivably a Manichean."[41] Whatever its possible origins, the tale does exist in a Hunaynian version,[42] and it is far from being the "rather silly story" that Arberry thinks it is.[43] Since the Tûsian version is but an abbreviated form of Hunayn's narrative, it is the latter that will be more significant for gender analysis.

"Hunayn ibn Ishâq said": thus the Arabic text begins. There was once a king, named Hirmânûs, who wanted a son. But this king stayed away from women, hating their company. When his sage/physician proposed to him that for the sake of having a male offspring who would take over the kingdom, this king should have sexual intercourse with a beautiful woman, the ruler refused. Instead, the sage/physician devised a way by which a son would be born from the king's semen. This infant was called Salâmân. A beautiful eighteen-year-old woman, named Absâl, became his wet nurse and brought him up. The king was extremely pleased by the creation from his semen of a son who came about without sexual intercourse with women, and he rewarded the wise man with a promise to fulfill his wish. When the wise man described his desire, a special building for the eternal rest of the soul that would be virtually indestructible and inaccessible but to the wise, the king ordered that two such edifices be built, one for the wise man and one for himself, in which they would be buried.

Meanwhile, Salâmân had completed his period of suckling, and the king wanted to separate him from Absâl. The young boy was unhappy about this, so the king decided to leave him with her until he reached

[39] Al-Tûsî, commentary on Ibn Sînâ, *al-Ishârât*, 4:52. It is the adoption of this story with a self-consciously Muslim tradition that brings it within the purview of our story.

[40] These stories have later Persian versions and analogues, but I am limiting my discussion to Arabic texts. Persian materials pose other civilizational problems.

[41] A. J. Arberry, *FitzGerald's Salâmân and Absâl* (Cambridge: Cambridge University Press, 1956), pp. 40–41.

[42] Hunayn ibn Ishâq, "Qissat Salâmân and Absâl," translated from the Greek, in Ibn Sînâ, *Tis' Rasâ'il* (Cairo: Maktabat Hindiyya, 1908), pp. 157–168. See the summary of this story in Corbin, *Avicenne*, pp. 243–252.

[43] Arberry, *FitzGerald*, p. 39.

puberty. But puberty led to the young man's falling in love with "the woman," and most of his time was spent with her instead of in the service of the king and kingdom. At this point, the king gave his son a lecture on women and on the pitfalls of associating with them. The conclusion: Salâmân should pull himself away from "the whore Absâl," for whom he has no need and from whose company he derives no benefit. Rather, the king would arrange for him to marry a young woman from the celestial world. On Absâl's advice, the young man rejected his father's counsel. After another round of royal advice that did not substantially alter Salâmân's behavior, the king asked his advisers about eliminating Absâl, an action from which the wise man attempted to dissuade him. Someone hearing the king's words alerted Salâmân, and he asked Absâl's advice on what to do. The two decided to flee to "what was beyond the Sea of the Maghrib." The king had an instrument through which he could see the various regions and peoples of the globe. Thus was he able to locate the two, taking pity on them and giving them what they needed to live. But eventually, the king became angry with their desire, and he blocked it through a technique he knew in such a way that each of them would yearn for, and be able to see, the other, without at the same time reaching that beloved. The young man, now aware of the extent of his father's anger, returned, apologetic, to him.

The king warned his son that he did not like Absâl "the whore" and that attachment to her was incompatible with being a ruler. To illustrate his point that the female was like a weight attached to the young man's foot that would prevent him from acceding to the throne, the king ordered that the experiment be actually done and that the two be attached in the way he had described. They were released at night. The two lovers clasped hands and threw themselves in the sea. The king, however, ordered that Salâmân be saved, which he was, while Absâl was drowned. Salâmân was distressed, and the wise man took on the task of bringing him back into the fold. This was eventually managed: the young man's attention was turned away from Absâl and his fancy concentrated on Venus through various techniques, including his dressing like Absâl, the appearance of Absâl's form to him on a daily basis to keep him company, and his revealing to the wise man all that he saw. Eventually, he took over the kingdom. He ordered that the story be written down and placed at the head of his father's tomb.[44]

This adventure of Salâmân and Absâl has been analyzed as a philosophical allegory. And it would seem, as with Ibn Tufayl's extended narrative, that all the parts fit. Al-Tûsî, in fact, himself undertakes the exe-

---

[44] Hunayn, "Qissat Salâmân," pp. 157–168. For al-Tûsî's summary version, see al-Tûsî, commentary on Ibn Sînâ, al-Ishârât, 4:50–52.

gesis of his text. The king is the active intellect, Salâmân is the rational soul, Absâl is the animal corporeal faculty, and so forth.[45] Though Corbin has effectively criticized this Tûsian presentation, his own is an equally philosophical and mystical interpretation.[46]

My gender-conscious analytical procedure differs. The philosophico-allegorical reading of any of these texts is a latent, encoded reading. However, its truth value, unlike that of a Freudian latent reading, derives from its conscious meaning. The allegorical decoding proceeds according to consciously applied rules, such as the female's being the equivalent of the physical corporeal faculty. This coding is an allegorical language that operates according to given principles and can be understood by any philosophically aware reader.

The reading I propose is not latent, but manifest. However, unlike the Freudian system, in which the latent represents the unconscious, the situation here is the opposite. In these philosophico-mystical allegories, it is the manifest that represents an unconscious, because unintended, level of meaning. This procedure begins by restoring the manifest meaning, deriving from it at the same time a latent, unconscious signification. The philosophico-mystical text will undergo an initial uncoding to permit the gender-conscious decoding. In the terminology of Arabic philosophy and mysticism, the interpretation will be exoteric (zâhirî) rather than esoteric (bâtinî), but it will nevertheless signal a hidden level of the text.

The analytical situation has similarities to that used with *Hayy ibn Yaqzân*. There, the gender exploration demanded an analytical jump, also leading to a type of bâtinî understanding, but based, initially, on the manifest meaning of the story.

Like Ibn Tufayl's male utopian vision, the Hunaynian/Tûsian text also fantasizes a world without women. One of Hayy's birth accounts was a tale of spontaneous generation, with no biological need for the female. In Salâmân's case, procreation is also aggressively asexual. But the procedure is unusual, to say the least, representing a sort of male parthenogenesis, a virtual biological impossibility. This is the privilege of fantasy, however. Sexuality is once again separated from procreation.

Although the female may be removed as a life-giving force, her mere presence is enough to lead astray the most noble of heroes. It is Absâl's role as wet nurse that creates problems. One wonders, however, why the text had to resort to a human female to fulfill the necessary nurturing. It would certainly have been much neater to have a gazelle or some other animal fill this function, as our thoughtful narrator so cleverly did in Ibn Tufayl's narrative. After all, if the human female is not needed for procre-

[45] Al-Tûsî, commentary on Ibn Sînâ, *al-Ishârât*, 4:52–53.
[46] Corbin, *Avicenne*, pp. 253–258.

ation, why should she be needed for nursing the infant? Simply, the problematic "mother" is at work again.

Intriguing as well is the transformation effected in Absâl's role. From a beautiful young woman of eighteen, she is transformed into a whore. The metamorphosis comes about through her relationship with Salâmân. This female nurturer, or substitute mother, is painted as particularly odious since she does not shun the advances of the male she is rearing. In al-Tûsî's version, she even encourages her admirer.[47] Instead of object of love, she is dubbed a "whore." Perhaps we should not be overly surprised: after all, in his first speech to his son, the king had warned him that women were "the tricks/stratagems of evil."[48] The word used here is *makâyid*, from the same root as *kayd*, that ubiquitous concept whose perimeters directly or indirectly encompassed the actions of women from Zulaykhâ through ʿAʾisha to the ʿifrît's woman in *The Thousand and One Nights*.

From nurturer, Absâl moves to temptress. In both roles, she is defined through her body. The only solution to the problem is her physical destruction. Thus it is that in the dramatic attempted double suicide, the young man is actively saved while the female is just as purposefully annihilated. The lover's obsession with his beloved must be diverted. The physical corporeality of the woman is exchanged for an image. This averts the danger, once more reaffirming that it is woman's body that leads men astray.

Other, more deep-seated mental constructs surface in this Salâmân-and-Absâl story. The initial premise that sets the entire process in motion is the king's desire for a son who would take his place, without his ever having to come in direct contact with a woman. The terms used all signify sexual intercourse: from *mulâmasa* and *dâjaʿa* in Hunayn ibn Ishâq to *yubâshir* in al-Tûsî.[49] Since the sage/physician took it on himself to work out the procedure of male parthenogenesis, the reader must assume that direct contact with a woman is not only sexual but includes merely being in her womb. But why this total aversion to the female? As with ʿAʾisha, whose intrusion into the male world of politics earned her the dubious honor of association with Joseph's seductress, so with the female in the complex world of Salâmân and Absâl. She must be excluded from the male universe of governing and ruling. Her presence soils this exclusive world of men.

To ensure that this message is clear and that woman indeed does not mix with politics, the narrator brings the two together again in the nar-

---

[47] Al-Tûsî, commentary on Ibn Sînâ, *al-Ishârât*, 4:51.
[48] Hunayn, "Qissat Salâmân," p. 161.
[49] Ibid., pp. 159, 160; al-Tûsî, commentary on Ibn Sînâ, *al-Ishârât*, 4:51.

rative (obviously with the aim of ensuring their separation). The explosive nonmixture of politics and woman turns into a leitmotiv in the text, and specifically in the ruler's discourse. A royal misogynist, this obsessively concerned father does not cease to remind his son (and consequently the reader) of women's evil nature, inherently linked to their bodies. When Salâmân returns to the paternal presence, his father warns him that he will not accede to the throne as long as his relationship to Absâl is literally and metaphorically tying him down. After Absâl's physical destruction and her complete elimination from Salâmân's emotional world, he becomes ready for governing because, as the narrator so thoughtfully reemphasizes, of his separation from her.[50]

In Hunayn ibn Ishâq's version of the story, Absâl plays an active role in guiding Salâmân and dissuading him from following his father's advice. In that sense, she could be conceived of as a viable threat or even alternative to the ruler. In the Tûsian variant, on the other hand, she is less tangible: when she is first presented, neither her beauty nor her age is mentioned. Her passivity does not, however, extend to the sexual domain: she encourages the young man.

All's well that ends well: Salâmân is cured of his passion for Absâl, whom he has replaced with the form of Venus. Cross-sexual dress, his wearing Absâl's clothing, is part of his therapy. It is as ruler that Salâmân orders that the story be written on gold. In this light, his adventure comes close to that of Shâhriyâr in *The Thousand and One Nights*. Both are cured, though obviously the reasons for the treatment differ in the two cases. For both, the threat of female sexuality has to be conjured away. Both kings, once the cure is effected, become legendary rulers. And both their stories are set down in writing for posterity.

This last act is important for its literary and gender implications. As with the *Nights*, it is a male who determines the preservation of the story and its writing in gold. Though the text is initially hidden, it is eventually uncovered and the immortalizing deed brings the amorous and sexual adventures of one individual into the public domain. The message is clear: the story must not be forgotten. Woman's trickery permeates once again the Muslim unconscious, as Absâl joins the pantheon of her wicked sisters.

Salâmân and Absâl are, in this first story of al-Tûsî borrowed from Hunayn ibn Ishâq, a problematic male-female couple. Al-Tûsî's second narrative involves a more traditional Islamic duo, two males. In this tale, Salâmân and Absâl (now a male) are brothers. Absâl was the younger of the two, had been brought up by his brother, and grew up to be beautiful, intelligent, learned, pious, and courageous. Salâmân's wife fell in love

[50] Al-Tûsî, commentary on Ibn Sînâ, *al-Ishârât*, 4:52.

with him and told her husband to let Absâl mingle with his children so they could learn from him. But the younger brother balked at his older brother's suggestion/order, not wanting to mix with women. So Salâmân told him that his wife was like a mother to the young man. Absâl went in to see the woman, who treated him nicely and revealed her passion to him. Absâl shrank away from this, and she realized that he would not obey her. So she told Salâmân to marry his brother to her sister, at the same time telling her own sister that she was marrying her to Absâl, not so he could belong to her exclusively, but so that she could share him with her. Then she told the young man that her sister was a virgin, that she was shy, and that he should not go in to see her (*dakhala ʿalâ*, which also means "to sleep with her," "to consummate the marriage") during the daytime, nor should he talk to her until after she became familiar with him.

On the wedding night, Salâmân's wife stayed in her sister's bed. When Absâl went in to her, she was unable to control herself and began to hug him. Absâl was suspicious and said to himself that virgins did not behave in this way. The sky at that point became overcast and lightning allowed him to see the face of Salâmân's wife. So he went out, intending to leave her.

Absâl then announced to his brother that he wished to conquer lands for him. He took an army and did just that. He returned to his homeland, assuming that the woman had forgotten him. But instead she was back to her pronouncements of love. Absâl refused her advances.

When an enemy appeared, Salâmân sent his brother to fight him. But the woman paid the military leaders to abandon him during battle, which they did. The enemies overtook the young man, wounded him, and left him for dead. However, a "wet nurse from among the wild animals felt compassion for him" and gave him of her milk, and he was cured.

Absâl then returned to his brother, who meanwhile had become surrounded by enemies and was sorrowful over the loss of his brother. Absâl reached him, took over the army, fought the enemy, and imprisoned its leaders, returning the kingdom to his brother. The woman, however, had Absâl poisoned. Salâmân, saddened over the death of his brother, left his kingdom, and after God revealed to him the facts of the case, he poisoned the woman and her cohorts.[51]

Once again, al-Tûsî interprets the tale.[52] Salâmân's role has not changed from what it was in the first story: he still represents the rational soul. Rather, it is the now-masculine Absâl who has undergone a total transformation, becoming the speculative intellect. Clearly, one can view

[51] Ibid., pp. 53–55.
[52] Ibid., pp. 55–58.

this complex narrative as a philosophical allegory, in which case some of the same forces operating in the first Tûsian tale make an appearance here as well.

This Salâmân-Absâl adventure resembles in its complexity a *Thousand and One Nights* tale. Like the two brothers in the frame of the *Nights* (and the two brothers of Ibn al-Batanûnî), Salâmân and Absâl are a close-knit pair, the younger one even having been brought up by the older one. Absâl's qualities, enumerated one after the other, are reminiscent of the positive characteristics that differentiated Shahrazâd from other women.[53] The same forces are operating for Absâl. His beauty, intelligence, piety, and courage make his victimization at the hands of Salâmân's wife that much more dramatic. He is a young man who shuns the company of women, refusing as he does his brother's suggestion that he mingle with the children.

The woman is, in fact, the aggressive and central character in this narrative. Despite her textual centrality, however, she remains nameless, the two brothers being the only ones endowed with so specific an identity. This onomastic presence signals the importance of the male couple as a unit. This nameless woman plots and connives to get her desires. It is her initial longing that sets the entire plot in motion and keeps that plot going. All of her actions are negative: from her initial suggestion for Absâl to mix across the genders, to the revelation of her passion, to the marriage arranged for her sister, to the second aborted seduction, to the attempted murder, and to the final poisoning. She is never daunted by Absâl's rejections of her advances.

The woman's odious behavior is perhaps most visible in the actual seduction scene. She substitutes herself for her sister on the couple's wedding night. Absâl's virtuousness when faced with the temptress is what earns him a place in Islamic mentalities alongside the Qur'ânic Joseph. And it is thanks to the lightning that Absâl recognizes the woman and escapes the seduction attempt.

Coming close to Joseph in his reaction somehow pulls Absâl away from the response of his literary cousins, those men in the *Nights* who, when faced with the perfidy of women, kill them. Of course, the major difference here is that it is not Absâl's wife who is at issue but her sister. Nevertheless, his is an aggressive reaction. Rather than channeling his energy into a destruction of the female, Absâl directs it toward military conquest. Eventually, he is the one who is destroyed.

Absâl's military reactions in the text are set off against those of his brother, Salâmân, who turns out to be a fairly weak character, most often following his wife's directions. His qualities are not enumerated as are

[53] See chapter 1 above.

those of his younger sibling. Nevertheless, he does perform one nonpassive act: poisoning the guilty female.

Once again, woman's sexuality is problematic. Her inability to control her body and her passion is what leads to her eventual annihilation. Her words of caution to Absâl about her sister's nature and behavior contribute to the young man's suspicions when he is faced with this woman's sexual aggression. Her words betray her body.

The two Tûsian Salâmân-and-Absâl stories both center on couples. In the first, it is a male Salâmân who forms a heterosexual unit with the female Absâl. In the second, both Salâmân and Absâl are males, and their relationship is homosocial in nature. These two couples, emerging as they do out of a philosophical framework, nevertheless participate in the larger gender politics of medieval Islamic civilization. They echo the Joseph story, on the one hand, and *The Thousand and One Nights*, on the other. Superimposing the two Salâmân-and-Absâl stories from al-Tûsî uncovers a revealing pattern. It is not just that Absâl is sexually ambivalent, male or female according to the case, but that there are two Salâmân-and-Absâl couples, onomastically identical but opposite in nature. What better way than this game of identity and difference between the two Salâmân-and-Absâl couples to show the fundamental tension between the male homosocial couple and its heterosexual competitor?

At the same time, thematic elements radiate outward from both Salâmân-and-Absâl stories in concentric circles, extending to other philosophical texts. When Absâl the male warrior is abandoned on the battlefield for dead, he is rejuvenated by a "wet nurse" animal who literally gives him "the nipple of her breasts" to feed on.[54] With its emphasis on the body, this incident is more graphic than the rescue scene in Ibn Tufayl's *Hayy ibn Yaqzân*. There, especially in the biological birth account, the infant's initial encounter with the gazelle exploits the same terminology.[55] Although the structural dynamics differ between the two deliverance scenes (one hero is an infant, the other an adult),[56] both humans are delivered from sure death by an animal who fills the role of surrogate human caretaker.

More important, the narrative of the Salâmân-and-Absâl heterosexual couple participates in that phenomenon referred to by S. H. Nasr as "sacred geography." Nasr elaborates this when discussing the Eastern Illuminationist philosophy of Shihâb al-Dîn al-Suhrawardî (d. 587/1191), whose text I shall analyze momentarily. In this system, the Orient is the world of pure light, whereas the Occident is the world of darknesss or

[54] Al-Tûsî, commentary on Ibn Sînâ, *al-Ishârât*, 4:55.
[55] Ibn Tufayl, *Hayy*, p. 123.
[56] Cf. Corbin, *Avicenne*, p. 261 n. 364.

matter.[57] The ill-fated couple escapes to an area beyond the Sea of the Maghrib, for all intents and purposes the Occident in the system of sacred geography.

Both Salâmân-and-Absâl stories represent flights from the female, whose existence can only threaten to destroy the harmony of a male-centered universe. In one case, the woman is the object of love who, nevertheless, must be ultimately destroyed. In the other case, the woman is the pursuer who never attains her quarry. She is also destroyed.

The Salâmân-Absâl duo is but one end of the continuum in the gender war posited by Ibn Tufayl. The problematic heterosexual couple is only one possibility for the articulation of these troublesome dynamics. The *Hayy ibn Yaqzân* of Ibn Tufayl points to the other extreme. This is equally true of the two other texts devoted to this mythical individual.

The first-person male narrator of Ibn Sînâ's *Hayy ibn Yaqzân* addresses his "brothers," informing them of his intention to tell the story of Hayy ibn Yaqzân. A beautiful old man, bearing various signs of divine glory, appears to the narrator and his friends while they are on an outing. This old man, who then takes up the narration, identifies himself as Hayy ibn Yaqzân, whose occupation is touring the different regions of the world. His face is directed toward his father, who is alive (hayy), and from whom the old man has learned the keys of the various sciences. It turns out that the science of physiognomy can reveal a great deal. Hayy proceeds to inform the original narrator that his various companions are disreputable characters: one is a liar, one is a thief, and the third, a glutton. The original narrator discovers that this is indeed the case, and he attempts to change them. When he informs Hayy that he wishes to perform the same voyages, he is told that this is impossible. Instead, Hayy himself undertakes a detailed description of the various regions, at the end of which he invites the initial narrator to follow him to the last region described.

Ibn Sînâ's text appears in the form of a monologue. Once the old Hayy ibn Yaqzân undertakes his exposition of the various climes, there is no more dialogue. His descriptions end with the ideal kingdom in which a king rules, like a father figure, over the inhabitants. Gender dynamics are seemingly (on the surface, at least) sacrificed to male homosocial dynamics. The latter, however, always exist indirectly in a dialectical relationship with gender questions. The opening of the text evokes homosocial bonding as the narrator addresses those metaphorical "brothers" already familiar to us from the introduction of many a medieval Arabic text.[58] Female society is shunned, if not occulted, and the only woman who ap-

---

[57] Seyyed Hossein Nasr, *Three Muslim Sages: Avicenna—Suhrawardî—Ibn 'Arabî* (Cambridge: Harvard University Press, 1964), pp. 64–66.

[58] See chapter 4 above.

pears is the beautiful female ruler who governs a carefree people. Her role is apparently benign. But this striking creature also appears as the seductress of the ruler of a kingdom whose inhabitants like to kill and mutilate. The Arabic word for the seduction is very telling. *Futina bi*, to be seduced by, is in the passive.[59] The woman is the source of the action, the man its object. More important, this verb is also the grammatical root that gives us *fitna*, that key concept which holds pride of place alongside (if not above) *kayd* in defining the dangers that woman, and specifically woman's body, evokes in the medieval Arabo-Islamic mental universe.[60]

If Ibn Sînâ's *Hayy ibn Yaqzân* is the most cerebral and abstract of the three *Hayy* narratives, it nevertheless contains in germ many of the concepts that will prove to be important in the later tales. Al-Suhrawardî's work, known as the "The Story of the Occidental Exile," is set in the form of an extended anecdote and makes allusion in its opening section both to the tale of Hayy ibn Yaqzân and to that of Salâmân and Absâl.[61]

Al-Suhrawardî's first-person male narrator, much like his antecedent, the narrator in Ibn Sînâ's *Hayy*, specifically addresses his story to "some of our honored brothers." This Suhrawardian protagonist was on a bird-hunting trip with his brother, ʿAsim, when they reached the city of Qayrawân (presumably, the city of that name in Tunisia). Upon discovering the identity of the two and of their father, Hâdî ibn Abî al-Khayr al-Yamânî, the inhabitants of that city surrounded them, chained them, and imprisoned them in an extremely deep well. Above the well was a castle with high towers. The two were told that they could go up to the castle at night but must return to the well during the daytime. The well had layers of darkness so that one could scarcely see one's hand. The prisoners received news of their homeland and continued in this constant up-and-down between the well and the castle. A hoopoe finally came to them with directions from their father on the exact steps to follow in order to escape. The letter was very specific, detailing all that would happen.

Directions from the father include the destruction of the family and the killing of the wife. During the boat ride homeward, the narrator takes the wet nurse who had suckled him and throws her in the water. Arrival at the father's abode does not, however, solve all problems. The father, a

[59] Ibn Sînâ, "Risâlat Hayy ibn Yaqzân," in Ibn Sînâ, *Rasâ'il*, ed. Mehren, p. 11.

[60] On the importance of fitna, see chapter 2 above.

[61] Al-Suhrawardî, "Hayy ibn Yaqzân," in *Hayy ibn Yaqzân*, ed. Amîn, p. 124. The Arabic text does not contain the reference to "Salâmân and Absâl" but repeats the reference to *Hayy* twice. The English translation, on the other hand, contains the reference. Given the context, the English translation would appear more correct. See Suhrawardi, *The Mystical and Visionary Treatises of Shihabuddin Yahya Suhrawardi*, trans. W. M. Thackston, Jr. (London: The Octagon Press, 1982), p. 100. This translation is not from the Arabic original but from a Persian version. See, also, A.-M. Goichon, "Hayy b. Yakzân," *EI².*

venerable old man, informs the narrator that, despite his escape, he must return to his occidental exile and imprisonment. He will, however, be able to leave at will and eventually will escape for good. The patriarch continues by explaining the hierarchy of forefathers: his father inhabits a mountain above his, and the line of ancestors continues until it ends with that ancestor "who has neither forefather nor mother." In the middle of this praise of the greatest ancestor, the narrator finds himself back in prison in the Maghrib. But for some inexplicable reason, he feels some pleasure. He weeps and prays, grieving at the separation and feeling that the rest was but a fleeting dream. The narrator closes his story, much as he began it: with invocations to the deity and a reference to the title of the work.[62]

Clearly, this tale is an allegory. It can be read as the imprisonment of the soul in the body and the difficulty of access to the various spheres of divine reality. It is, in this sense, an initiatic tale, in which the voyage plays a crucial role. It also illustrates quite eloquently the sacred geography so crucial in these philosophical texts.[63]

Yet even within that level of a first allegorical reading, the gender issues are prominent. In fact, gynocide is a major motivating force in the male-female relationships. The directives of the father are clear: destroy the family and kill the wife. The narrator takes it upon himself to dump his wet nurse overboard. He chooses to do this "when we reached a place where the waves were clashing."[64] This destruction of the wet nurse is particularly violent. The weather conditions are harsh. The reader knows that she will not be saved as was the infant Hayy when his mother dumped him in the water. The two acts are parallel: the same expression is used in both, *fī al-yamm*.[65] As for the wife, the order is explicit and specific: kill her. This is nothing but an invitation to murder. There is more at issue than the wife's being a symbol of concupiscence.[66] The women in this story are only present to be eliminated. Even the narrator's sister is removed, with phraseology echoing the *Qur'ān* and specifically a verse that speaks of what befalls evildoers.[67] The different varieties of female relationships are present: maternal, marital, and sibling. And the male narrator must be detached from each.

More important, the ubiquitous homosocial relationship is at play. The

[62] Al-Suhrawardî, "Hayy," in *Hayy ibn Yaqzân*, ed. Amîn, pp. 122–127. For an English translation, see Suhrawardi, *Mystical and Visionary Treatises*, pp. 100–108.

[63] Corbin, *Avicenne*, pp. 40–52.

[64] Al-Suhrawardî, "Hayy," in *Hayy ibn Yaqzân*, ed. Amîn, p. 125.

[65] Ibid. For this expression in Ibn Tufayl and its relationship with the Moses story in the *Qur'ān*, see chapter 4 above.

[66] See Suhrawardi, *Mystical and Visionary Treatises*, p. 102, translator's note v.

[67] Al-Suhrawardî, "Hayy," in *Hayy ibn Yaqzân*, ed. Amîn, p. 126; *al-Qur'ān*, Sûrat Yûnus, verse 27.

two brothers, much like the two brothers in *The Thousand and One Nights*, are off on a hunting trip. It is this trip that initiates the entire adventure leading to their imprisonment and to the eventual destruction of the female. That the presence of the woman is a negative element in the all-male universe is well illustrated by the father's exposition of the forefathers. He eventually reaches the greatest ancestor "who has neither forefather nor mother." Being the forefather (*jadd*) is not identical to being the biological father (*ab*), who would be, after all, the logical counterpart of the mother. And this was what we had with the spontaneous-generation birth account in Ibn Tufayl's *Hayy ibn Yaqzân*. This ancestor must also be woman-free, and specifically of the woman as procreator.

This gender reading represents only one set of possibilities. Luce Irigaray has demonstrated quite eloquently that more hides behind philosophical texts.[68] This is certainly the case for al-Suhrawardî. The bottomless dark well in which the brothers are imprisoned is essentially a vaginal structure. The castle with its high towers is the opposite, a symbol of the phallic. The multiple "births" suggest the inability to escape the female. Instead, the male finds himself dragged repeatedly back into the vagina. In most stories of initiation, once the hero has achieved his goal, he is not made to return to his initial position. In this tale of al-Suhrawardî, however, there is a sense of fragility, as the male is recurrently brought back to the womb. His inability to escape the female only reinforces the other misogynist elements in the story.

Al-Suhrawardî is, in his own way, advocating a society of men. Eventually, we are led to understand, the male narrator will be able to realize his goal of escaping from the imprisonment in the well (read: vagina). After all, the father has predicted this, and he is the strongest and most positive figure in the story. He is responsible for the escape plans, for ordering the destruction of the female, and for returning the narrator to his original state of exile.

This strong father figure is an element shared by most of these philosophico-mystical allegories. In the Salâmân-Absâl heterosexual love story, this unbending misogynist was responsible for the breakup of the couple and the destruction of the female. In Ibn Sînâ's *Hayy ibn Yaqzân*, the old man is as much a father figure as he is a spiritual guide. When this Hayy describes the ideal kingdom at the end of his monologue, its ruler is described as a father and the people as his children and his descendants.[69]

The fragility of al-Suhrawardî's male adventure brings us close to the

---

[68] Luce Irigaray, *Spéculum de l'autre femme* (Paris: Les Editions de Minuit, 1974), pp. 299–457.

[69] Ibn Sînâ, "Hayy," in *Hayy ibn Yaqzân*, ed. Amîn, p. 49.

arbitrary temporariness of Ibn Tufayl's male utopia. Neither is a triumphant text. After all, the Suhrawardian narrator is made to return to his imprisonment at the end of the tale, and his temporary pleasure is but a fleeting dream, as he himself describes it.

These texts are not marginal but rather central narratives for the Islamic mystical and philosophical worldview. Their strongly antifemale nature marks a central current of Sufism.[70] In fact, the narrators all, with no exception, describe the female principle as negative and as something that must be escaped.

The Sûfî allegory of which all these works form a part, and in turn help to define, operates around two major and interrelated axes. On the one hand, it is not particularly optimistic and its conclusion is far from being an erotic grand finale. On the other, its gender dynamics promote all-male fellowship, while being strongly antifemale. Hence, it is in contrast with the mysticism of erotic union, which parallels the mystic experience with erotic attraction (as well as with other forms of intoxication).[71] Nevertheless, the contradiction between these two systems of mystical allegory is reduced somewhat by the sexual ambivalence of the characterization of the beloved in mystical as well as much profane love poetry. A heterosexual couple or a homosexual one? It is not always clear.

The dream of a world without sex is tied in the Islamic mental universe to that of a world without women. The wish to separate creation or procreation from sexuality brings the Islamic view close to that of its Christian cousin. In both cultures, sexuality is not without pitfalls and ultimately participates in the creation of a distinctive misogynist view. An Islamic misogynist worldview implies the absence of the female, preferably a total absence. There is concomitantly no obsession with virginity. The dream of a virgin mother, so central to Christian misogyny, is alien to its Islamic counterpart. All this, of course, is in the realm of the imagi-

---

[70] Leila Ahmed, "Feminism and Cross-Cultural Inquiry: The Terms of the Discourse in Islam," in *Coming to Terms: Feminism, Theory, Politics*, ed. Elizabeth Weed (New York: Routledge, 1989), pp. 143–151, stresses another interpretation when she argues that "Sufism—or certain strands within early Sufi thought—" was essentially gender free, using the life of the famous mystic Râbi'a al-'Adawiyya as her chief example. On gender and sexual politics across the entire Sûfî tradition, see, also, Annemarie Schimmel, *Mystical Dimensions of Islam* (Chapel Hill: University of North Carolina Press, 1975), pp. 426–435; Annemarie Schimmel, "Eros—Heavenly and Not So Heavenly—in Sufi Literature and Life," in Marsot, *Society and the Sexes*, pp. 119–141. On Râbi'a, see, also, the discussion by Nawâl al-Sa'dâwî, *'An al-Mar'a* (Cairo: Dâr al-Mustaqbal al-'Arabî, 1988), pp. 133–144. Ahmed's discussion effectively forms part of a feminist Islamic school which argues that original Islamic institutions were more open to women than later "orthodox" traditions, an issue which is beyond our purview here.

[71] See, for example, A. J. Arberry, *Sufism* (London: Unwin Paperbacks, 1979), pp. 113–118.

nation, of mental structures, and these need not always mirror social reality. Yet these two variant misogynies do seem related to fundamental civilizational impulses. Where European Christian civilization has celebrated virginity and emphasized purity, Islam has opted for seclusion. On the level of social practice as on that of mentalités, homosociality takes precedence over heterosexuality.

Woman's body is indeed problematic. The medieval Arabic male-generated text assures us of this. The literary narratives deal with this physicality, often permitting the female to participate in the discourse. Yet her speech remains tied to the seductive power of her body. The geographical and philosophical worlds, also literary creations, are more exclusively masculine, occulting the corporeal female and centering their energies on the formulation of an alternative male reality. It is no wonder that modern feminist authors in the Arab world, to achieve their right to literary speech, must begin by reconquering their bodies.

CHAPTER 6

Nawâl al-Saʿdâwî and the Escape from the Female Body: From Handicap to Gender

THE MEDIEVAL male scriptors, those geographers, cosmographers, philosophers, or litterateurs who controlled the prose texts, were obsessed with the female body and woman's access to discourse. It was a philosopher-physician, the twelfth-century Ibn Tufayl, who radically eliminated the female in his male utopian vision. It is perhaps no accident that the most vocal contemporary Arab feminist should also be a physician. The Egyptian Nawâl al-Saʿdâwî is without doubt the most articulate activist for woman's causes in the Arab world. Nowhere, also, is the importance of the literary body more evident than in Nawâl al-Saʿdâwî's corpus.

Virtually no form of modern prose is a stranger to Dr. al-Saʿdâwî's pen: novels, plays, short stories, autobiography, prison memoirs, and travel literature. Her programmatic and theoretical works on sexuality threaten and vex readers just as much as does her literary corpus.[1] Speaking of one of al-Saʿdâwî's franker discussions, Hisham Sharabi notes that "it is difficult to explain to the non-Arab reader the effect ... [al-Saʿdâwî's prose] can have on the Arab Muslim male."[2] More than any other Arab woman writer, al-Saʿdâwî has broken the barriers. She is conscious of the literary tradition weighing on her and in her first novel, *Memoirs of a Female Physician*, recasts and replies to the classic autobiography in modern Arabic letters, that of the blind Egyptian modernizer, Tâhâ Husayn. The forces that make literary bedfellows of al-Saʿdâwî and Tâhâ Husayn are not merely literary historical. They derive also from cultural mental structures that intimately link women and the blind. In Arabic civilization, and therefore also Arabic letters, gender intertwines with physical handicaps in provocative ways. Of all physical limitations, it is blindness that places itself most squarely at the cultural intersection

---

[1] Nawâl al-Saʿdâwî, *al-Unthâ Hiya al-Asl* (Cairo: Maktabat Madbûlî, 1983); Nawâl al-Saʿdâwî, *al-Marʾa wal-Jins* (Cairo: Maktabat Madbûlî, 1983); Nawâl al-Saʿdâwî, *al-Marʾa wal-Sirâʿ al-Nafsî* (Cairo: Maktabat Madbûlî, 1983); Nawâl al-Saʿdâwî, *al-Rajul wal-Jins* (Beirut: al-Muʾassasa al-ʿArabiyya lil-Dirâsât wal-Nashr, 1980); Nawâl al-Saʿdâwî, *Qadiyyat al-Marʾa al-Misriyya al-Siyâsiyya wal-Jinsiyya* (Cairo: Dâr al-Thaqâfa al-Jadîda, 1977). Dr. al-Saʿdâwî's most famous work is *The Hidden Face of Eve*.

[2] Hisham Sharabi, *Neopatriarchy: A Theory of Distorted Change in Arab Society* (New York: Oxford University Press, 1988), p. 33.

with gender, transforming and redirecting the latter into new areas, such as the language of the body.

In the case of twentieth-century Arabic letters, mental structures are not, obviously, all of recent origin. Arabic novels, poems, and stories of the past century draw not only upon the literary but also the more general cultural heritage of classical civilization. It is, therefore, not surprising that continuing classical and traditional Arabic mental structures should be central to the understanding of modern Arabic writing.[3] The relations between the areas of gender and blindness can best be understood as the expression, in a contemporary literary medium, of traditional, but still viable, mental structures. A comparative analysis of Tâhâ Husayn's *al-Ayyâm* and a work of Nawâl al-Sa'dâwî will permit the investigation of these critical areas.

Why Tâhâ Husayn and Nawâl al-Sa'dâwî? At the outset, they would seem to be an unlikely pair. Indeed, the comparison would shock many a contemporary Arab intellectual: on the one hand, a male literary giant, dubbed "the dean of Arabic letters" (*'amîd al-adab al-'arabî*); on the other hand, probably the most controversial feminist writer in the Arab world. Born in 1931, al-Sa'dâwî was raised in the Egyptian countryside and attended a variety of public schools before going on to the Faculty of Medicine of the University of Cairo. But despite her success in science courses, al-Sa'dâwî early acquired a literary vocation, writing her first stories while still a teenager. Since receiving her medical degree, Dr. al-Sa'dâwî has practiced in the areas of public health (she was briefly national public health director), thoracic medicine, and psychiatry. Over the years, medicine has been increasingly replaced by her second career: that of political activist and writer. Though she still sees a few psychiatric patients, it is this second role that absorbs most of her energies and has produced most of her fame.[4] She is principal animator of the Arab Women's Solidarity Association.

[3] For relations between classical and modern literature, see, for example, Fedwa Malti-Douglas, "Blindness and Sexuality: Traditional Mentalities in Yûsuf Idrîs' 'House of Flesh,' " in Malti-Douglas, *Critical Pilgrimages*, pp. 70–78; Sasson Somekh, "al-'Alâqât al-Nassiyya fî al-Nizâm al-Adabî al-Wâhid," *al-Karmil* 7 (1986): 109–129.

[4] Allen Douglas and Fedwa Malti-Douglas, "Reflections of a Feminist: Conversation with Nawal al-Saadawi," in *Opening the Gates: A Century of Arab Women's Writing*, ed. Margot Badran and Miriam Cooke (London and Bloomington: Virago and Indiana University Press, 1990), pp. 394–404. Dr. al-Sa'dâwî's controversial corpus has recently provoked a critical (in both senses of the term) Freudian analysis. Jûrj Tarâbîshî, *Unthâ Didd al-Unûtha* (Beirut: Dâr al-Talî'a, 1984). This work has been partially translated by Basil Hatim and Elisabeth Orsini as *Woman against Her Sex: A Critique of Nawal el-Saadawi* (London: Saqi Books, 1988). Al-Sa'dâwî penned a reply to this criticism that was published in the same volume. The major thrust of Tarâbîshî's work is to identify Freudian-defined neurotic conditions in the characters toward the conclusion that al-Sa'dâwî's work does not liberate

A practicing physician and political activist, imprisoned under Sadat in 1981, Dr. al-Sa'dâwî has deliberately chosen to break with the traditions of Arabic letters and adopt a simple yet powerful style, to make her work accessible to a wider Arabic readership. Many critics angrily deny literary importance to her considerable and varied literary corpus. Yet this is the sort of criticism that seems often like a tribute. One of Egypt's most distinguished academic critics (the name has been concealed to protect the guilty) privately said how much he admired her controversial latest novel, *Suqût al-Imâm* (The Fall of the Imam).[5] Unfortunately, he added, he felt that he could not say so in print. Had he done so, we might point out, his life might have been threatened, as was al-Sa'dâwî's, and he might today be living with a twenty-four-hour guard on his building, as does al-Sa'dâwî.

This, indeed, is the paradox of Nawâl al-Sa'dâwî's literary reputation. Though she is shunned by the official media, her books are published in Lebanese and Egyptian editions and eagerly sought by tens of thousands of readers across the Arab world. Moreover, more is at stake here than a question of relative literary merit. The male's visual handicap and the female's femininity bring the two together inextricably. Both are defined through the body.

One of the most important works that the modern blind Egyptian intellectual Tâhâ Husayn has left us is his three-volume autobiography, *al-Ayyâm* (The days). It tells the story of his struggle with blindness and his educational ascent from early childhood to adulthood and success—to his

women. Methodological problems aside, it can be noted that he does not provide a systematic understanding of the sexual or social issues in al-Sa'dâwî's work. See, also, Sumayya Ramadân, "al-Radd 'alâ Kitâb *Unthâ Didd al-Unûtha*," in *al-Fikr al-'Arabî*, pp. 125–131. On al-Sa'dâwî, see, also, Evelyne Accad and Rose Ghurayyib, *Contemporary Arab Women Writers and Poets* (Beirut: Institute for Women's Studies in the Arab World, 1985), pp. 49–50; Heong-Dug Park, "Nawâl al-Sa'adâwî [*sic*] and Modern Egyptian Feminist Writings," Ph.D. diss., University of Michigan, 1988; Issa J. Boullata, *Trends and Issues in Contemporary Arab Thought* (Albany: State University of New York Press, 1990), pp. 127–131; Barbara Harlow, *Resistance Literature* (New York: Methuen, 1987), pp. 138–139. For contrasting review articles, see Fedwa Malti-Douglas, "An Egyptian Iconoclast: Nawal el-Saadawi and Feminist Fiction," *The American Book Review* 11, no. 3 (July–August 1989): 5, 8; Sabry Hafez, "Intentions and Realisation in the Narratives of Nawal El-Saadawi," *Third World Quarterly* 11, no. 3 (July 1989): 188–198. I am currently completing a book on Nawâl al-Sa'dâwî and her fiction.

[5] Nawâl al-Sa'dâwî, *Suqût al-Imâm* (Cairo: Dâr al-Mustaqbal al-'Arabî, 1987), translated by Sherif Hetata as *The Fall of the Imam* (London: Methuen, 1988). Nawâl al-Sa'dâwî has recounted this event to me on many an occasion during 1988 and 1990. The critic in question happens to be someone I greatly admire. When in 1988 (soon after the publication of *Suqût al-Imâm*), the editor of a literary page for one of Cairo's most respected dailies (again the name must be occulted) proposed to me that I review any recently published book for his page, I suggested al-Sa'dâwî's *Suqût al-Imâm*. He very subtly discouraged me from the endeavor.

thirty-third year.[6] Nawâl al-Saʿdâwî's *Mudhakkirât Tabîba* (Memoirs of a female physician), similarly, tells the story of a young Egyptian girl, through her medical training, once again to successful adulthood—this time, to the age of thirty.[7]

Yet there is an essential generic difference between these two texts. *The Days* is, without question, an autobiography, indeed the most famous autobiography in modern Arabic letters. *Memoirs of a Female Physician*, however, is really a novel. Though its title and first-person narration suggest an autobiography (especially for those who know that its author is a female medical practitioner), the text nowhere formally presents itself as an autobiography. Those crucial generic features identified by Philippe Lejeune as constituting the autobiographical pact are nowhere present.[8] Despite some similarities, the life described is not that of the author. *Memoirs* is a fictional autobiography, a novel that adopts the external form, but not the textual reality, of autobiography.

Thus, both Tâhâ Husayn's text and that of Nawâl al-Saʿdâwî function as equivalents on the level of mental structures. They both recount a life, and, on this level, the story (in Genette's sense)[9] of the female physician approaches that of the male writer. Al-Saʿdâwî's female Bildungsroman (to use Annis Pratt's phrase) parallels Husayn's autobiographical "education."[10] The realism and autobiographical fiction of *Memoirs* only function because its discourse operates on the same referential level as that of an autobiography. The narration of *The Days* in the third person and that of *Memoirs* in the more typically autobiographical first does not interfere with this basic equivalence. That it is the fictional autobiography which adopts the first person, and not the true autobiography, is not co-

[6] Tâhâ Husayn, *al-Ayyâm*, vol. 1 (Cairo: Dâr al-Maʿârif, 1971), vol. 2 (Cairo: Dâr al-Maʿârif, 1971), vol. 3 (Cairo: Dâr al-Maʿârif, 1973). The three volumes have been translated into English as Taha Hussein, *An Egyptian Childhood*, trans. E. H. Paxton (Washington: Three Continents Press, 1981); Taha Hussein, *The Stream of Days*, trans. Hilary Wayment (London: Longman, 1948); and Taha Husayn, *A Passage to France*, trans. Kenneth Cragg (Leiden: E. J. Brill, 1976). Though the three volumes of the Arabic were originally published over forty years, they form a clear unity. See Fedwa Malti-Douglas, *Blindness and Autobiography: al-Ayyâm of Tâhâ Husayn* (Princeton: Princeton University Press, 1988).

[7] Nawâl al-Saʿdâwî, *Mudhakkirât Tabîba* (Beirut: Dâr al-Adâb, 1980). The first chapter has been translated by Fedwa Malti-Douglas as "Growing Up Female in Egypt," in *Women and the Family in the Middle East: New Voices of Change*, ed. Elizabeth Warnock Fernea (Austin: University of Texas Press, 1985), pp. 111–120. The entire text has been translated as Nawal El Saadawi, *Memoirs of a Woman Doctor*, trans. Catherine Cobham (San Francisco: City Lights Books, 1989).

[8] For the textual features that constitute and identify autobiographies, see Philippe Lejeune, *Le pacte autobiographique* (Paris: Editions du Seuil, 1975), esp. pp. 13–46.

[9] Gérard Genette, *Figures III* (Paris: Editions du Seuil, 1966), pp. 72, 146.

[10] See, for example, Annis Pratt, *Archetypal Patterns in Women's Fiction* (Bloomington: Indiana University Press, 1981), pp. 13–37 (chapter written with Barbara White).

incidental. *Memoirs* needs the first person to reinforce its autobiographical fiction. *The Days*, since it exploits other aspects of the autobiographical pact, has the luxury of dispensing with first-person narration.[11]

Memoirs opens with the statement of a continuing and long-standing conflict between the protagonist and her femininity. This struggle, expressed as beginning even before the narrator has become conscious of her physical origin or of her humanity, occupies most of the narrative and sets the stage for the other conflictual relationships that dominate the first chapter. These sentiments extend to her female body as well, giving rise to resentment and hatred of its physical peculiarities.

The heroine is first in her class, and, rejecting her family's marriage designs, she decides to enter the Faculty of Medicine. Science takes on a great appeal for her, but eventually this cedes place to nature, as she moves to a peaceful country village. The accompanying partial resolution permits the heroine to make peace with other figures in her life.[12]

Yet there is still something missing. The novel then chronicles the young woman's relationships with men. The first, with an engineer, ends in disaster. The second, with a physician, also fails. It is only the third, with an "artist" (actually a composer), that permits the female physician to finally come to terms with her career, her sexuality, and her relations with men.

The saga of Tâhâ Husayn also introduces the hero first as a young child. He grows up in the village, is educated in the Qur'ânic school, and then proceeds to the Azhar (the international Muslim citadel of traditional learning), for what should lead to a traditional career for a blind individual, Azhar professor or *Qur'ân* reciter. But, instead, Tâhâ[13] fights the traditional system and moves on to the secular university. From there, again over the objections of university officials, he goes on to study in France, returning with a doctorate and a French wife. He comes back to his home country to take up a career as professor in the university.

But like the text of Nawâl al-Sa'dâwî, that of Tâhâ Husayn is also one of conflict. Tâhâ fights two parallel battles, one with the limiting social roles set by society for him as a sightless individual and the other with a pessimism and rejection of life linked to his personal identification with

[11] See Lejeune, *Le pacte*, pp. 13–46; Malti-Douglas, *Blindness and Autobiography*, chapter 6.

[12] On the general importance of nature for such resolutions, see Pratt, *Archetypal Patterns*, pp. 16–24. This is paralleled in a short story, "I Learned Love," where village life teaches the physician-narrator that people are all alike and she, subsequently, learns to love. Nawâl al-Sa'dâwî, "Ta'allamt al-Hubb," in Nawâl al-Sa'dâwî, *Ta'allamt al-Hubb* (Cairo: Maktabat al-Nahda al-Misriyya, 1961), pp. 7–17.

[13] Tâhâ Husayn refers to the historical individual, the author of *The Days*, whereas Tâhâ refers to the central character of *The Days*.

the famous blind ʿAbbâsid poet, Abû al-ʿAlâʾ al-Maʿarrî (d. 449/1057). Again, as well, *The Days*, like *Memoirs*, closes with the resolution of these problems.

Both *The Days* and *Memoirs of a Female Physician* tell stories of conflict and conquest. In each text, the protagonist surmounts the obstacles set for him or her by society to go on to a successful, personally fulfilling career. Both hero and heroine must break social barriers to do so, social barriers associated with physical realities, based, of course, on the body. For both protagonists, biology is destiny; physical realities are supposed to dictate social and professional roles. And it is these roles that both Tâhâ and the young woman first rebel against and finally succeed in escaping. As a child, the heroine of *Mudhakkirât Tabîba* hates

> the ugly, limited world of women, from which emanated the odor of garlic and onion.
>
> No sooner would I escape to my small world than my mother would drag me to the kitchen, saying, "Your future lies in marriage . . . You have to learn to cook . . . Your future lies in marriage . . . Marriage! Marriage!"
>
> That loathsome word that my mother repeated every day until I hated it . . . And I never heard it without imagining in front of me a man with a big belly inside of which was a table of food . . .[14]

It is a combination of education and the social power of medicine that allows the heroine to escape from the prison of domesticity and the powerlessness of the female state. (Blindness has also been seen as a prison, and even by Tâhâ Husayn, but not, interestingly enough, in *al-Ayyâm*.)[15]

The young Tâhâ also shows an aversion to the traditional roles set out before him as a sightless individual. Blind itinerant *Qurʾân* reciters are described in contemptuous language. Even the more attractive alternative, the highest goal his father could conceive for him, that of teacher in the Azhar, is consistently seen as too limiting. Yet what else does society offer, Tâhâ muses, for blind people like himself? In this case also, however, it is education, now in the secular university, that allows the young man, despite the prejudices and frequent noncooperation of university officials, to finally escape the constricting social roles which had been placed upon him.[16]

And, at the same time, the two protagonists must also come to terms

---

[14] Al-Saʿdâwî, *Mudhakkirât*, p. 10; al-Saʿdawi, "Growing Up," p. 114. In *al-Marʾa wal-Jins*, p. 50, al-Saʿdâwî cites an almost identical passage from "a diary of a ten-year-old girl." The provenance of material from various sources, even including the autobiographical, does not change the autonomy and integrity of the fictional text. It is, of course, not our task here to examine the compositional process of the author.

[15] Malti-Douglas, *Blindness and Autobiography*, pp. 15, 83, 90.

[16] Ibid., pp. 75–90.

with the ways in which their physical peculiarities have been presented to them, as limiting factors. The woman's femaleness, just as much as the man's blindness, regulates her behavior. Hence, both these two statuses are perceived, in the works in question, as types of physical marginality, though, of course, only one of these (blindness) is statistically marginal, while the other (femaleness) is essentially marginal in its social definitions.[17] In both cases, therefore, the resolution of conflict is also an escape from socially defined marginality.

The Days chronicles the saga of a blind individual, and *Memoirs*, that of a woman. Yet there are, in addition to the basic similarity in personal quest, many further points of convergence between the two texts.

When, in the opening chapter of al-Saʿdâwî's text, the narrator defines the limiting or negative nature of her femininity, she does so through a comparison with her brother:

And there was only one meaning for the word "girl" in my mind . . . that I was not a boy . . . I was not like my brother . . .

My brother cuts his hair and leaves it free, he does not comb it, but as for me, my hair grows longer and longer. My mother combs it twice a day, chains it in braids, and imprisons its ends in ribbons . . .

My brother wakes up and leaves his bed as it is, but I, I have to make my bed and his as well.

My brother goes out in the street to play, without permission from my mother or my father, and returns at any time . . . but I, I do not go out without permission.

My brother takes a bigger piece of meat than mine, eats quickly, and drinks the soup with an audible sound, yet my mother does not say anything to him . . .

As for me . . . ! I am a girl! I must watch my every movement . . . I must hide my desire for food and so I eat slowly and drink soup without a sound . . .

My brother plays . . . jumps . . . turns somersaults . . . but I, whenever I sit and the dress rides up a centimeter on my thighs, my mother throws a sharp, wounding glance at me.[18]

---

[17] See chapter 2 above.

[18] Al-Saʿdâwî, *Mudhakkirât*, pp. 5–6; al-Saʿdawi, "Growing Up," pp. 111–112. Cf. Malek Chebel's description for the Maghreb: "Thus compared to the complete liberty of expression left to the male body, that of the young girl is very early submitted to a repertory of prohibitions. . . . The young boy can roll around in all directions, raise his legs in the air, proceed to a complete uncovering of his body, and appreciate precociously its possibilities and its limits. The girl, in contrast, can neither lie down as she would probably have a tendency to do, imitating her little brother or creating original positions, nor raise her legs in the air, nor open her thighs, nor spread her knees when she is seated, nor jump if she is

Not only is the heroine defined by what she cannot do, by her unfreedom, but, perhaps even more important, her femininity is conceived not as an essence but as a difference. And this difference is essentially grounded in and articulated through the body. The first object the narrator focuses on is hair: hers (chained, imprisoned) versus her brother's (free). Braids and ribbons are normally external signs of femininity. Al-Saʿdâwî's narrator has effected a change of registers: external signs of femininity are turned into acts of confinement for the young girl. Perhaps it is not accidental, then, that her first overt act of rebellion should consist of her going to a beauty shop to have her hair cut. "Woman's crown" falls at her feet. Hair remains an obsession for the female narrator. When she dissects a woman's body during her medical education, the same terminology is applied to the head of hair on the corpse. As Nancy Huston has shown, there has been a link between hair and sexuality from time immemorial.[19] Under al-Saʿdâwî's pen (might we also add scalpel?), the combination takes on special meaning, helping to circumscribe what is and what is not the female body.

This self-definition in relation to others, who are placed in a superior position, is also visible in *The Days*. When the narrator presents Tâhâ's family, he explains that the hero felt differentiated from his siblings. His parents did not treat him as they did his brothers and sisters. They were allowed things that he was not permitted. His siblings treated him cautiously, and he sensed that "other people were superior to him." Most important, he heard his brothers "describing things of which he had no knowledge, so he knew that they could see what he could not see."[20] Though this is not the first reference to the hero's blindness in the text of *al-Ayyâm*, it is the first that clearly indicates his inability to see. If we except an ambiguous allusion in the first chapter, the only preceding reference is to the hero's "dark eyes," into which his mother put drops. Thus, not only is the young Tâhâ different, but the reality of his blindness as a physical handicap is defined by the contrast with his brothers.[21]

Parallels go further than the way in which the central problems of the female and blind protagonists are formulated. Similarities also extend to the manner of resolution. In both *The Days* and *Memoirs*, nature plays an important role in healing the wounds of the protagonists, and in leading them to a rebirth. After the heroine of *Memoirs* completes her medical

---

older." Malek Chebel, *Le corps dans la tradition au Maghreb* (Paris: Presses Universitaires de France, 1984), p. 23.

[19] Nancy Huston, "The Matrix of War: Mothers and Heroes," in *The Female Body in Western Culture: Contemporary Perspectives*, ed. Susan Rubin Suleiman (Cambridge: Harvard University Press, 1986), p. 120.

[20] Tâhâ Husayn, *al-Ayyâm*, 1:17–18.

[21] For the development of the idea of the hero's blindness in the first volume of *al-Ayyâm*, see Malti-Douglas, *Blindness and Autobiography*, chapter 1.

studies, she replaces the god of science with that of nature. In the countryside, she stretches her gaze from the "wide, peaceful, green fields to the pure, blue sky." "I surrendered to the rays of the sun and let them fall on my body." When a light breeze blows the covering from her legs, she is not hit by "that old terror which I used to feel when my legs were bared." This environment, in effect, permits the heroine to escape not only from the constraints of the city but from those associated with her femininity and her body as well. She disregards, for example, all of her mother's advice on how a girl should eat: she fills her mouth with food and drinks audibly, actions she was not permitted to perform as a girl and which, as we saw, distinguished her from her brother. But more than that, these actions, now performed with unrestrained physicality, show once again the limitations that a female body places on its subject. Most important, however, nature brings about a rebirth: "I felt at that moment that I was born anew."[22] The presence of nature in the female Bildungsroman is certainly nothing new. Annis Pratt and Barbara White have amply shown its predominance. "Nature," to quote them, "becomes an ally of the woman hero, keeping her in touch with her selfhood, a kind of talisman that enables her to make her way through the alienations of male society."[23]

This thematic complex of nature and rebirth is also central to *The Days*. In the third volume of the autobiography, Tâhâ meets his future wife in France; and this meeting revolutionizes his existence. When first introduced, she is merely a voice, but one that alters Tâhâ's world. The voice is compared to "that sun which came on that spring day" and transformed the city into light.[24] Nature begins to have a completely different meaning for the hero. The voice "used to speak to him of the sun, when it filled the earth with light, and of night when it filled the earth with darkness." The young woman turns "his darkness" into "light."[25] He, like the heroine of *Memoirs*, feels that he has begun a life which has no relation with his previous one, that "he has been created anew."[26]

But for each central figure, al-Saʿdâwî's and Tâhâ Husayn's, this creation anew has to be seen in the context of another character in the narrative, one whose literary role is that of catalyst in the process of resolution. For Tâhâ, the radical change in his outlook could not have been effected without the presence of this other party, embodied in "the voice," that of the woman "through whose eyes" he is able to see.[27]

For the young physician in *Memoirs*, it is only with the help of the artist

[22] Al-Saʿdâwî, *Mudhakkirât*, pp. 42–47.

[23] Pratt, *Archetypical Patterns*, p. 21.

[24] Tâhâ Husayn, *al-Ayyâm*, 3:85.

[25] Ibid., pp. 114–115.

[26] Ibid., pp. 102, 112. For a fuller discussion of this transformation and its significance for the work as a whole, see Malti-Douglas, *Blindness and Autobiography*, chapter 3.

[27] Tâhâ Husayn, *al-Ayyâm*, 3:113.

at the end of the story that we get a full resolution of the conflict presented in the first line of the novel. This resolution in *Memoirs* did not, however, come about easily or without a price. Two relationships with males had to be eliminated before the third one proved to be a success. The first of the two failures described in *Memoirs* fits Pratt's archetypal patterns only too well, but with one major difference. In the prenuptial stages of the relationship, the man initially offers more than he is willing to deliver. The woman is lured into what she believes is a relationship of mutual equality, and the marriage proves to be the opposite. This is the first part of the archetypal structure in which al-Saʿdâwî's heroine finds herself. But unlike the protagonists discussed by Pratt, the narrator of *Mudhak-kirât* will not allow her health (read: her body) to atrophy. Rather, she leaves her husband and continues her quest.

Thus it is that she finally meets the right mediator. And in both her case and in that of Tâhâ, the mediator is a member of the dominant or "normal" social group: for Tâhâ, a sighted individual, and for the young physician, a male artist. And by his presence and acceptance, the mediator then testifies to the new, nonproblematic status of the marginal. The artist, like the voice, permits the full resolution of the personal and social conflicts provoked by the marginality of the hero. A similar set of images (including the light/darkness metaphor) involving nature and a rebirth through the intercession of a third party can be seen in Helen Keller's autobiography.[28]

It is perhaps not coincidental, either, that both the blind hero and the female protagonist dwell on their ability to be like everyone else, if not better. The narrator of *Memoirs* ends the first chapter by insisting that she will show her mother "that I am smarter than my brother, than man, than all men . . . and that I am capable of doing all that my father does, and still more."[29] Similarly, *The Days* explains that during Tâhâ's stay in France, he came into contact with something which "awakened in him hopes that had never occurred to him. He knew that he could be like other people, rather *better than* many people."[30] The physical difference will be not only conquered but redefined in such a way that it will provide the path to superiority rather than inferiority. The body will be the conquered and not the conqueror.

These similarities in narrative structures and expressions reflect an essential parallel between the sagas recounted by these two texts. There is, however, a point at which the parallels become identity. This point is verbal. One term crystallizes the central issues of both works.

[28] Helen Keller, *The Story of My Life* (New York: Airmont Publishing Company, 1965), p. 19.

[29] Al-Saʿdâwî, *Mudhakkirât*, p. 21; al-Saʿdawi, "Growing Up," p. 119.

[30] Tâhâ Husayn, *al-Ayyâm*, 3:88, emphasis mine.

One of the most central, provocative, and emotionally laden words in Nawâl al-Saʿdâwî's *Memoirs of a Female Physician* is *ʿawra*. In literary Arabic, this word signifies at the same time something shameful, defective, and imperfect; the genitals; and something that must be covered.[31] Should the girl's dress ride up while she was sitting, her mother "would give her a sharp look" and she would hide her "*ʿawra*." "*ʿAwra*! Everything in me is *ʿawra*, though I am a child of nine years!"[32] After her awakening through the medium of nature, now that she no longers feels that "terror" when her legs are bared by a breeze, the young physician wonders how her mother had been able to instill in her "that loathsome sensation that my body was *ʿawra*."[33]

In al-Saʿdâwî's text, therefore, the initial *ʿawra* of the private parts is made to expand and apply to the heroine's body in its entirety. In large part, the concept of *ʿawra* contributes to the sense of difference that the young woman feels and which sets her apart, marginalizing her.

This very idea of *ʿawra*, interestingly enough, also distinguishes the blind hero of *The Days*. When Tâhâ was on board the ship to Europe, he discarded his traditional Egyptian Azharî dress for European garb. But, according to the narrator, he only forgot one thing, "that blind sight of his," and his eyelids that opened on "darkness." It was then that he remembered that Abû al-ʿAlâʾ al-Maʿarrî (with whom he had been identifying himself) used to say, "Blindness is an *ʿawra*." At this point in the text, Tâhâ begins wearing dark glasses, to cover his eyes. Yet the narrator does not put this concept aside but repeats twice more that blindness is an *ʿawra*, extending the shame from earlier actions that set the protagonist apart as a blind individual (such as his eating and drinking in isolation in order not to evoke the pity or sarcasm of the sighted) to this latest indignity, having to cover his eyes with dark glasses.[34]

ʿAwra is, thus, for both figures, a sign whose signifieds expand outward in concentric circles from a physically circumscribed reality to the dilemmas of the hero and heroine themselves. The identity of the signifier, of course, associates the signifieds.

The primary referents of *ʿawra* are physical: the private parts of the heroine of *Memoirs*, the blind eyes of the hero of *The Days*. But it is

---

[31] Hans Wehr, *A Dictionary of Modern Written Arabic*, ed. J. Milton Cowan (Ithaca: Spoken Languages Services, 1976), p. 656; Ibn Manzûr, *Lisân al-ʿArab* (Cairo: al-Dâr al-Misriyya lil-Taʾlîf wal-Tarjama, n.d.), 6:290–299; al-Zabîdî, *Tâj al-ʿArûs*, vol. 13, ed. Husayn Nassâr (Kuwait: Matbaʿat Hukûmat al-Kuwayt, 1974), pp. 154–170; Ibn Sîda, *al-Muhkam wal-Muhît al-Aʿzam fî al-Lugha*, vol. 2, ed. ʿAbd al-Sattâr Ahmad Farrâj (Cairo: Matbaʿat Mustafâ al-Bâbî al-Halabî, 1958), pp. 245–249.

[32] Al-Saʿdâwî, *Mudhakkirât*, pp. 6–7; al-Saʿdawi, "Growing Up," p. 112.

[33] Al-Saʿdâwî, *Mudhakkirât*, p. 46.

[34] Tâhâ Husayn, *al-Ayyâm*, 3:96, 100; Malti-Douglas, *Blindness and Autobiography*, pp. 55–57.

obvious that it also stands for the femininity of the female physician and the blindness of Tâhâ. ʿAwra can make this semiotic leap because it is, in fact, part of a physico-moral discourse in Arabic culture—a discourse of the body. In this discourse, a physical reality, which in and of itself possesses no necessary moral or social meaning, is invested with a moral value. This, in turn, dictates social conclusions. It is in the nature of such physico-moral discourses to occult the middle step in this process, to make it appear as if the first principle, the physical reality, dictates the third, the social conclusion. The concept of ʿawra, however, with its moral essence (that which is shameful) clearly links the physical referent to the social conclusion (that which must be covered).

ʿAwra is central to the predicament of both hero and heroine, the key cultural reality against which they rebel, embodying both their sense of physical shame and inadequacy, on the one hand, and the social restrictions placed upon them, on the other. But the coincidence of the term ʿawra does more than signify a similarity in the situations of the two protagonists: it links and mutually defines them. When their physical realities are viewed through the lens of ʿawra, they are elevated to a level of moral abstraction at which they become equivalent. Tâhâ's eyes become like pudenda that must be covered, while the female physician's entire body takes on the notions of shame and imperfection associated with a physical handicap like blindness. It should be borne in mind that what we are discussing here is the conceptualization of a radical feminist novel, not the official positions of the society. Many would argue that woman's body must be covered because of its high value and attractiveness, that it is a hidden treasure. Of course, one could reply with Terry Eagleton that "for women of any epoch, the pedestal is never very far from the pit."[35] More pertinently, the valuation of that which is covered is not the perspective of the heroine of *Memoirs* or that of the work as a whole. That is why ʿawra is exploited as a negative term and the baring of the body is associated with "terror."

But whence comes this identity between blind man and sighted woman? Is it merely a modern sociological perception of shared marginality? Certainly, other modern texts reflect this sameness. In a particularly effective short story, the Syrian woman writer, Ghâda al-Sammân, brings the same two categories together when her female protagonist goes out for a walk at the end of the narrative. She encounters a blind man in the street.

> I see a man in the distance. He is walking slowly at the end of the road. He comes towards me. Nearer. With a stick he taps the ground. My companion

[35] Terry Eagleton, *The Rape of Clarissa: Writing, Sexuality and Class Struggle in Samuel Richardson* (Minneapolis: University of Minnesota Press, 1982), p. 15.

in the deserted street . . my companion in the brazen city, the companion of my wanderings at dawn . . in a dawn that will not brighten. He comes nearer. Lost, he wanders towards me, he does not see me . . He is blind. My companion is a blind man, who taps the ground with his stick, walking along unseen ways. Dawn and dusk are all one to him. I feel a strong link between him and me . . I walk beside him . . He does not hear my footsteps . .

I walk beside him and feel my way along with my glances as he feels his with his stick. He walks and talks to himself—it does not matter what he is saying. I also mutter and talk to myself. We walk on and on and at a distance we look like two friends.

A fearful satisfaction fills me. Together we represent the closest of human ties . . no pretences, no forced conversation.[36]

The blind man becomes the heroine's alter ego. Associations of a heroine and a blind man are also developed in Andrée Chedid's novel *Le sommeil délivré*, especially an argument of social equivalence. Twice, we are told: "At that hour. . . . The village belongs [is] to children, to women, and to the blind man."[37] Assia Djebar compares the veiled female to the blind person: "Render her invisible. Transform her into a being more blind than the blind."[38]

The narrator of *The Days* himself pointed to the origin of this mental structure when he authorized the association of blindness with ʿawra not primarily through the predicament of the hero but through the words of the medieval poet Abû al-ʿAlâʾ al-Maʿarrî. Indeed, the equivalence, or even identity, of the blind man and the sighted female is such a well-established mental structure in classical Arabic civilization that it can be identified in several different cultural contexts.

I have already had occasion to elaborate the notion that one of the most important sources for the medieval Arabic literary consciousness is that category of works referred to as adab works.[39] Analysis of how woman became a character type in this complex system of literary and social characterization helped to elucidate woman's discourse, in particular as it intersected with her body.

The relations between social groups, like the blind and women, are most clearly evident in the subcategory of encyclopedic adab works. Each

---

[36] Ghâda al-Sammân, "Ghajariyya bi-lâ Marfaʾ," in Ghâda al-Sammân, *Lâ Bahr fî Bayrût* (Beirut: Manshûrât Ghâda al-Sammân, 1981), p. 81. The translation is taken from Ghada el Samman, "Street Walker," trans. Azza Kararah; rev. Lewis Hall, in *Arabic Writing Today: The Short Story*, ed. Mahmoud Manzalaoui (Cairo: Dar al-Maaref, 1968), p. 326. On Ghâda al-Sammân, see Hanan Awwad, *Arab Causes in the Fiction of Ghâdah al-Sammân 1961/1975* (Quebec: Editions Naaman, 1983).

[37] Chedid, *Le sommeil*, pp. 129, 140.

[38] Assia Djebar, *L'amour, la fantasia* (Paris: Editions Jean-Claude Lattès, 1985), p. 138.

[39] See chapters 2 and 3 above.

topic in these multisubject collections, we should remember, is defined not only in its own terms but also in reference to its textual neighbors. In the arrangement of subjects, semiotic principles operate, including the syntactic, the relative position of an item in a sequence. A syntactic organization loosely reflecting a hierarchy of social status tends to predominate, with the most important subjects preceding the less dignified ones. The second semiotic principle operative in encyclopedic adab works, and closely related to the first, is the syntagmatic, the relationship between a given subject and its immediate neighbors in a chain with which it forms a syntagm.[40]

Syntactically, within the adab social hierarchy, both the women and the blind are placed toward the end of the encyclopedic collections, usually along with other physically or socially marginal types. This is the case, for example, in Ibn Qutayba's prototypical encyclopedia, the ʿUyûn al-Akhbâr.[41] Hence, on one level, the women and the blind are relegated to a similar social status.

But it is syntagmatically that the special relationship between women and the blind surfaces most clearly. In Ibn Qutayba's work (in which the women bring up the rear), the blind are actually embedded in the "Book of Women." In this book, material on women precedes and follows the material on the blind and other handicapped.[42] A similarly close association exists between the two groups in al-Nuwayrî's fourteenth-century encyclopedia. Here, the anecdotal chapter on the blind is placed between that on women and that on beggars.[43] The relationship between blindness and beggary is evident. Many beggars were blind (or pretended to be).[44] That between the blind and women is less obvious and depends upon the mental structure of equivalence.

Clearly, then, in these literary works, women and the blind are relegated to the same mental universe: one of physicality, relative physical imperfection, and social marginality. The intimate connection between

[40] I have discussed this issue in detail elsewhere. Malti-Douglas, *Structures of Avarice*, pp. 14–17.

[41] Ibn Qutayba, ʿUyûn, 4:1–147.

[42] Ibid.

[43] Al-Nuwayrî, *Nihâyat al-Arab*, 4:18–23.

[44] Alongside the relatively small number of genuine blind beggars, we find a large number of falsely blind beggars, beggars who feign blindness. See, for example, al-Jâhiz, *Bukhalâʾ*, p. 53; al-Bayhaqî, *al-Mahâsin wal-Masâwî*, ed. Muhammad Abû al-Fadl Ibrâhîm (Cairo: Matbaʿat Nahdat Misr, n.d.), 2:415–416; al-Tanûkhî, *Nishwâr al-Muhâdara*, ed. ʿAbbûd al-Shâlijî (Beirut: Dâr Sâdir, 1971–1973), 2:358; al-Hamadhânî, *al-Maqâmât*, ed. Muhammad ʿAbduh (Beirut: Dâr al-Mashriq, 1968), pp. 78–81. See, also, the excellent study by C. E. Bosworth, *The Medieval Islamic Underworld: The Banû Sâsân in Arabic Society and Literature* (Leiden: E. J. Brill, 1976), vol. 1, especially pp. 39ff.

these two socially marginal groups in the medieval Arabic consciousness is not, however, limited to the literary sphere.

In the introductory essays to his biographical dictionary of the blind, al-Safadî discusses the reliability of the blind as transmitters of Prophetic traditions. The problem is linked to the possibility of confusion arising from the hearing process. Islamic legists noted that when the wife of the Prophet, ʿAʾisha, and other holy women in early Islam transmitted ha-dîths, they did so from behind a curtain. Their hearers would then transmit on their authority. It is well known, al-Safadî notes, that in this case, the state of the sighted woman is the same as that of the blind man. Similarly, on the pilgrimage, the legal status of the guide (qâʾid) of the blind man is the same as that of the male guardian (mahram) of the woman.[45] When legal comparisons are needed, it is with women that they are made. In al-Suyûtî's epitome of Shâfiʿî jurisprudence, for example, al-Ashbâh wal-Nazâʾir, the status of the sightless is explicitly related to that of women.[46]

The association between women and handicaps might seem at the out-set to be a universal phenomenon. To quote Mary Ann Doane, "Disease [here, I would substitute handicap] and the woman have something in common—they are both socially devalued or undesirable, marginalized elements which constantly threaten to infiltrate and contaminate that which is more central, health or masculinity."[47] What distinguishes the Arabo-Islamic tradition is the mode of articulation of the nexus handicap/woman. Rather than a syntagmatic relationship in which the woman be-comes closely associated with disease, if not its carrier, we observe a par-adigmatic relationship in which women and the blind become inter-changeable phenomena. For example, the well-known Western association of hysteria with women more commonly produces hysterical women than an equivalence between hysterical men and normal women. A similar pattern obtains with other diseases. In the Arabo-Islamic con-text, blind women, while not completely absent in historical and some limited literary sources, are textually rare and do not become cultural foci or topoi. In the modern West, by contrast, the syntagmatic addition of blindness and womanhood is quite common. From André Gide's *La sym-phonie pastorale* to Marc Baconnet's *Midi, la nuit*, blindness reinforces

---

[45] Al-Safadî, *Nakt*, pp. 50, 62. On the mental structures governing the blind in medieval Islam, especially in the Mamlûk period, see Malti-Douglas, "*Mentalités* and Marginality," pp. 211–237.

[46] See, for example, al-Suyûtî, *al-Ashbâh wal-Nazâʾir fî Qawâʾid wa-Furûʿ Fiqh al-Shâfiʿiyya* (Cairo: ʿIsâ al-Bâbî al-Halabî, n.d.), pp. 273–276.

[47] Mary Ann Doane, "The Clinical Eye: Medical Discourses in the 'Woman's Film' of the 1940s," in Suleiman, *The Female Body*, p. 152.

the feminine frailty of a heroine.[48] In Rayner Heppenstall's *The Blaze of Noon*, a blind-deaf female establishes a relative weakness and dependence vis-à-vis the blind male hero.[49] The paradigmatic relationship between blind man and sighted woman seems unique to Arab culture.

The classical Arabic tradition, however, contains more than literary or legal equivalences. As we saw, it is also the origin of the multireferential concept of ʿawra itself. This word is derived from the radicals ʿayn-wâw-râʾ, which can signify the related meanings of the loss of an eye or the performance of a base act.[50]

The relationship of the eye to the genitals is, however, more than lexicographical. Abdelwahab Bouhdiba, in his provocative work *La sexualité en Islam*, cites the polymath Fakhr al-Dîn al-Râzî (d. 606/1209) to the effect that the sight of the genitals of a sexual partner makes one blind.[51] The erotic manuals also link the sexual act to the visual one. Al-Nafzâwî, for example, advises that copulation before breakfast weakens sight and will cause blindness to be inherited.[52] And it is certainly not a coincidence that the names of the male sexual organ include *al-aʿwar*, "the one-eyed," and *abû ʿayn*, "he of the one eye."[53] The concept of ʿawra is, furthermore, extended to areas that are not, at first glance, primarily sexual. The voice of a Muslim woman, for example, is ʿawra. In addition, both the lexicographers Ibn Manzûr (d. 711/1312) and al-Zabîdî (d. 1205/1791) cite the hadîth "Woman is an ʿawra."[54] The position of the legist Ahmad

---

[48] André Gide, *La symphonie pastorale* (Paris: Gallimard, 1925); Marc Baconnet, *Midi, la nuit* (Paris: Gallimard, 1984).

[49] Rayner Heppenstall, *The Blaze of Noon* (London: Allison and Busby, 1980).

[50] Ibn Manzûr, *Lisân*, 6:290–299; al-Zabîdî, *Tâj*, 13:154–170; Ibn Sîda, *al-Muhkam*, 2:245–249. Cf. Bouhdiba, *La sexualité*, p. 52. Cf., also, Chebel, *Le corps*, p. 25, who speaks of "la 'partie aveugle' du corps (el-âwra)" (the "blind part" of the body).

[51] Bouhdiba, *La sexualité*, p. 51. Cf. Khatibi, *La blessure*, p. 157.

[52] Al-Nafzâwî, *al-Rawd*, pp. 22, 24.

[53] Ibid., p. 24. Chebel, *Le corps*, p. 57, lists "l'aveugle" (the blind one) as one of the names given by al-Nafzâwî for the penis. None of the versions available to me lists this.

[54] Bouhdiba, *La sexualité*, pp. 51, 53. Ibn Manzûr, *Lisân*, 6:296; al-Zabîdî, *Tâj*, 13:161. On the identification of eyes with genitals in the West, see, for example, Donald D. Kirtley, *The Psychology of Blindness* (Chicago: Nelson-Hall, 1975), pp. 31–33; William R. Paulson, *Enlightenment, Romanticism, and the Blind in France* (Princeton: Princeton University Press, 1987), p. 82. It is noteworthy that in the Western tradition, blind men are not made the equivalent of women. Instead, they are desexualized. See Kirtley, *Psychology*, pp. 21, 27–30, 39, for example; Pierre Henri, *Les aveugles et la société* (Paris: Presses Universitaires de France, 1958), pp. 36–37, 56, 16, for example. The relationship of blindness and sexuality will be discussed further below.

This question is distinct from the idea put forward by feminists like Luce Irigaray, that male sexuality is essentially "scopic," that is, visual-dominant. The heroine of *Memoirs* must respond within the visual context that demands covering. On the other hand, Husayn's autobiographical hero clearly objectifies, reduces, and dominates his love/sex object, but he does so in a completely nonvisual way. See, for example, Moi, *Sexual*, pp. 143–145.

ibn Hanbal (d. 241/855) is more categorical: he simply states, "Everything in woman is an ʿawra."[55] Such extensions would by no means surprise the narrator-heroine of *Memoirs*.[56]

Clearly, then, the medieval Islamic mental universe brings together women and the blind. Equally clearly, this was seen to be operative in the two contemporary texts as well. But the relationship of Nawâl al-Saʿdâwî to her predecessor, Tâhâ Husayn, is more complex than this linkage itself. It extends from the plane of mental structures to that of literary history.

In *The Anxiety of Influence*, as well as other work, Harold Bloom argues that the literary text, in particular the poem, functions in a dialectic with earlier texts. For him, there is an Oedipal relationship between earlier and later writers, similar to that between fathers and sons. The son must, in some sense, overcome the father.[57] The gender-defined (and, hence, limited) nature of Bloom's interpretive model is now a commonplace in gender criticism. Annette Kolodny has certainly made it clear that Bloom is working within a single, dominant literary tradition, and that his conclusions cannot be applied easily to authors, like female writers, who may feel themselves alienated from the dominant, male-oriented, tradition.[58] Rather than an anxiety of influence, one might better speak of an "anxiety of authorship," to use Gilbert and Gubar's formulation.[59]

A woman writer, especially if she is also a feminist, is obliged not only to imitate but also, in a certain sense, to negate her literary predecessors insofar as these are seen as constituting a masculine tradition against which she is rebelling. Such a perspective is plainly applicable to the two texts at hand.

Within the Arabic literary tradition, both medieval and modern, women have traditionally held a less prominent position than their male counterparts. This does not mean that women were considered outside

[55] Ibn Hanbal, *Ahkâm al-Nisâ'*, pp. 29ff.

[56] Al-Saʿdâwî herself expands the boundaries of ʿawra when, in a short story entitled "And Love Died," the narrator declares that "weakness is an ʿawra." Nawâl al-Saʿdâwî, "Wa-Mâta al-Hubb," in Nawâl al-Saʿdâwî, *Hanân Qalîl* (Beirut: Dâr al-Adâb, 1986), p. 83.

[57] Harold Bloom, *The Anxiety of Influence: A Theory of Poetry* (New York: Oxford University Press, 1973). For a discussion of Bloom's other developments on this subject, see Annette Kolodny, "A Map for Rereading: Gender and the Interpretation of Literary Texts," in *The New Feminist Criticism: Essays on Women, Literature and Theory*, ed. Elaine Showalter (New York: Pantheon Books, 1985), pp. 46–62.

[58] Kolodny, "Map for Rereading," in Showalter, *Feminist Criticism*, pp. 46–62. And for a masterful and wide-ranging feminist revision of the Bloomian thesis, see Sandra M. Gilbert and Susan Gubar, *The Madwoman in the Attic: The Woman Writer and the Nineteenth-Century Literary Imagination* (New Haven: Yale University Press, 1979).

[59] See, for example, Gilbert and Gubar, *Madwoman*, pp. 49–51.

the pale of literature and culture. There certainly have been prominent women poets, like the pre-Islamic al-Khansâ' and the medieval Andalusian Wallâda, as well as women mystics and scholars. But these individuals were really exceptions, both exceptional women and exceptions as literary figures. Most female poets, of course, were the Islamic equivalents of geishas, the singing slave girls. Their social marginality and dubious respectability were evidenced by the distinctive treatment they always received in biographical and literary sources.[60] Thus, if one were to name the literary classics of medieval (and, it could be argued, modern) Arabic literature, few (if any) women writers would be included. Arabic literature is a masculine tradition, and this is especially true of prose writing. A woman belletrist working within this tradition reacts to it, whether or not one wishes to cast this reaction into Bloomian-Oedipal, or other Freudian, terms.

This is particularly true of Nawâl al-Saʿdâwî's *Memoirs of a Female Physician*. The text is a feminist response to the autobiography of Tâhâ Husayn, itself one of the most widely read works in the Arabic literary tradition. Al-Saʿdâwî read *The Days* at a young age and was greatly angered by its antifemale bias. When I first asked Dr. al-Saʿdâwî in 1983 how she felt about Tâhâ Husayn's *The Days*, I was surprised by the vehemence of her answer. I have subsequently discussed this issue at length with her on numerous occasions, both in Cairo and in the United States, and it is clear that the autobiography of Tâhâ Husayn made a considerable (though not necessarily positive) impression on her. Of course, such implicit rewriting is distinct from Nawâl al-Saʿdâwî's explicit rewriting of Tawfîq al-Hakîm's famous play *Izîs* with her own feminist version, under the same title.[61] Her reaction to Tâhâ Husayn's text is not by any means fanciful. *Al-Ayyâm* is a sexist, if not misogynist, text.

The two female characters that play a major role in the autobiography are Tâhâ's mother and his wife. The mother is the symbol of tradition, in its most aggressively ignorant and destructive sense. It is she who places the painful drops in the young Tâhâ's eyes. She carries the blame for his blindness through her ignorance of modern medicine and her unwillingness to call in a physician for her ailing children. Her role is assimilated to that of all mothers (hence, all women): "And what child does not complain! It is only a day and a night, then he awakens and is cured. And if his mother does concern herself with him, she belittles the physician or

---

[60] See chapter 2 above.

[61] For a further discussion of antifemale elements in Tâhâ Husayn's autobiography, see Malti-Douglas, *Blindness and Autobiography*, chapters 1 and 5. Nawâl al-Saʿdâwî, "Introduction," in Nawâl al-Saʿdâwî, *Izîs* (Cairo: Dâr al-Mustaqbal al-ʿArabî, 1986), pp. 6–16. For al-Saʿdâwî's negative appraisal of the gender politics of some other Husaynian texts, see al-Saʿdâwî, *ʿAn al-Marʾa*, pp. 99–101.

ignores him. She relies on that criminal knowledge, the knowledge of women and their likes." When Tâhâ's brother, afflicted with cholera, lies on his deathbed, the father calls in a doctor, while the mother prays. Her prayers, a traditional response, are placed in clear opposition to the scientific intervention of the physician. Associations of tradition with the female and with therapeutic inefficacy are, of course, not unique to *al-Ayyâm*. We find them in the equally eloquent autobiography of the blind Indian-American Ved Mehta.[62] In the Egyptian odyssey, they come together with the description of the wife to create the antifemale bias which permeates that classic of modern Arabic literature.

The treatment of Tâhâ's French spouse, while superficially more positive, does nothing to rectify the sexist view of women. She is initially presented by the third-person narrator as a voice, devoid of a name and a body. It could be argued, of course, that this is primarily due to the central character's visual handicap, since he learns to acquire knowledge largely through his hearing. But as I have shown in my study of *al-Ayyâm*, third-person narration is a textual ruse that can permit the intervention of a sighted narrator—that is, one possessing the ability to see—to counter the blind central character. And this sighted narrator often shows his powers of physical visual description.[63] Tâhâ's companion is barely developed as a character and remains always subordinated to the hero. When she ceases to be merely a "voice," it is to become Tâhâ's "eyes."

Nawâl al-Sa'dâwî's reaction to *al-Ayyâm* is, hence, quite gender-conscious. *Memoirs*, the first novel she authored and which represented a sort of rite de passage for her as a writer,[64] effectively reverses the dynamics of the Husaynian text, recasting them from the point of view of a female protagonist. This, of course, reverses the sexual politics of Tâhâ Husayn's autobiography. But it does not do so by negating the male author's central problematic. Instead, a new figure, the woman, has been substituted for the original one, the blind man. And it is the classical Arabic mental structure of the equivalence of these two physico-social types that permits this paradigmatic literary relationship. Sexual politics are reversed; social politics of marginality are preserved. Here, we can see the dialectical relationship between the feminist's novel and the autobiography of her male predecessor. Even the manner of the literary rebellion itself is based on the shared classical tradition of mental structures governing blindness and gender. If a sighted woman can borrow the textual strategies of a blind man, it is because she, like him, has been linked to a devalued body.

[62] See, for example, Ved Mehta, *Vedi* (New York: Oxford University Press, 1981), p. 15.
[63] Malti-Douglas, *Blindness and Autobiography*, pp. 93–112.
[64] Nawâl al-Sa'dâwî, personal communication, Cairo, Egypt, July 1983.

CHAPTER 7

Nawâl al-Saʿdâwî and Empowerment through Medicine

IN IBN TUFAYL'S mystical allegory, the violent dissection of the gazelle/ mother was a crucial step for the young hero's onset of consciousness. In Nawâl al-Saʿdâwî's *Memoirs of a Female Physician*, dissection, but this time of a human body, plays an equally important role, in this case for the heroine's gender consciousness. It is no accident that both the eleventh-century Andalusian writer and the twentieth-century Egyptian feminist were/are physicians. For this contemporary woman writer, medicine, science, and the physician are placed in a dialectical relationship with the feminist problematic of gender and power. The physician's science is sublimated first into social power in the battle between the sexes and, second, into the discursive authority, the power of comprehension and description, that the medical practitioner shares with the writer. For Nawâl al-Saʿdâwî, medicine and its literary articulation are inextricably tied to woman's body and to the expressive ability of woman's literary voice. But as a branch of science, medicine also plays a key mediating role in a set of creative tensions between control and compassion, society and nature, and, finally, in a reformulation of the idea of the two cultures, science and art.[1] Medicine turns into the literary locus for discussions of science, art, and gender.

Several of the most sophisticated and most influential writers of the contemporary Arab world are, or have been, practicing physicians. There is a societal reason for this: in the Egyptian educational system, the best secondary school graduates frequently entered the Faculty of Medicine, since this path was at once the most demanding and the most prestigious. Among male authors in this group, the best known is certainly the Egyptian fiction writer Yûsuf Idrîs. Others include the Syrian ʿAbd al-Salâm al-ʿUjaylî, and the Egyptians Mustafâ Mahmûd and Sherif Hetata. In the oeuvre of each of these men, medicine and/or the physician play an important role.[2]

---

[1] C. P. Snow, *The Two Cultures and A Second Look* (Cambridge: Cambridge University Press, 1986).

[2] Mahmûd and Hetata have yet to receive major critical attention. On Yûsuf Idrîs, see P. M. Kurpershoek, *The Short Stories of Yûsuf Idrîs* (Leiden: E. J. Brill, 1981); Sasson Somekh, *Lughat al-Qissa fî Adab Yûsuf Idrîs* (Acre: Matbaʿat al-Sarûjî, 1984); and the intro-

Much the same phenomenon exists, of course, in the fiction of medical practitioners in the West, like Richard Selzer, William Carlos Williams, and others. In sharp contrast to her Western colleagues, the Egyptian feminist doctor makes relatively little of disease and cure, shifting attention instead to the social role of medicine and the physician. Striking, indeed, is her de-emphasis of the therapeutic process. Often, fictional situations that could lead to the medical treatment of physical maladies are short-circuited and resolved without professional intervention.[3] The therapeutic, essentially healing, relationships that physicians have with patients in, for example, the prose of William Carlos Williams or Richard Selzer are not present here.[4] This Sa'dâwian de-emphasis denudes medicine and science of part of their magical, technological power.

If the medical interaction between physician and patient is not the primary concern in these narratives, then what is? The most pervasive function of medicine (and the physician) in the Sa'dâwian fictional corpus is that of power, most often sexual.[5] Woman's body and woman's voice become pawns in the Sa'dâwian narrative medical discourse. Corporal dynamics shift: from her role as healer, the woman physician is transformed into a mediator of discourse.

Al-Sa'dâwî's first novel, *Memoirs of a Female Physician*, sets forth the major issues related to medicine and the physician that dominate the rest of her fictional corpus. The canonic implications of this text have already been investigated.[6] When the protagonist decides to attend the Faculty of Medicine, she is quite conscious that her decision is motivated by the respect and awe she witnessed her family manifesting toward the physician.

---

duction in Sasson Somekh, *Dunyâ Yûsuf Idrîs min Khilâl Aqâsisihi* (Tel Aviv: Dâr al-Nashr al-'Arabî, 1976). On 'Abd al-Salâm al-'Ujaylî, see Fedwa Malti-Douglas, "al-'Anâsir al-Turâthiyya fî al-Adab al-'Arabî al-Mu'âsir: al-Ahlâm fî Thalâth Qisas," trans. 'I. al-Sharqâwî, *Fusûl* 2, no. 2 (1982): 21–29.

[3] See, for example, Nawâl al-Sa'dâwî, "Lâ Shay' Yafnâ," in Nawâl al-Sa'dâwî, *Lahzat Sidq* (Beirut: Dâr al-Adâb, 1986), pp. 77–82; Nawâl al-Sa'dâwî, "Min Ajl Man," in Nawâl al-Sa'dâwî, *Hanân Qalîl*, pp. 123–127.

[4] For some of these relationships, see William Carlos Williams, *The Doctor Stories*, comp. Robert Coles (New York: New Directions Books, 1984); Richard Selzer, *Rituals of Surgery* (New York: Harper's Magazine Press, 1974).

[5] Tarâbîshî, in *Unthâ*, sees medicine chiefly as the limiting point between life and death: "Was it [medicine] not chosen as a profession because it permits its practitioner to live with death on a daily basis and to stand night and day on the threshold separating it and life?" (p. 66). This point is an excellent example of the methodological pitfalls of Tarâbîshî's approach. One *could* choose medicine for this reason, but there is no real evidence in al-Sa'dâwî's corpus, nor does Tarâbîshî adduce any, for such an interpretation. An important thematic element, like medicine, must be interpreted according to its function in a particular work or corpus. Only then can such conclusions be tested against other interpretive schemata, Freudian or otherwise.

[6] See chapter 6 above.

The medical school experience, which consists partly of dissecting cadavers, brings her to the conclusion, proven by science, that woman is like man, and man like animals. "Woman has a heart, a brain, and nerves, exactly like man. And an animal has a heart, a brain, and nerves, exactly like a human."[7] The body as physical entity is the great equalizer.

Memoirs also chronicles three childhood sexual encounters between the heroine and members of the opposite sex. The first involves a doorkeeper who approaches her when she is sitting on a bench and attempts to explore her sexual parts with his hand. She stands up in terror and runs away.[8] The second episode involves a friend of the heroine's father's. She is asked to meet him, as a matrimonial prospect. When her father announces that she is first in her class, she expects the guest to show some admiration. But all she sees is the man scrutinizing her body, to finally settle on her chest. She runs out of the room, again in terror.[9] The third encounter is with her cousin, with whom she played as a youngster. They take a walk together and decide to run a race. As she is about to win, however, he pulls her down and prepares to kiss her. For a moment, she wishes that he would embrace her fiercely, but when she comes back to her senses, she becomes angry and slaps him.[10]

These three childhood encounters display the same dynamics: physical violation, be it overt or covert, of woman's body. The first example, with the doorkeeper, is clear. The second, that with the father's friend, is more complex. Normally, this encounter would be viewed as entirely licit, or at least free of violation. But the narrator does not experience it this way, and that is why she runs away with the same terror. Despite its socially licit nature, this encounter must be understood as an illicit one, also representing a physical violation, though more subtle than that by the doorkeeper. The narrator's ultimate reaction to her cousin's attempt to kiss her is to slap him. She, willy-nilly, has interpreted his advances, despite her own initial desire, as physical transgression.

Despite their various degrees of social licitness, these three incidents are all treated in the text as more or less open forms of physical violation, as unwanted male sexual power over woman. In the heroine's adult experiences, however, it is she who determines the outcome of the encounters, who initiates and terminates relationships with the males. The balance of power has shifted.

In the narrator's first adult relationship, leading to marriage with the engineer, she eventually leaves him when he attempts to block her career. Her second involvement, this time with a physician, is also a frustrated

---

[7] Al-Saʿdâwî, *Mudhakkirât*, p. 32.

[8] Ibid., p. 9; al-Saʿdawi, "Growing Up," pp. 113–114.

[9] Al-Saʿdâwî, *Mudhakkirât*, p. 12; al-Saʿdawi, "Growing Up," p. 115.

[10] Al-Saʿdâwî, *Mudhakkirât*, pp. 17–19; al-Saʿdawi, "Growing Up," pp. 118–119.

one and ends as well with her decision to leave him. It is only with the third male, a composer, that the heroine achieves a successful relationship.

The rite of passage that separates childhood from adult status is the heroine's medical training. Medicine equals power, and it is this power that, in fact, instigates the narrator to attend the medical faculty in the first place. Medicine gives the male attribute of power to the female.

Al-Saʿdâwî's position here can be seen most clearly when compared with that in a story by the Egyptian male physician writer Yûsuf Idrîs. In "On Cellophane Paper," a woman, disgusted with her marital situation, experiences a change of attitude when she watches her husband perform a delicate surgical procedure.[11] If for Yûsuf Idrîs medicine can act as the means for the establishment of the male gender's power over womankind, for Nawâl al-Saʿdâwî it becomes the means through which a woman escapes the roles traditionally assigned to her sex. In another of al-Saʿdâwî's novels, *al-Ghâʾib* (The absent one), the female protagonist is prevented from entering medical school by her poor examination scores. This was the career her mother had wished for her, since men were "useless."[12]

Yet there is more to medicine in *Memoirs* than sexual power. At first, the heroine conceives of it as science and as an all-powerful deity. But her view changes as she sees one of the physician-instructors slap a patient, and she decides that this medicine, at least, lacks compassion. In effect, the narrator projects the male-female division directly onto medicine, pairing off science versus art, and coldness versus compassion. It is only because the female physician is able to overcome her obsession with medicine as power that she is equally able to transcend her focus on the male-female power struggle and come to terms with both her femininity and medicine. This last is now seen as both science and art, reason and compassion.

One of the interesting elements in this system is that while the female physician-heroines integrate these two aspects of medicine, the male physicians do not. Indeed, in *Memoirs*, and in the work of Nawâl al-Saʿdâwî generally, there are really two types of physician. While the female physicians are capable of compassion, their male counterparts are generally coldhearted embodiments of science. There are only two short stories in Nawâl al-Saʿdâwî's fictional corpus in which the male physicians play a central role without their being opposed to female medical practitioners

[11] Yûsuf Idrîs, "ʿAlâ Waraq Sîlûfân," in Yûsuf Idrîs, *Bayt min Lahm* (Cairo: Dâr Misr lil-Tibâʿa, 1982), pp. 31–51, translated by Roger Allen as "In Cellophane Wrapping," in *In the Eye of the Beholder: Tales of Egyptian Life from the Writings of Yusuf Idris*, ed. Roger Allen (Minneapolis and Chicago: Bibliotheca Islamica, 1978), pp. 169–189.

[12] Nawâl al-Saʿdâwî, *al-Ghâʾib* (Cairo: Maktabat Madbûlî, n.d.), p. 18.

in the same narrative. And both form part of al-Sa'dâwî's first published collection of short stories, *Ta'allamt al-Hubb* (I learned love). In one, "Shay' Akhar" (Something else), the reader is treated to a day in the life of Dr. Rajab, economically not as well off as his neighbor, whose Cadillac the physician admires with envy. Dr. Rajab insults his staff, has too many patients and not enough beds, and feels that he has wasted seven years in medicine.[13] In the other text, "Hâdhihi al-Marra" (This time), the male physicians function as objects of desire for the nurses, who see them as an escape from the poverty and squalor of their lives.[14]

The arbitrariness of making the female physician caring and her male counterpart not can be seen when this pattern is compared with the strategy of Sherif Hetata, also a physician-writer (and the husband of Nawâl al-Sa'dâwî). In *The Eye with the Iron Lid*, for example, he pairs off two male medical practitioners, one coldhearted and cowardly, the other courageous and compassionate.[15]

Nawâl al-Sa'dâwî develops the sexual politics of medicine in two ways: first, by using it as a vehicle for women to regain their lost power; and second, by making it the focus of her own call for the integration of traditionally male and female qualities.

This complex of elements is not, however, restricted to *Memoirs of a Woman Physician*. In *Two Women in One*, the author develops similar themes. The heroine is a student in medical school and is torn between her medical training and her career as an artist. The same dichotomy is set up in the young woman's relationships with men: on the one hand, there is the medical doctor, the professor at the Faculty of Medicine, and on the other, the young man who encourages the heroine in her artistic endeavors.[16]

The thematic nexus of science and art, elements that pull in opposite directions, pervades the fictional narratives of Nawâl al-Sa'dâwî and tears her heroines apart.[17] In one short story, "A Special Letter to an Artist Friend," the first-person narrator, not surprisingly a physician, speaks of the conflict that has plagued her since birth. She wanted to become an

---

[13] Nawâl al-Sa'dâwî, "Shay' Akhar," in al-Sa'dâwî, *Ta'allamt*, pp. 71–88.

[14] Nawâl al-Sa'dâwî, "Hâdhihi al-Marra," in al-Sa'dâwî, *Ta'allamt*, pp. 52–61.

[15] Sherif Hetata, *al-'Ayn Dhât al-Jafn al-Ma'danî* (Cairo: Dâr al-Thaqâfa al-Jadîda, 1981), translated by Sherif Hetata as *The Eye with the Iron Lid* (London: Zed Press, n.d.).

[16] Nawâl al-Sa'dâwî, *Imra'atâni fî-Mra'a* (Cairo: Maktabat Madbûlî, 1983), translated by Osman Nusairi and Jana Gough as *Two Women in One* (London: al-Saqi Books, 1985).

[17] This dichotomy of art and science among physician writers is by no means peculiar to Nawâl al-Sa'dâwî's fiction. See, for example, Theodora R. Graham, "The Courage of His Diversity: Medicine, Writing, and William Carlos Williams," *Literature and Medicine* 2 (1983): 15. See, also, D. Heyward Brock, "An Interview with Dannie Abse," *Literature and Medicine* 3 (1984), especially, p. 18.

artist and wonders what drove her to become a physician.[18] That medicine precludes art is also visible in the novella *al-Khayt* (The thread). The patient in this text simply tells the female physician, "You are a physician and not an artist."[19]

But this conflict is perhaps most eloquently expressed by the female physician in the short story "Kullunâ Hayârâ" (All of us are confused). Here, the narrator reveals that she erred in choosing medicine. "I should have been an artist, or a poet, or a writer." The Faculty of Medicine is the "Faculty of Illness, and Moaning, and Death."[20] Much the same assessment is made by the heroine in the short story "Hînamâ Akûn Tâfiha" (When I am worthless). Here, the physician-narrator expresses her disgust at both her financial and her social status when she wonders how she could possibly have lost her way and entered the Faculty of Medicine.[21] The idea of medicine as death is extended to the accoutrements of the physician. In *Two Women in One*, for example, the metal stethoscope hanging around a physician's neck is likened to a hangman's noose. And this very same image is repeated in *Memoirs*.[22]

Medicine becomes, thus, a focus for conflicts and choices in the lives of young women. But these conflicts and choices revolve around medicine as a total system and especially as a career. The relationship of physician with patient, and hence also of physician with cure, is generally subordinate in the texts. This tendency is increased by the emphasis on the period of medical training.

But Nawâl al-Saʿdâwî explores the relations of power, medicine, and the female condition in other ways than simply by centering on medicine as a career. This she does by focusing on the physician-patient relationship in a significant, and eminently characteristic, literary procedure.

In some highly innovative texts, Nawâl a-Saʿdâwî exploits a narrative technique that, though it brings her close to her medieval literary ancestor, Shahrazâd, is most unusual in modern Arabic letters. This is a technique of embedding or enframing. A female physician, acting in her professional capacity, becomes the initial narrator who enframes a story told, eventually, by the patient.

Woman at Point Zero is without a doubt one of al-Saʿdâwî's most

---

[18] Nawâl al-Saʿdâwî, "Risâla Khâssa ilâ Sadîq Fannân," in Nawâl al-Saʿdâwî, *Mawt Maʿâlî al-Wazîr Sâbiqan* (Cairo: Maktabat Madbûlî, 1980), pp. 73–87, translated by Shirley Eber as "A Private Letter to an Artist Friend," in Nawal El Saadawi, *Death of an Ex-Minister*, translated by Shirley Eber (London: Methuen, 1987), pp. 97–111.

[19] Nawâl al-Saʿdâwî, *al-Khayt*, in *al-Khayt wa-ʿAyn al-Hayât* (Cairo: Maktabat Madbûlî, 1972), p. 41.

[20] Nawâl al-Saʿdâwî, "Kullunâ Hayârâ," in al-Saʿdâwî, *Taʿallamt*, pp. 144–148.

[21] Nawâl al-Saʿdâwî, "Hînamâ Akûn Tâfiha," in al-Saʿdâwî, *Hanân Qalîl*, p. 113.

[22] Al-Saʿdâwî, *Imraʾatâni*, p. 119; al-Saʿdâwî, *Mudhakkirât*, p. 35.

powerful novels. Its external narrator is a psychiatrist working in a women's prison. She begins the narration by explaining her interest in the case of one of the prisoners, a prostitute convicted of murder and awaiting execution. The bulk of the novel then consists of the narration of her own life by the convicted killer. The physician is drawn to this woman—realizing, at the end of the novel, that she herself is no better than the prostitute.[23]

The physician-narrator begins her literary frame with the assertion that "this woman is real, of flesh and blood."[24] This "real" woman, the voice that will enter the narrative and control her own saga, is defined first and foremost through her body. Her name, Firdaws, means Paradise. This richly allusive onomastic presence is contrasted with the narrator's namelessness. The physicality that initially defines Firdaws in the psychiatrist's frame will maintain her narrative.

But the reality of this prostitute-murderer is problematic: her narrative entrance and exit are couched in uncertainty. When the female jailer runs to the psychiatrist to announce to her the good news that Firdaws will talk to her, the physician likens the jailer's voice to the voices one hears in dreams: "And her mouth also became big, and her two large lips move in front of my eyes like two panels of a large door that is opening and closing, and then opening and closing."[25] The lips/panels of the mouth/door with their repeated opening and closing are an eloquent metaphor for the oral process that will follow. The female jailer is but a herald of things to come. In fact, the psychiatrist will enter Firdaws's narrative through her mouth/door.

But the jailer's large lips, when combined with her large mouth, also stand for woman's vagina. Firdaws's narration is announced through woman's body, and it is through, and for, the body that she will articulate her own saga. The vaginal metaphor is extended as we discover that the narration takes place in a hermetically empty cell, a womblike structure whose window and door are closed. The two women are the only things in it.

The dreamlike state introduced with the jailer is extended to the process of internal narration itself. The psychiatrist sits on the ground of the jail cell. She is "like someone who moves while asleep." The ground under her is cold, but with a coldness that does not reach her body, "like the coldness of the ocean in a dream." Firdaws's voice is "like those voices which we hear in dreams." They seem to come from afar, though they are

[23] Nawâl al-Saʿdâwî, *Imraʾa ʿind Nuqtat al-Sifr* (Beirut: Dâr al-Adâb, 1979), translated by Sherif Hetata as *Woman at Point Zero* (London: Zed Press, 1983). See, also, Accad and Ghurayyib, *Contemporary*, pp. 52–55.

[24] Al-Saʿdâwî, *Nuqtat al-Sifr*, p. 5.

[25] Ibid., p. 11.

near, or they sound close though they are far off.[26] There is great uncertainty in their provenance (from up or down? from the left or the right? from the earth or the sky?), which reinforces the uncertainty of the dreamlike state. When Firdaws's narration comes to an end, her voice "stopped suddenly as voices in a dream stop." The psychiatrist moves her body "like someone who moves while asleep." Though Firdaws's voice disappears, its echo remains "like those voices which we hear in dreams." Once again, where these voices come from seems uncertain. The identical phrases that introduced Firdaws's narration bring it to a close.[27] In this vast uncertainty, one thing is certain: we have come full circle.

Countering these dreamlike qualities is the psychiatrist's insistence that the woman whose story is about to unfold (in the opening of the frame) or has already unfolded (in the closure of the frame) is "real." She is "of flesh and blood."[28]

The tension between dream and reality lies at the heart of the frame, in its form as both prologue and epilogue, of *Woman at Point Zero*. Has the reader simply been witness to a dream? More important, what is the relationship of dream and reality? Reality is associated with "the flesh and blood" of Firdaws, a corporeality that defines her as a body. It is her voice that belongs to the ethereal and uncertain realm of dreams. Woman's body is pitted against woman's voice. And the two interact in a narrative game that overturns the reality of the body, flanked as it is by the uncertainty of the voice. That voice emanating from the world of dreams is responsible for the narrative. The narrative is what is "real" for the reader, and for the psychiatrist-listener. The flesh and blood, the elements of Firdaws's corporeality, will be destroyed when the death sentence is carried out.

Woman at Point Zero is a searing feminist indictment of male-female relations. Firdaws travels the different paths of a woman's life. She has a secondary school degree and is married at a young age to an old man. She is repeatedly abused by men. She becomes a prostitute but reforms her ways and works in an office as a secretary. She falls in love but becomes disillusioned when the object of her affections marries the boss's daughter. Firdaws returns to the streets, becoming a successful and sought-after object of men's desires. A pimp's attempts to run her existence lead to her killing him. One of the most important leitmotivs of the novel is woman's body. Who controls it? Who owns it? Does Firdaws have a right to it? Firdaws's narrative is a verbal attempt to reclaim her body. But society is more powerful, we learn. This female body will be ultimately annihilated.

[26] Ibid., pp. 13–14.
[27] Ibid., p. 114.
[28] Ibid., pp. 14, 114.

Were it not for the persistent psychiatrist, Firdaws's story would have been destroyed with its protagonist. "Let me speak and do not interrupt me," entreats the prisoner at the outset of her narrative, "for I have no time to listen to you."[29] Firdaws takes control, and the physician becomes the passive recipient of the discourse.

Telling her story, we discover, is essential to Firdaws's existence, ephemeral though it may be. When she meets the madam who will train her in the world's oldest profession, Firdaws learns that all men are identical, no matter what their name. She tells this newfound friend her story. The madam treats her to a bath, combs her hair, dresses her. Firdaws's body becomes "soft like the body of a child born an instant ago." When she opens her eyes and sees herself in the mirror, "I realized that I was born anew, with a soft clean body."[30] Just as recounting her tale to the madam permits her to shed the old Firdaws, expounding her saga to the psychiatrist will also bring about a rebirth of sorts, this time in the form of narrative.

Firdaws's discourse is oral. It is her physical voice that transmits her story. The voice of many other Sa'dâwian heroines is epistolary. The female physician-narrator of the novella *The Thread* tells the reader, in the frame, that she had had the occasion to see a woman with strange symptoms. The physician later receives a letter from this patient, outlining the events from her perspective. The physician and medicine are then seen through the eyes of this patient, who has had a neurotic relationship with her father. The patient, addressing the physician—external narrator, spends an inordinate amount of time explaining that her being a physician precludes her being a woman, that she is incapable of feeling, and then poses the question: can medicine turn a human being into a stone?[31] The patient's neurosis clearly connects this cold "scientific" aspect of medicine with patriarchy.

In both *The Thread* and *Woman at Point Zero*, the doctor is reflected through the patient, and in the two works, the patients receive more narrative space than their physicians. In addition, in these two cases, both the physicians and their patients are women. But the patients are deliberately set up as social opposites of the doctors. In both narratives, however, the sense of the speech (oral or epistolary) of the patients is an attempt to call this separation into question. In this way, both *The Thread* and *Woman at Point Zero* cast doubt on the role of the physician as an embodiment of science and wisdom, superior to, and standing outside of, the patient.

---

[29] Ibid., p. 15.
[30] Ibid., p. 61.
[31] Al-Sa'dâwî, *al-Khayt*.

It is not, however, coincidental that external and internal narrator, doctor and patient, are both women. The literary linkage reflects their common embodiment of the female condition. Physician and patient alike are caught in the coils of sexual politics.

The Thread and *Woman at Point Zero* show us, in a sense, only half the picture. Another Sa'dâwian text also exhibits this technique, but here, the internal narrative has nothing medical about it and could, in fact, stand on its own without the external narration by the physician. In "The Man of the Buttons," the physician-narrator tells us that she published a story entitled "My Husband, I Do Not Love You,"[32] to which one of her readers replied by expressing her dislike of the narrator's story and presenting her own story.[33]

This internal epistolary voice is named Firdaws, like the narrating Firdaws of *Woman at Point Zero*. The Firdaws of the short story is not a prostitute or a murderer, but she does cross paths with the Firdaws of the novel. For both women, the marital state becomes the occasion for a scorching criticism of male-female relations, in general, and of man's body, in particular. Both husbands, we discover, made a habit, out of miserly concern, of watching their wives eat.[34] The short story narrator has an obsession with a physical characteristic of her husband's: the *zabîba* (literally, raisin), the prayer bump on a Muslim's forehead that results from the forehead's repeatedly touching the ground during the ritual five daily prayers. This black zabîba is visible in the dark and constantly hits her own forehead when "that thing" occurs.[35] The novelistic Firdaws, more violent than her literary cousin in the short story, similarly centers on a facial characteristic: a tumor on her husband's lower lip. The physical aspects of this tumor are graphically described, as can be done only by a physician's pen. "Under his lower lip was a big tumor with a hole in its middle that would dry in a few days. On other days, like a rotten tap, red drops like blood or yellow or white drops like pus would fall from it."[36] The pus oozing from the sore evokes disgust both on Firdaws's part and on that of the reader, as the old man, over sixty years old, approaches his young wife, not yet nineteen, to kiss her. When the sore was not dry, "a stink resembling the stink of a dead dog" would

---

[32] There is, in fact, a story by that title in al-Sa'dâwî's collection *Ta'allamt*, pp. 135–143.

[33] Nawâl al-Sa'dâwî, "al-Rajul Dhû al-Azrâr," in Nawâl al-Sa'dâwî, *Kânat Hiya al-Ad'af* (Cairo: Maktabat Madbûlî, 1979), pp. 115–124, translated by Shirley Eber as "The Man with Buttons," in Nawal El Saadawi, *She Has No Place in Paradise*, trans. Shirley Eber (London: Minerva, 1989), pp. 103–111.

[34] Al-Sa'dâwî, "al-Rajul," in al-Sa'dâwî, *Kânat*, p. 122; al-Sa'dâwî, *Nuqtat al-Sifr*, p. 50.

[35] Al-Sa'dâwî, "al-Rajul," in al-Sa'dâwî, *Kânat*, pp. 118, 120.

[36] Al-Sa'dâwî, *Nuqtat al-Sifr*, p. 50.

emanate from it and the young woman would move away her lips and her nose.[37] Both Firdawses overtly connect the male physical oddity to the sexual act, as woman's body becomes but a tool at the hands of her husband. Both protrusions are felt as the male body comes close to that of the female.

The Firdaws of the zabîba calls into question the "real" aspect of the Firdaws in *Woman at Point Zero*. More important, the juxtaposition of the two female characters assures the fictionality of both accounts. One Firdaws relates her saga in a jail cell, the other through a letter.

If these internal narratives could have stood on their own, without need for an external physician-narrator, what is the function of the embedding? First and foremost, the external first-person narrator adds a second subjectivity to that of the internal narrator. More important, these embedded texts turn the narrative authority over to the physician, who becomes ultimately responsible for their transmission. Furthermore, by having embedded narratives that are not directly related to any medical questions, the text extends the power of the physician beyond the medical into the general. This can be seen in another story in which the physician-narrator decides to recount the story of a woman whom she had seen while practicing in Jordan.[38]

In all four cases of embedded narratives, the stories, both internal and external, are about women. In all four cases, as well, a physician-narrator presents the saga of a woman who might not, by her social situation, have the opportunity for literary self-expression. The physician, in her role as a figure of social power, serves as the literary medium through which the other voices can speak.

Here again, of course, medicine as power for individual women is set against a larger context of relative female powerlessness. But something far more subtle and more culturally encompassing is being intimated. Nawâl al-Saʿdâwî has fused the social power of the physician with that of the narrator. As cultural critics (first among them in time and importance Michel Foucault) have shown repeatedly, medicine acts as a special discourse, itself a form of power.[39] Like the writer, the physician interprets a reality, codifies it, explains it. To other physicians, he reports and transmits it. In the Saʿdâwian corpus, the social power of the physician merges into that of the writer.

In "A Story from a Female Physician's Life," a third-person narrator introduces the text: "Dr. S. wrote in her diary." This is followed by the

[37] Ibid., pp. 50, 52.

[38] Nawâl al-Saʿdâwî, *ʿAyn al-Hayât*, in al-Saʿdâwî, *al-Khayt*, pp. 59–112.

[39] See, for example, Michel Foucault, *Histoire de la folie à l'âge classique* (Paris: Editions Gallimard, 1972) and *Naissance de la clinique: Une archéologie du regard médical* (Paris: Presses Universitaires de France, 1963).

first-person narrative of Dr. S. and the permanent disappearance of the third-person narrator from the story. This is an odd coincidence, indeed—the initial S. standing, among other things, for al-Saʿdâwî. This is most plausible, given that the greater number of the Egyptian feminist's fictional texts are narrated in the first person. Dr. S. in this unusual framing proceeds to recount the story. A young girl is sitting in her clinic, flanked by a tall young man, her brother. The brother entreats the physician to examine his sister, wishing to reassure himself about her, "since we are marrying her off to her cousin next week." The girl cuts her brother off, insisting that she does not love this man and does not wish to marry him. The brother, however, responds that she does not want to marry him for "another reason, Doctor . . . I think you understand," a clear allusion to the possibility of her having lost her virginity. Observing the fright in the young girl's eyes, the physician asks the brother to leave the room in order that she may undertake the examination. Alone with the physician, the young girl begs her to save her from this brother, who would kill her. The physician decides that she cannot examine the patient without her permission. She tells the young woman that she will inform her brother that this is outside of her bounds. The patient objects, insisting that her brother will simply take her to another doctor. She then asks the physician to claim that she examined her and that she was "honorable." Her brother, she adds, will kill her otherwise. But she is in love with another man and will marry him in a month. She swears to the physician that nothing dishonorable has occurred between them. Examining her conscience and her medical codes, the physician calls in the brother and declares to him that his sister is honorable. As she explains it, she believes that the girl is indeed honorable. "Medicine can only distinguish between disease and nondisease. It cannot distinguish between honor and dishonor." The brother is made to apologize to his sister for doubting her, and the two leave. The physician then writes her own oath: "I swear that my humanity and my conscience will be my rules in my work and my art," adding, "I put down my pen and felt an ease I had not felt for a long time."[40]

The framing technique here serves to introduce the physician's written words. If it were absent, however, it would not alter the essential plot of the story. Hence, its presence is quite eloquent. This physician needs a third-person narrator as an intermediary who introduces the actual writing process itself. The recording of the story in writing differs from the oral and epistolary enframed narratives analyzed, although like them it requires mediation. Like the other protagonists whose sagas needed to be

---

[40] Nawâl al-Saʿdâwî, "Qissa min Hayât Tabîba," in al-Saʿdâwî, *Hanân Qalîl*, pp. 117–121.

narrated by the physician, these two characters, peasants, are individuals who would not have access to the written word. The female physician is in all these cases the means through which silent voices can tell their stories.

But the framing of Dr. S.'s story highlights an important element that redefines the other enframed narratives. The "Dr. S. writes in her diary" is followed by the account of a clinic visit: the two characters enter and pose the problem for the physician, the physician makes her "diagnosis," the two leave, and the physician writes her concluding words. The story functions as a medical case history. The frame emphasizes this. Seen this way, the other physician-mediated narratives take on a different cast. They also become case histories of sorts.

The brother-sister combo is reminiscent of the brother-sister duo in Ibn Tufayl's *Hayy ibn Yaqzân*. The sister in this twentieth-century short story resembles Hayy's mother, frightened as she is by her brother. Twice she repeats to the physician that her brother will kill her. The question of the girl's honor is the motivating force behind the visit to the physician. The female body must be certified as honorable before it can be handed on to the would-be husband. But this male knows little about women's solidarity. He is attempting to control woman's body, which becomes a pawn in intricate social gender games. The physician, however, is able to defeat this man's desire and give the young woman back her body. We are far from the medieval ludic anecdote in which a slave girl was asked whether she was a virgin or not. There, her wit eliminated her apparent physical imperfection.[41] Here, it is medicine as power over body and word that comes to the rescue.

In the Sa'dâwian short story, the brother's concern for his sister's virginity is preeminent. Her body is a commodity whose honor, if absent, will surely lead to her death. In his short story "al-'Urs al-Sharqî" (The Eastern wedding), the Syrian male writer Zakariyyâ Tâmir savagely attacks the marital customs that turn the female into a commodity. There, the price of the young girl is agreed on, so much per kilo, and she is taken to the marketplace and weighed in.[42] Tâmir comes close to al-Sa'dâwî who even in her first novel likened the vocabulary used in the marriage ceremony to that used in the rental of an apartment, store, or other property.[43] The marriage-as-commerce metaphor is repeated when the narrator of *Memoirs* wonders if people expect her to sit and wait while some

[41] See chapter 2 above.

[42] Zakariyyâ Tâmir, "al-'Urs al-Sharqî," in Zakariyyâ Tâmir, *al-Ra'd* (Damascus: Manshûrât Maktabat al-Nûrî, 1978), pp. 71–79.

[43] Al-Sa'dâwî, *Mudhakkirât*, pp. 66, 71.

man decides to come and buy her as one buys a cow.[44] Woman's body is seen as a commercial object, whose value is linked to its "honor."

Dr. S.'s new oath with which she closes her case history calls for humanity and conscience not only in her work but in her art as well. Medicine and art are once again brought together in an eloquent proclamation. But it is through medicine that she has saved a sister from the death threats of her brother. Social justice becomes fused with the physician's art, understood in the broadest sense.

The universalization of social power is also its dissolution through the transcending of the oppositions dominating al-Saʿdâwî's corpus and her heroines. It is not a coincidence that medicine escapes the dilemma of power (by becoming the point of fusion of science and art) in the context of a literary corpus—and a life—in which the role of medical practitioner has become fused with that of artist. Medicine becomes a space of purification, the locus where the raw social power of science is transmuted into the acceptable social power of art. As such, it is the ultimate woman's trick, but a modern one this time: linking individual with collective emancipation.

[44] Ibid., p. 76.

CHAPTER 8

Subverting the Male Body: ʿAbla al-Ruwaynî and the Poetics of Cancer

THE PROJECT of female empowerment behind Nawâl al-Saʿdâwî's fictional corpus derived much of its power from the juxtaposition of woman's body and woman's discourse. Hers are controversial and much-contested literary tactics (she is often accused of doing nothing but repeating the same feminist message incessantly throughout all her work). Female physicality must be actively recuperated through a corporal discourse. Medicine permitted woman to accede to the rank of man and to grant speech to narrative voices previously consigned to silence.

For ʿAbla al-Ruwaynî, it is not medicine but its nemesis, disease, specifically cancer, that subverts the patriarchal literary tradition and permits ascendancy over the male voice. It is the control of the male body and its ultimate destruction that will gain her literary voice for the female. Al-Ruwaynî's work, *al-Janûbî: Amal Dunqul* (The Southerner: Amal Dunqul), belongs to a subgenre of autobiographical writings: the text in which a woman writes of her late husband.[1] Visions of the self are traditionally sought, of course, in strictly autobiographical writings. But this memoiristic subgenre is crucial for a woman's self-vision. Subverting the laudatory and eulogistic implications of such memoirs, *The Southerner* constructs a hidden, though feminist, autobiography. Its strategy involves two overlapping phases: at once the construction of the heterosexual couple and its revolutionary redefinition and then, under the sign of cancer, the ultimate role reversal and replacement of the male by the female.

The text of *The Southerner* presents a story some of whose aspects might seem superficially familiar: a meeting between a man and a woman, a marriage, and a tragic death. But al-Ruwaynî's text treats these elements in a revolutionary and, to a certain extent, unfamiliar way. Subsequently, the components of the story take on a new signification, providing the text of *The Southerner* with a particularly effective internal tension that transports the work beyond the limits of mere memoirs.

ʿAbla al-Ruwaynî's late husband, Amal Dunqul, was, until his dra-

[1] ʿAbla al-Ruwaynî, *al-Janûbî: Amal Dunqul* (Cairo: Maktabat Madbûlî, n.d.).

matic death at age forty-three from cancer, the poet laureate of Egypt.[2] Amal hailed from a small village in Upper Egypt; hence the reference in the title to the South. We shall return to the title below. *The Southerner*, a work in three parts, and which purports to be a tribute to the great man, in fact chronicles and centers on 'Abla's and Amal's relationship, beginning with their meeting and ending with Amal's death.

This text belongs to a specific literary genre, that of personal memoirs revolving around an individual other than the author himself. We are not dealing here, strictly speaking, with an autobiography or even a biography, but rather with a special type of memoir. And this despite the fact that the autobiography and the memoir, as literary types, approach one another, through their literary and structural dependence on personal experience and on the special knowledge of the author/narrator. The reader normally associates this special knowledge with the common use in these texts of the first-person pronoun, leading him to the belief that the text is presenting an intimate (and dare we say true?) picture of the events in question. It is partly as a result of these literary criteria that both memoirs and autobiographies create a special pact (I borrow here Philippe Lejeune's concept from his *Le pacte autobiographique*)[3] among the reader, the author, and the text. Focusing on both the narrator and an external subject, the text of *The Southerner* hesitates between the two genres of memoir and autobiography.

In the context of Arabic literature, in particular, and the Middle East in general, we have numerous autobiographical writings. The genre was a flourishing one in the medieval Islamic period and continues to be important in the modern Middle East. It encompasses spiritual autobiographies, like that of the eleventh-century al-Ghazâlî; educational odysseys, like that of the twentieth-century Salâma Mûsâ; and accounts of personal sagas, like that of Tâhâ Husayn.[4] But the Arabic autobiographical canon is predominantly a male one. Certainly, for the heyday of Arabic literature—that is, the classical period—no women's autobiographies come to mind whatsoever. The male scriptor, as I have amply shown, dominated the medieval prose literary endeavor. Yet classical Arabic poetic production included the female voice, and this from the pre-Islamic period on-

---

[2] Amal Dunqul's poetry has been collected in Amal Dunqul, *al-Aʿmâl al-Shiʿriyya al-Kâmila* (Beirut: Dâr al-ʿAwda, 1985). On Amal Dunqul's poetry, see the special issue of the literary journal *Ibdâʿ* that was dedicated to his memory: 1, no. 10 (1983). See, also, Jâbir Qumayha, *al-Turâth al-Insânî fî Shiʿr Amal Dunqul* (Cairo: Hajar lil-Tibâʿa wal-Nashr wal-Tawzîʿ, 1987).

[3] Lejeune, *Le pacte*, pp. 13–46. For Lejeune's later thoughts on this, see Philippe Lejeune, "Le pacte autobiographique (bis)," *Poétique 56* (1983): 416–434.

[4] For an overview of the Arabic autobiographical tradition, both classical and modern, see Malti-Douglas, *Blindness and Autobiography*, pp. 9–11.

ward. In fact, in the Jâhiliyya (the pre-Islamic) period, women had a poetic genre allocated to them (the rithâ' or *marthiya*), that of mourning the menfolk in the tribe, such as their brothers and fathers. Al-Khansâ' is perhaps the most famous of these women poets, having immortalized her brother, Sakhr (and herself, of course) through the verses she composed in mourning for him.[5] For the modern period, the female autobiographical voice is a bit louder. But the autobiographical texts authored by women are far less numerous than those by men. In addition, their literary impact has been even more negligible than their number. And the same is true of women's memoirs.

Therefore, the very act of authorship of *The Southerner* is an ambiguously revolutionary one and represents, in a sense, a break in the Arabic literary canon. While it could be seen as a modern marthiya of sorts, designed with a full consciousness of the Arabic literary tradition, it is a subversive one giving dominance to the female voice. If it evokes one tradition, it is to subvert others.

Memoirs written by the husband or wife of the work's subject represent a subgenre in the larger memoiristic genre and are far from being new in Western literature. Most often, the form is exploited by the female spouse of a famous husband, be he a politician or a media personality. In a sense, the famous male's death becomes the vehicle that permits the literary creativity of the female. Marital relations differ, by their nature, from relations of friendship, for example, and it is the characteristics of marital relations in particular that prove the most important in 'Abla al-Ruwaynî's narrative. That a widow should write of her husband is not considered problematic in the West. That a widow should do the same in a Middle Eastern context, however, is. This hesitation is related to the historical construction of the heterosexual couple.

Al-Ruwaynî's text emphasizes first and foremost the couple and its dynamics as a heterosexual unit. The Arabo-Islamic emphasis on the male couple and male homosociality has been amply demonstrated. Of course, heterosexual love and heterosexual lovers are portrayed, but when such couples are treated, it is most usually as star-crossed lovers, like Laylâ and Majnûn, 'Antar and 'Abla. Thus, reactions to 'Abla al-Ruwaynî's narrative act were frequently vehement: critics and friends of the deceased poet questioned her right to author the work. Many a sophisticated Arab male critic explained to me that a writer's friend would know him far better, and would be a more authoritative source on his life and feelings than his wife could ever be. In modern Arab society, this position is not unreasonable. Even in *The Southerner* itself, homosociality has deep roots. Amal Dunqul and the Palestinian poet Ahmad Dahbûr had a

---

[5] See Nicholson, *Literary History*, pp. 126–127.

strong friendship. When Amal went to Beirut for a poetry festival, Ahmad Dahbûr screamed when he saw him approaching: "I cannot believe my eyes . . . My heart is almost stopping."[6] The identity of the two initials (A.D./Amal Dunqul, A.D./Ahmad Dahbûr) has powerful metaphorical force. Al-Ruwaynî, we shall see, has a long way to go in her subversive heterosexual project.

'Abla al-Ruwaynî's work stands as a major marker at the crossroads of this subgenre of widows' memoirs. A generic link could be posited between this literary masterpiece and the earlier work of Suzanne Tâhâ Husayn, also a work written by a widow and dealing with her late husband, the blind intellectual and literary giant, Tâhâ Husayn. The influence of his classic autobiography, al-Ayyâm (The days), on the contemporary feminist literary corpus has already been analyzed.[7] While studying in France, Tâhâ Husayn met and married a French woman, who returned with him to Egypt. She never learned Arabic and maintained her allegiance to the Catholic church. After the death of her husband, she was encouraged by a French scholar, Jacques Berque, to set pen to paper and write her reminiscences of her famous husband. This manuscript, written in French but never published in that language, was then translated into Arabic under the title Ma'ak (With you).[8] It is not a coincidence that its origin is doubly Western. Now in its second edition in the Arab world, it is widely read.

Al-Ruwaynî's "biography" of her late husband also set in motion other similiar works in Arabic. After its appearance, other Egyptian literary widows, if we may call them that, began proposing such works on their famous husbands. This was the case with Samîha Ghâlib, the television personality, whose husband, Salâh 'Abd al-Sabûr, was in his lifetime the acknowledged greatest poet of Egypt in particular, and, for many, of the Arab world in general.[9] Munâ Qattân, the surviving wife of the famous political caricaturist and popular poet Salâh Jâhîn, did, unlike Samîha Ghâlib, author a work on her relationship with her late husband.[10]

The text of the Syrian Marie Seurat, Les corbeaux d'Alep, hangs ambiguously between a Western and an Eastern widow's memoir. Her husband, Michel Seurat, was a greatly respected (and much loved among those who knew him, including the present writer) young French scholar

---

[6] Al-Ruwaynî, al-Janûbî, p. 51.

[7] See chapter 6 above.

[8] Suzanne Tâhâ Husayn, Ma'ak, trans. Badr al-Dîn 'Arûdakî (Cairo: Dâr al-Ma'ârif, 1964). Badr al-Dîn 'Arûdakî, the translator, explained to me (July 23, 1987) that the original French manuscript was never published.

[9] Samîha Ghâlib herself spoke to me of this project on numerous occasions between 1984 and 1988, but it remains unfinished.

[10] Munâ Qattân, Ayyâm ma'a Salâh Jâhîn (Cairo: Maktabat Madbûlî, 1987).

who died as a hostage in Lebanon. She herself was born in Aleppo, and the work, though written in French, tells as much about the Middle East as it does about France.[11]

Marie Seurat's saga, like that of ʿAbla al-Ruwaynî, contains much drama. On the one hand, a kidnapped husband who becomes the subject of enormous media attention in an attempt to get him released, but who dies in captivity nevertheless. His is a very private death (one account has it that he died in the trunk of a car while being transported from one location to another). On the other, a husband who dies a dramatic and public death of cancer. Amal Dunqul's bout in the hospital was an event in which almost every Arab intellectual participated, directly or indirectly. Many were the days that one could visit Amal in the Cancer Institute in Cairo and run into the greatest names in literature and the arts. Cameras were invariably flashing in the waiting area outside his room. His dying process was a public event and his wife but one of the participants. These two widows are trying both to reclaim their husbands and to make their own statements, but with very different agendas.

These factors are important for distinguishing the work of ʿAbla al-Ruwaynî from that of her supposed literary precursor, Suzanne Tâhâ Husayn. The first difference, and perhaps the most superficial, is that involving the language of composition of the two books. Suzanne Tâhâ Husayn's *With You* was originally written in French. It places itself, hence, in the context of the French literary tradition, despite the fact that the subject of the text is a great Arabic litterateur, whose nickname is ʿAmîd al-Adab al-ʿArabî, The Dean of Arabic Letters. Tâhâ Husayn comes to possess in his widow's memoirs a European cast: he vacations in the French Alps, he listens to European classical music, he consorts with European intellectuals, and so forth. ʿAbla al-Ruwaynî's poet is a quintessentially Arabic one: for example, the works that have influenced him hail from within the Arabic tradition itself, and he listens to Arabic music. This difference between the two works is, from the point of view of literary genre or structure, the least important. Suzanne Tâhâ Husayn, upon having decided to author a set of memoirs about her late husband, had to make basic choices in the relationship between herself as writer and her husband as "written about." And ʿAbla al-Ruwaynî, of course, faced identical literary questions.

Another difference between the two texts lies in their titles. The title of a work possesses great importance: the French critic, novelist, and *cinéaste* Alain Robbe-Grillet has noted that it represents the true beginning of any text, since it comprises the first words a reader encounters.[12] The title

---

[11] Marie Seurat, *Les corbeaux d'Alep* (Paris: Gallimard, 1988).

[12] Colloque de Cerisy, *Robbe-Grillet: Analyse, théorie*, vol. 1 (Paris: Union Générale d'Editions, 1976), p. 165.

subsequently influences a reader's expectations of the nature of any text. The title *With You* points to the presence of another character interacting with the subject of the narrative. This is obvious from the use of the preposition *with* and the second-person pronoun *you*. As the French linguist Emile Benveniste noted, the presence of the second-person pronoun (here, the *you*) creates a relationship with the first-person *I* (or the grammatical speaker), even when this last pronoun is not overtly present in the text.[13] What this means for the case at hand is that the grammatical narrative-voice *I* (referring to the voice of the hero's wife) is present in the title of the work through the presence of the pronoun *you*. Hence, two characters are evoked by the title of the work: the hero of the text and its narrator. In addition, the preposition *with* links these two characters. The *you* (second-person pronoun) in the title implies someone who is addressed. Commonly in autobiographical situations, the *you* refers to the reader. But here, this pronoun refers to the subject of the book, Tâhâ Husayn. The reader becomes almost a listener, as it were, to a dialogue between Suzanne Tâhâ Husayn and her late husband.

And the presence of the two characters, the hero and the narrator, in the title of *Ma'ak* is extremely significant. We encounter it on the first page (and a number of other locations) in the text. After two epigraphs (the first from the Bible and the second from the Syrian poet Nizâr Qabbânî), we read the words of the hero: "We did not live to be happy." The reaction of the female narrator follows directly: "When you said these words to me in the year 1934, I was astonished."[14]

A number of points emerge from this textual beginning. First, the opening words of the text are attributed to the hero: he then possesses a voice in the text. He is not merely a subject of the narrative but appears as an active speaker in it. Second, the response of the female narrator points to the relationship already analyzed in the title. *Ma'ak* foregrounds its hero in such a way that he becomes an important vocal participant in his wife's narration.

The title of the second work, *The Southerner: Amal Dunqul*, points first and foremost to the poet, the subject of the text. The reader is under the illusion that he is dealing with one independent character, the poet Amal Dunqul. And by not indirectly alluding to another character, the title leads the reader to further believe that the text will provide him with an objective portrayal of its protagonist. Compared with the content of the work, it can be seen either as a form of self-censorship or as a cover for subversion.

The title, *The Southerner*, however, is even more provocative from an

---

[13] Emile Benveniste, "La nature des pronoms," in Emile Benveniste, *Problèmes de linguistique générale, I* (Paris: Gallimard, 1966), pp. 251–253.

[14] Suzanne Tâhâ Husayn, *Ma'ak*, pp. 5–6.

intertextual perspective. One of the last poems Amal Dunqul authored, and which appeared shortly before his death, was entitled "al-Janûbî" (The Southerner). Therefore, the title of ʿAbla al-Ruwaynî's prose narrative harks back to Amal Dunqul's poem and, in a sense, provides him with a voice.

But more significant still is the fact that the poem "al-Janûbî" was autobiographical. Hence, *The Southerner*, as title, creates a fundamental multifaceted tension in ʿAbla al-Ruwaynî's scriptoral project conceived in its entirety. This tension occurs among the three referents at hand. First of all, we have the supposed biography of Amal Dunqul by ʿAbla al-Ruwaynî, which is the book entitled *al-Janûbî*. Second, and because of the intertextuality, there is the autobiography of Amal, through "al-Janûbî" as a poem. Finally, the tension is augmented by the fact that the project of this memoir as a whole can be seen as a hidden autobiography of ʿAbla al-Ruwaynî.

The widow's narrative encourages these tensions and ambiguities: the text opens with a passage by the foremost short-story writer, Yûsuf Idrîs, which plays the role of a eulogy for Amal. This epigraph is followed by the title of the first chapter, "A Substitute for Suicide." The first words following this enigmatic title read: "The attempt to discover a true entrance to Amal Dunqul's personality is difficult since we collide in it with a completely contradictory world, which reflects a sharp dualism, each of whose two sides destroys the other. . . . He is the thing and its opposite."[15]

All of this leads us to believe that the text is about the character Amal Dunqul. Even the narrator herself appears to be presenting her reader with a true objective vision of this complex character. This objectivity is, however, but a literary ruse helping to create the textual tension characteristic of ʿAbla al-Ruwaynî's narrative, centering as it does not simply on one character, Amal Dunqul, but equally on his widow, ʿAbla al-Ruwaynî.

The relationship between the couple (male and female) in *The Southerner* is more important, in effect, than the analogous relationship in *Maʿak*. In the latter work, the relationship is presented in the first lines and then treated synchronically, whereas *The Southerner* treats the same phenomenon diachronically, the formation of the couple becoming a crucial element in the work. In reality, many of the expressions in the opening sentence of the narrative are more easily applicable to Amal *and* ʿAbla taken together than to Amal alone. The "dualism" is characteristic of the text in its entirety, and the "contradictory world" is a better representation of the couple than it is of the male alone. Even the pronoun *we*, referring in principle to the narrator, uncovers more than simply this

---

[15] Al-Ruwaynî, *al-Janûbî*, p. 5.

seemingly naive voice. The opening lines, which center literally on one character, awaken us to the binarism or duality that will govern the work in its entirety.

Many components of *The Southerner* testify to its being an artistic and literary work. Perhaps the most obvious is the use of anachronism: the narrative presents events out of the order in which they occurred. Gérard Genette has made a distinction between the story—the totality of events and their arrangement as they took, or might have taken, place—and the narrative—the arrangement of events as these appear in the text. Clearly, the narrative does not have to agree with the story, and vice versa.[16] For example, the fourth chapter of ʿAbla al-Ruwaynî's text provides the elegy of the poet Fârûq Shûsha written for Amal Dunqul.[17] Naturally, this elegy was not composed until Amal Dunqul's death, which in fact occurs only at the end of the story (and the narrative).

Furthermore, these anachronisms need not refer to future events ("prolepses," in Genette's terminology). They can just as easily refer to events that took place in the past with relation to the story. This type of anachronism is an "analepsis" in Genette's system (a system I shall not by any means exploit to its full here).[18] Suffice it to say that al-Ruwaynî's narrative contains analepses as well. When we read, for example, about the blood analysis that will define the type of cancer, the narrative presents the explanation of the physician during the first surgical operation for the disease. This is clearly an analepsis, since this particular blood analysis took place after the first surgical operation. But these anachronisms demonstrate the composed nature of the text. This is not a direct and objective picture of Amal Dunqul but a self-conscious literary work.

The text of *The Southerner* can be divided into three parts. The first opens with a semi-introductory chapter about the poet and then continues with the account of the meeting between the poet and the female narrator, the development of their relationship, as well as the poet's relations with other individuals. The second part treats the subject of marriage and the relationship of the two central characters inside and outside the house. It is in this part that we read about the importance of poetry, the visit of the narrator to Upper Egypt (Amal Dunqul's home), and the events that led to the death of the great Egyptian poet Salâh ʿAbd al-Sabûr. The third—and final—part of *The Southerner* treats of the experience with cancer and the demise of the hero, Amal Dunqul.

The first part of the book contains six chapters, one serving as an introduction to the book as a whole, and the subsequent five presenting the

---

[16] Genette, *Figures III*, pp. 72, 146.

[17] Al-Ruwaynî, *al-Janûbî*, p. 49.

[18] Genette, *Figures III*, pp. 92–114.

first section of the narrative. The second and third parts of *The South-erner* are also each composed of five chapters, thus providing the text with a clear, virtually classical, organization.

The first part of the book treats the meeting between the male hero and the female narrator and the beginning of their relationship. To appreciate the revolutionary dynamics of ʿAbla al-Ruwaynî's narrative, we can ask: what are the traditional social rules that govern a meeting between a man and a woman in the modern urban Middle East (after all, the social back-ground against which this narrative is set)? Normally, the male plays the more active role and the female in no sense initiates the relationship. But when the text of *The Southerner* presents the meeting and the beginning of the relationship between male poet and female narrator, it reverses the sexual roles. The second chapter treats this subject and is entitled "The Search for the Pharaonic Warrior."[19] Aside from the connection of Amal Dunqul to Pharaonic Egypt (a connection whose implications we will not consider here), several important points emerge clearly from this compli-cated title. It becomes clear that the character undertaking the search is the narrator herself, since the warrior sought is the hero. But how is this search undertaken? As the text explains, the narrator seeks Amal Dunqul in the Café Riche to conduct an interview with him. The Café Riche is a café in central downtown Cairo long known as a gathering place for in-tellectuals, artists, and critics. It is said that this is the location where Gamal Abdel Nasser and the Free Officers plotted the 1952 revolution.[20] The poet becomes the character being searched for, a passive figure in the game of encounter. The "Warrior" in the title is superficially Amal Dun-qul: we are told subsequently that his name is Muhammad Amal Fahîm Muhârib Dunqul, according to his identity card. The Arabic name Mu-hârib means "warrior." But the character who really fights is ʿAbla. The irony is particularly rich given the name of the heroine-author. Two of the most famous heterosexual lovers in the Arabic literary tradition were the aforementioned ʿAntar and ʿAbla. But ʿAntar distinguished himself first and foremost as a great warrior. In *The Southerner*, ʿAbla has be-come ʿAntar.

From the beginning of the chapter, the reader is made aware that con-ducting and writing this interview with the poet was not an easy matter. The narrator herself says that she thought about "running all the red, green, and yellow lights" when she decided to write about him.[21] The path she chose to meet the poet was indeed revolutionary and nontradi-tional. When she was told that publishing the interview would be diffi-

[19] Al-Ruwaynî, *al-Janûbî*, pp. 17–24.

[20] Now, the Café Riche has become popular among Western tourists, and the intellectuals are gradually abandoning it for another café.

[21] Al-Ruwaynî, *al-Janûbî*, p. 17.

cult, she saw this as a challenge to which she rose. Making this decision even more dramatic and risky was the fact that it was made while ʿAbla was still in her training period at the newspaper and had not yet received her appointment. She conquered all the difficulties and succeeded in placing the interview in the newspaper, *al-Akhbâr*.

This initial meeting with the doomed poet generated an interesting set of firsts for the female narrator. The Café Riche was the first coffeehouse she had ever entered. When Amal proposed they go to a quiet place for the interview, it was a bar he had in mind. And this was the first time she entered a bar. It was also the first newspaper interview she conducted in which the subject was drinking beer.[22]

These firsts are all made to seem virtually illicit by the narrator. In an Islamic culture, the bar, of course, speaks for itself. But even among secularized, liquor-drinking Egyptians, the association of alcohol with women has a flavor of impropriety. In case we had any doubt about the licitness of her entering the coffeehouse, the narrator clearly expresses her anxiety and embarrassment at this act.

These entries into forbidden locations, into forbidden territory, mark most importantly a critical crossing, a rite de passage, that the narrator goes through. She has crossed a boundary that not only brings about the meeting between the two characters but that in a sense gives her the right to undertake the entire scriptoral project. The masculine image of entry is by now far from being textually alien to this precocious narrator. After all, it was she who spoke, in the previously cited first sentence of the work, of "the entrance" to Amal's personality.

And these processes help the narrator to emerge on a par with the hero. But the two are not only equal; they are opposites. The narrator says, for example, that she searched for Amal during the time which she knew, and that was morning. He, however, was a being who did not appear in the morning but in the evening. So she left him a note; he contacted her in the morning, and their meeting took place in the evening.[23] Both characters abandon their personal habits and customs to permit this historic encounter.

To better understand the presence of these two powers in the text, we can examine the first appearance of the first-person narrator. How does the female narrator initially enter the text as a character? The text opens with the pronoun *we*.[24] But this is the *we* of the author. When the grammatical speaker appears for the second time, it is the *I* of the character.

In the introductory chapter in the first part of the book, the text pre-

---

[22] Ibid., p. 21.
[23] Ibid., p. 19.
[24] Ibid., p. 5

sents Amal's personality as a means of introducing this extremely complex character: he loves life, he is anarchic, he is hard, and so forth. When the *I* enters for the first time, it is thus: "He likes to a degree to wipe my tears in moments of violent fighting. And I tear his clothing and tear him."[25] The two powers are present but in interesting and variable ways. He wipes her tears, whereas she tears him and his clothing. The female narrator's first entrance as a character into the text is that of an active participant. Their relationship is defined initially by violence and fighting.

The equality between the two characters plays an important role not only on the verbal level of the text but on that of its deep structure. This can be seen through the role that writing plays in *The Southerner*. Clearly, Amal Dunqul is a famous poet. Writing fulfills an essential function in his identification and definition as an individual. And it is his role as poet that first instigates the journalist-narrator to conduct that decisive interview with him which reverses the traditional roles. The female narrator is a journalist, i.e., she too is a writer. Her role as journalist/writer brings her close to that of the hero of the text: the poet/writer. But she only truly becomes a writer after this initial rite of passage. It is the role as writer that permits her to surpass the traditional feminine role normally allocated a woman in an initial encounter with a male. Yet her role as writer serves another important function: it transforms the other character who is a writer, and therefore active, into someone written about, and therefore passive. And it is, in fact, this active role allocated to the female writer, involving as it does the conquest of severe difficulties by the journalist-narrator, that permits the writing of the very book we hold in our hands. Insofar as this book represents a personal testimony on the poet Amal Dunqul after his death, it also then represents a way for the narrator to bid adieu to the poet. Her relationship with him begins and ends with writing. It begins with Amal the written about and ends also with Amal the written about.

It was necessary, in a sense, for the narrator to take possession of the role of writer in the first encounter because, to a certain extent, she did not possess it initially. But this does not by any means imply that ʿAbla the narrator has complete control over the position of writer in the text or that writing has become completely her domain. *The Southerner*, in general, divides the role of writer between the two characters. ʿAbla remains a narrator in the process of writing, while Amal participates in the process of writing first through his life as poet and second because the work discusses a great deal of his poetry.

But Amal also participates in the process of writing in yet another way: through a literary technique already mentioned and which points to the

[25] Ibid., p. 9.

concept of writing in its essence—intertextuality. The narrator exploits other written texts in her own narration, most of them lines of poetry, largely composed by the poet Amal Dunqul. And these verses play specific roles in *The Southerner*: repeating the content of the text, clarifying it, or commenting on a given event.[26] Amal Dunqul's verses provide him with a voice in the text. He then becomes a character with two presences: his narrative presence as a hero in the plot, and his presence as a poet through the process of writing and intertextuality, which, in turn, endows him with an active voice in the text.

Intertextuality, however, has a role beyond that of the poetry inside the text. And here, as well, Amal Dunqul plays an important and active part. Each section of *The Southerner* is introduced by epigraphs, seemingly external to the plot of the story. The first section is preceded by the aforementioned text by Yûsuf Idrîs, the second section by Amal Dunqul's own poetry, and the third by words of the great living Egyptian poet Ahmad 'Abd al-Mu'tî Hijâzî, the man who, since Amal's death, has been considered the leading poet of Egypt.[27] These passages, serving as they do as introductions, govern the sections following them. The presence of Amal among two of his most prominent compatriots and contemporaries points to the significant role allocated to him, the hero of *The Southerner*. But in another way, the presence of Amal's poetry in its introductory capacity pulls him away from that initial role as hero and turns him into a textual authority governing the text from outside it. Subsequently, Amal is inside the narrative as subject but outside it as writer. And insofar as these introductory texts remain external to the narrative yet wield authority over it, the presence of Amal Dunqul the writer in those segments endows him not only with a certain amount of freedom from the narrator, 'Abla, but with an active role that almost equals hers.

The first part of *The Southerner* reverses traditional male-female roles. When the subject of marriage first surfaces, it is 'Abla who insists that it take place, Amal being reluctant because of his deplorable economic condition.[28] The marriage is indeed concluded, and the second part of the text, chronicling married life, continues the same sexual dynamics observed in the first part. The female narrator has not changed her fundamentally rebellious nature. On a visit to the house of the village chief in Upper Egypt, for example, Amal suggests to his wife that she wear the traditional black clothing "like any Upper Egyptian woman." She replies, "Impossible." The two then visit the house of the chief, with 'Abla wearing "a pair of pants and a long blouse." It is, in fact, Amal who attempts

[26] See, for example, ibid., pp. 76, 87, 103, 168, 169.
[27] Ibid., pp. 3, 73, 141.
[28] Ibid., pp. 69–71.

to conform to what he sees as the traditional forces operating in Upper Egypt. The incident with ʿAbla's clothing leads them both to realize that Upper Egypt is actually more open-minded than he had thought.[29]

Woman has always been one of the most important maintainers and carriers of tradition. And clothing has also always played a major role in this. Kate Millett observed this phenomenon and addressed it quite eloquently in her travelogue to postrevolutionary Iran.[30] It is not surprising, therefore, that clothing should form a locus for the rejection of the traditional role by our narrator.

Nor does the marital union change the sexual balance of power. ʿAbla would accompany Amal throughout the Egyptian capital, and Cairo knew them always as "inseparable."[31] This word, coming as it does from the sixth form of the verb, is quite crucial. This specific verbal form expresses a mutual relationship of activity between actors. They appeared "as two friends more than as a couple."[32] Such a statement, which might seem banal in America, is striking in the more homosocial context of modern Egyptian society, and of the Arabic literary tradition.

In the third section of the book, a fundamental change takes place in the balance of these two powers and in their marital dynamics. The catalyst that permits this change is the cancer with which the poet was afflicted. The disease, in fact, leads to the merger of the two characters and to the metaphorical consummation of the marriage. The third part of the book chronicles the strengthening of the marital bonds through the fatal disease, at the same time as it reasserts the role reversal effected in the opening two sections.

When the narrator speaks of the marital situation in the second section of *The Southerner*, she notes: "We exited from the traditional forms of marriage, as the street became our house. We would spend more time in it than we would spend inside our home."[33] In fact, finding a house was an extremely difficult problem, and the two kept moving "from one furnished apartment to another."[34]

But cancer changes this situation, when Room Number 8 at the Cancer Institute becomes "from the first day, our permanent abode."[35] Cancer is the element that brings about the couple's settling down permanently. The female narrator is kind enough to provide the reader with a detailed

[29] Ibid., pp. 129–133.

[30] Kate Millett, *Going to Iran* (New York: Coward, McCann & Geoghegan, 1982), p. 49.

[31] Al-Ruwaynî, *al-Janûbî*, p. 85.

[32] Ibid.

[33] Ibid.

[34] Ibid., p. 111.

[35] Ibid., p. 153.

description of the room, down to the things hanging on the wall.[36] But the importance of this room transcends its characteristic as an abode when it becomes, along with the cancer that led the two characters to that room, the fate of the married couple: "Room Number 8 on the seventh floor had an appointment with us, or perhaps we were the ones who had an appointment with it."[37]

Cancer plays a significant role in the marriage of the female narrator and the male hero, since it permits them to complete this marriage. Amal himself makes a distinction between this cancer and another "real" cancer, which is their separation.[38] More important, cancer transcends this completive role to textually become the child of this ill-fated marriage. The cancer appeared "exactly after the passing of nine months in our marriage: a small tumor in Amal's body, growing one day after the next."[39] The momentous nature of this occurrence is accentuated by its being the first event to be introduced with a specific date. That particular subsection in *The Southerner* which contains specific dates spans the period of the beginning of the cancer as a small tumor to the couple's finally getting a room at the Cancer Institute.[40] Nine months is, of course, the human gestation period, and textually the cancer has become the infant of this couple. Furthermore, the tumor grows in size in the body of the sick individual just as the fetus grows in size in a mother's womb. This literary image concords with what Susan Sontag writes in *Illness as Metaphor* when she speaks of cancer as a "demonic pregnancy."[41] This particular marriage does not in reality produce any children or even any pregnancies. And insofar as the husband dies, there will be no offspring. All this reinforces the image of the cancer as the true child of these two individuals. Even more revolutionary in 'Abla al-Ruwaynî's case is that the pregnant individual is the male, adding to the role reversal already noted in *The Southerner*.

This on the one hand. On the other hand, turning the man into the childbearer leads to a type of fusion of identity between female narrator and male hero. Their actions begin to parallel one another. When she calls out for a taxi to the Cancer Institute, Amal tells her: "You are pretty when you say 'Cancer.' He laughed so I would not cry and I laughed in turn so he would not be sad."[42] He is originally the sick member of the couple.

---

[36] Ibid.

[37] Ibid.

[38] Ibid., p. 151.

[39] Ibid., p. 145.

[40] Ibid., pp. 145–151.

[41] Susan Sontag, *Illness as Metaphor* (New York: Farrar, Straus and Giroux, 1978), p. 14.

[42] Al-Ruwaynî, *al-Janûbî*, p. 150.

But she also begins to play this very role in the narrative. After the physician announced to Amal that he had cancer, the first few weeks were quite difficult. The narrator says, "After this, the physician saw me laughing, so he thanked Amal because he was an excellent companion to the sick person, who was I."[43] The narrator has become the sick individual, just as the hero was the one bearing the child. The fusion between them is complete.

The same phenomenon appears elsewhere in the text. When the hero asks the narrator, "What will you do after my death?" she answers: "Nothing. Just like what you will do after my death."[44] This brief interchange indicates that the narrator has textually replaced the hero. She has not answered the question in the manner expected. Rather, she used the very words the hero employed in addressing her. On closer examination, it becomes clear that the question and answer are grammatically and syntactically identical. The death of the hero in the question is balanced by the death of the narrator in the answer. "What will you do" in the question is balanced by "what you will do" in the answer. The fusion is effected even in the dialogue.

This fusion of the two characters functions as the axis around which the third part of *The Southerner* revolves, just as the presence of the two equivalent powers was the axis for the first two sections. But what about the last appearance of the female narrator in the text? After all, if her entrance was significant, should not her exit be as well? This is on the last page of the last chapter:

> His face was calm as they closed his eyes.
> My calm was impossible as I opened my eyes.[45]

Here, not only are the two characters present, but they resemble each other. The same grammatical constructions are common to both statements, as are the words, a phenomenon similar to the previous example with the question and answer. But there is a difference in the case of the two statements. The second one, referring to the narrator, begins with "my calm," using a word taken from the first sentence, referring to the hero at the time of his death. The state of the female narrator and that of the male hero have become connected. But this connection is not fusion; it is, rather, a replacement. When they close his eyes, she opens hers. The vision of one has replaced the vision of the other, which has come to an end. The opening of the eyes clearly signals some kind of rebirth for the narrator. In fact 'Abla, in the immediately preceding passage, has seized

43 Ibid., p. 160.
44 Ibid., p. 183.
45 Ibid., p. 191.

the active role from her now-helpless husband. He tries to remove the intravenous feeder from his hand. The nurse and his brother prevent him. So ʿAbla, responding to the mute appeal of his eyes, removes the needle, ending his life.[46]

The last four lines of the narrative are written not as normal prose but rather as poetic lines. The female narrator has, in effect, not only been reborn but, in the process, become a kind of poet and replaced the hero-poet at the end of the text. His death permits her metaphorical birth.

The two very last lines represent the reactions of the cancer and death to the demise of the hero.

> And the cancer alone was screaming.
> And death alone was crying over its mercilessness.[47]

The imagery of cancer is crucial here. The disease has become an independent character with a voice of its own. It is anthropomorphized. Its reaction to Amal's death should not come as a surprise. After all, it was the narrator who informed the reader earlier that the cancer was their friend.[48] The hero's death represents, in a sense, a loss for the cancer as well. The cancer elsewhere was the shark that swallowed the rare fish.[49] Both Amal and the cancer have been placed in the same category of beings.

The first function of cancer in *The Southerner* was the completion of the marriage. But the cancer becomes, in a way that links it directly to this completion, the child of this union. The begetting of the child on the level of the plot concords with the anthropomorphization of the disease on the level of literary images. Death is also anthropomorphized in the last line, but this is a familar image.

It seems fitting that ʿAbla al-Ruwaynî's work, which began with a dualism, should end with one as well. It is equally fitting that what began as a kind of literary subversion should end as a virtual physical replacement. *The Southerner* begins with an authorial ruse. What pretends to be a tribute to a husband-hero turns out to be the literary expression of a widow-narrator. Physical replacement of one life with another, a replacement whose four phases were discovery, conflict, merger, and finally replacement, signifies a scriptoral replacement in which one writing voice takes over from another.

This differs markedly from Simone de Beauvoir's account of Sartre in

[46] Ibid., p. 190.
[47] Ibid.
[48] Ibid., p. 160.
[49] Ibid., p. 143.

La cérémonie des adieux.[50] Amal's body is not, as Alice Jardine describes for Sartre, "cut up by the violence of (Beauvoir's) discourse."[51] Yes. The male body has been subverted, and the male voice effectively silenced. But the violence is in the successful overturning of a set of expectations. The male body has been made the childbearer. Amal's silence is noted on many an occasion in the text. He is silent with his friends; he is silent when he is afraid; he has periods of poetic silence, in which he does not produce poems. ʿAbla had been blamed for this phenomenon, which she is careful to deny.[52] The poet, we also discover through the introductory comment by Yûsuf Idrîs, is already dead at the beginning of ʿAbla al-Ruwaynî's odyssey. Was he ever alive in the text? "Al-Janûbî" (The Southerner), the narrator does not forget to mention, was the last poem Amal composed in his ill-fated room in the Cancer Institute.[53] The title of the poem is the title of the book. It is as though this were the last breath of an already-dead poet. His is but a literary presence to allow the female voice to come to the fore. Is it an accident that the book ends with rough drafts of his poems? Can we trust this narrator who tells us in another place that Amal composed his poems in his head and that he did not have rough drafts of them?[54] The rough drafts are there to provide readers with an intimate picture of Amal Dunqul the poet, to make readers feel that they are penetrating the persona who is the poet. But the poet has been dead from the first page of the book that pretends to be his biography but which is actually a postmortem narrative. It is ʿAbla al-Ruwaynî's voice that we have been hearing.

[50] Simone de Beauvoir, *La cérémonie des adieux* (Paris: Editions Gallimard, 1981), pp. 13–176.

[51] Alice Jardine, "Death Sentences: Writing Couples and Ideology," in Suleiman, *The Female Body*, p. 91.

[52] See, for example, al-Ruwaynî, *al-Janûbî*, pp. 48–49, 124, 157.

[53] Ibid., p. 172.

[54] Ibid., p. 94.

CHAPTER 9

Problematic Birth: Fadwâ Tûqân and the Politics of Autobiography

ʿABLA AL-RUWAYNÎ subverted the male body and gave herself the attribute possessed in the beginning of the narrative by her "dead" husband, the poet Amal Dunqul. She ends the saga as a poet. The Palestinian poet Fadwâ Tûqân in her autobiography, *Rihla Jabaliyya, Rihla Saʿba* (Mountain journey, difficult journey), recounts her poetic odyssey and at the same time questions both the male and the female traditions in all their ramifications.[1] She at once englobes and recasts the rich Arabo-Islamic tradition that has given birth to the various gender relations and dynamics we have been examining in the previous chapters.

Unlike her two contemporary female scriptors, al-Saʿdâwî and al-Ruwaynî, Fadwâ Tûqân has a unique relationship to the Arabo-Islamic tradition. The centuries-long Arabic literary tradition, albeit male, did permit the female poetic voice to exist under carefully circumscribed conditions. As a poet, Fadwâ Tûqân has a long line of Arabic poetic women's voices with which to identify and against which to react. As a prose autobiographical writer, however, she carves out her own territory, creates her own literary voice. These two poles lead to literary tensions important to Tûqân's odyssey. The act of writing that generates the literary voice in this autobiography is problematic, indeed, tied as it is to both the corporal and poetic identity of the heroine. Fadwâ's[2] life in the text creates relationships (both literary and biological) that will at once recast and redefine familiar, and very old, ones.

---

[1] Fadwâ Tûqân, *Rihla Jabaliyya, Rihla Saʿba* (Amman: Dâr al-Shurûq lil-Nashr wal-Tawzîʿ, 1985). Selections from the autobiography have been translated by Donna Robinson Divine, " 'Difficult Journey—Mountainous Journey,' The Memoirs of Fadwa Tuqan," in *The Female Autograph: Theory and Practice of Autobiography from the Tenth to the Twentieth Century,* ed. Domna Stanton (Chicago: University of Chicago Press, 1987), pp. 187–204; reprinted in Badran and Cooke, *Opening,* pp. 26–40. But the translations have so many significant problems that they should only be approached with caution. For example, a reference to a musical instrument is misread as the word for God (Allâh) (p. 202): phrases are missing, sentences misconstrued (pp. 196–197), etc. The entire text of *Rihla Jabaliyya* has been translated as Fadwa Tuqan, *A Mountainous Journey: An Autobiography,* trans. Olive Kenny (London: The Women's Press, 1990).

[2] As with chapter 6, I am using the first name to refer to the character in the text and the full name for the author.

Poetry has been, and continues to be, perhaps the most sacred literary medium for the Arabs. And the name of Fadwâ Tûqân has long been associated with poetry. She was born in 1917 to an influential landowning family in Nablus in the West Bank. Nablus prides itself on its tradition of struggle and resistance, and for this its region was dubbed the "Jabal al-Nâr" (Mountain of Fire).

Fadwâ Tûqân's earliest work was predominantly intimate and, in Fadwâ's words, concerned the self and not the collectivity. After the 1967 War, however, her poetry showed a greater concern with the Palestinian cause and became more openly political.[3] Her poetic collections include *Wajadtuhâ* (I found it); *A'tinâ Hubban* (Give us love); *Wahdî ma'a al-Ayyâm* (Alone with the days); *al-Layl wal-Fursân* (Night and the horsemen), dedicated to "The Palestinian Freedom Fighter"; *Tammûz wal-Shay' al-Akhar* (July and the other thing); *Amâm al-Bâb al-Mughlaq* (In front of the locked door); and *'Alâ Qimmat al-Dunyâ Wahîdan* (On top of the world alone).[4] The title of this last collection is explained with reference to the novella *Mâ Tabaqqâ lakum*, by the Palestinian writer Ghassân Kanafânî.[5] Her autobiography was first published serially in 1978–1979 in *al-Jadîd*.[6] *Mountain Journey, Difficult Journey* is clearly defined as an autobiography (and not as a memoir) on the cover of the book. Tûqân, thus, joins the long line of Arabic literary personalities who felt the egotistical and narcissistic urge to bare their lives before readers.[7] It is, however, the male voice that dominates the classical or medieval genre.

In the modern period, the female voice begins to join that of the male. The modern autobiographical venture has attracted secular feminists as well as religious activists. The life story of Hudâ Sha'râwî, the first to

---

[3] See, also, Salma Khadra Jayyusi, *Trends and Movements in Modern Arabic Poetry* (Leiden: E. J. Brill, 1977), 2:563, 655–656, 657.

[4] Fadwâ Tûqân, *Wajadtuhâ* (Beirut: Dâr al-'Awda, 1974); Fadwâ Tûqân, *A'tinâ Hubban* (Beirut: Dâr al-'Awda, 1974); Fadwâ Tûqân, *Wahdî ma'a al-Ayyâm* (Beirut: Dâr al-'Awda, 1974); Fadwâ Tûqân, *al-Layl wal-Fursân* (Beirut: Dâr al-Adâb, 1969); Fadwâ Tûqân, *Tammûz wal-Shay' al-Akhar* (Amman: Dâr al-Shurûq, 1987); Fadwâ Tûqân, *Amâm al-Bâb al-Mughlaq* (Acre: Matba'at al-Jalîl, 1968); Fadwâ Tûqân, *'Alâ Qimmat al-Dunyâ Wahîdan* (Beirut: Dâr al-Adâb, 1973).

[5] Tûqân, *'Alâ Qimmat al-Dunyâ*, p. 62. Ghassân Kanafânî, *Mâ Tabaqqâ lakum*, in Ghassân Kanafânî, *al-Athâr al-Kâmila* (Beirut: Dâr al-Talî'a lil-Tibâ'a wal-Nashr, 1980), 1:153–233. For the translation of Kanafânî's novella, see Ghassan Kanafani, *All That's Left to You*, trans. May Jayyusi and Jeremy Reed (Austin: University of Texas Center for Middle Eastern Studies, 1990).

[6] Samîh al-Qâsim, "Introduction," in Tûqân, *Rihla*, p. 5; Divine, " 'Difficult Journey,' " p. 189. On the larger context of Palestinian women, see Donna Robinson Divine, "Palestinian Arab Women and Their Reveries of Emancipation," in *Women Living Change*, ed. Susan C. Bourke and Donna Robinson Divine (Philadelphia: Temple University Press, 1985), pp. 57–83.

[7] See chapter 8 above.

take off the veil in a dramatic public gesture at the Cairo train station in 1923, stands alongside Zaynab al-Ghazâlî's account of her religious struggle.[8]

Fadwâ Tûqân's project is dramatic and, in its own way, unique. Her saga is set against the backdrop of Palestine and the plight of the Palestinians. The political struggle is at once present and occulted, superseded most often by the gender vision of the narrator. Hers is not the cultural autobiography that Bernice Johnson Reagon sees in black women's life stories "because the story of a woman's selfhood is inseparable from her sense of community."[9] While in a sense Fadwâ's is conceived under the sign of "double jeopardy," since she is a woman living in occupied Palestine, she runs counter to the female group identification, as we shall see.[10]

Mountain Journey centers on the life of its protagonist from her birth until her return to Palestine after an educational stint in England. The actual biography of this heroine is framed (in the Arabic text) between an introduction by the renowned Palestinian poet Samîh al-Qâsim and an epilogue formed of fragments from Fadwâ Tûqân's diary, which carry the reader forward to the June 1967 War. Following Samîh al-Qâsim's introduction, Fadwâ Tûqân herself presents a prologue to her life story. Hence, the details of this life are hidden, as it were, behind two veils that the reader must cast aside before beginning the saga. On one level, these introductions distance the reader from the central body of the text, the actual life of its protagonist. But more important, the presence of the male poetic voice (Samîh al-Qâsim is a very influential literary figure), coming as it does before that of the female, appears to legitimize hers and in a sense gives her the right to speak. At the same time, it subordinates her voice to that of male poetic authority.

The question of gender and the narrative voice is a central one in *Journey*. For example, the narrator resorts to travelers' accounts to describe the city of Nablus and its inhabitants.[11] These travelers are males. And it

---

[8] Huda Shaarawi, *Harem Years: The Memoirs of an Egyptian Feminist*, trans. and introd. Margot Badran (London: Virago, 1986). On this text see, also, Leila Ahmed, "Between Two Worlds: The Formation of a Turn-of-the-Century Egyptian Feminist," in *Life/Lines: Theorizing Women's Autobiography*, ed. Bella Brodzki and Celeste Schenck (Ithaca: Cornell University Press, 1988), pp. 154–174. Zaynab al-Ghazâlî, *Ayyâm min Hayâtî* (Beirut: Dâr al-Shurûq, 1987).

[9] See the discussion of Reagon's ideas in Susan Stanford Friedman, "Women's Autobiographical Selves: Theory and Practice," in *The Private Self: Theory and Practice of Women's Autobiographical Writings*, ed. Shari Benstock (Chapel Hill: University of North Carolina Press, 1988), p. 43.

[10] For a discussion of double jeopardy, see Friedman, "Women's Autobiographical Selves," p. 47.

[11] See, for example, Tûqân, *Rihla*, pp. 39, 43.

is as males that they give credence to what follows, material presented in the female narrator's voice. Or, when Fadwâ receives letters from her cousin in England in which he describes his educational adventures and her own eventual trip to the West, the reader encounters direct quotations from the missives themselves.[12] Fadwâ, it is clear, answered her cousin's letters, but in this case her own letters are not quoted. Indeed, this constant intertextual presence of the male voice is disturbing. Is this the male control of discourse (a by-now-familiar Middle Eastern cultural reality) that can at times permit the female to take over? This would seem to be at the outset the major impact of Samîh al-Qâsim's introduction.

The male legitimizing aspect of al-Qâsim's introduction goes further, however. In extolling the particular qualities (courage, literary expression) of Fadwâ Tûqân's text, he explicitly compares her autobiography to Tâhâ Husayn's.[13] This is, in and of itself, eloquent. It is the male voice once again which legitimizes that of the female. But evoking the Egyptian modernizer in the context of the Palestinian poet creates that fundamental problematic I have analyzed in Arabic mentalities: the equation between "normal" female and blind male.[14]

The way the narrative is structured, however, sharply distinguishes Tâhâ Husayn's account from that of Fadwâ Tûqân. Though chronological in a rough sense, hers (narrated in the first person, the most superficial difference) is a fragmentary text, parts of it separated from others, with prolepses and analepses that would drive a chronologically minded reader wild. Here she comes closest to Roland Barthes's autobiographical project, without, of course, the photographs he includes, whose referential specificity is the opposite of elusiveness.[15] If, as Domna Stanton argues, such fragmentation is a frequent characteristic of female autobiography (in contrast to the more linear male mode),[16] then Tûqân's autobiographical project is a rejection and a subversion of the traditional male developmental autobiographical form in which a life and a life account take on shape and become a coherent whole. The instability of the subject is quite evident.[17]

Fadwâ Tûqân's special and subversive vision appears in the opening lines of her saga: "I came out of the darkness of the unknown into a world that was unprepared to accept me. My mother tried to get rid of me in

---

[12] See, for example, ibid., pp. 163–168.

[13] Al-Qâsim, "Introduction," in Tûqân, *Rihla*, p. 5.

[14] See chapter 6 above.

[15] Roland Barthes, *Roland Barthes* (Paris: Seuil, Ecrivains de Toujours, 1980).

[16] See Domna Stanton, "Autogynography: Is the Subject Different?" in Stanton, *Female Autograph*, pp. 11–12.

[17] Cf. Shari Benstock, "Authorizing the Autobiographical," in *The Private Self: Theory and Practice of Women's Autobiographical Writing*, ed. Shari Benstock (Chapel Hill: University of North Carolina Press, 1988), p. 21.

the first months of her pregnancy with me. She tried and repeated the attempt. But she failed."[18] This beginning is strangely reminiscent of that presented by the first-person narrator of al-Sa'dâwî's autobiographical novel, *Memoirs of a Female Physician*.[19] Both acts of entry into the world become problematic events. But al-Sa'dâwî's female narrator is in revolt against her femininity, and the narrative chronicles an eventual resolution of this conflict. The focus remains individual, on the heroine's experience.

The opening of Fadwâ Tûqân's *Journey*, however, radically shifts attention from the child to her mother, who sought to deny her birth. This striking nonevent, this aborted abortion, foregrounds a woman's lack of control over her own body; it makes motherhood into a problem. Motherhood, a quasi-sacred activity and the life dream of virtually all Middle Eastern women—and their only access to status[20]—is demystified and subverted. The repeated unsuccessful attempts to eliminate the fetus add failure and impotence to the rejection of motherhood. In the process, not only is the ideal of motherhood itself subverted, but so also are the mother herself, her power, and the idea of matriarchy. *Mountain Journey* is a matriphobic text.[21] The narrator explains in great detail the travail associated with her mother's bearing ten children and the father's desire for progeny and hostility to abortion. One might wish to argue for the disculpation of the mother here, the abortion attempt being a reaction to the multiple births she has already experienced. The reader is not privy to the mother's "reality," of course, since it is Fadwâ who controls the narration.

The attempted abortion also undercuts the heroine of the text herself. Linking her birth to a nonevent calls her being into question; and what should normally have been a joyous event becomes the opposite. If the young Fadwâ's existence is, thus, effectively sundered from the romantic myths of biological maternity, it is nevertheless linked with another set of fictions, those of literature, which is posed as an alternative parentage. Her name, we are given to understand, was taken from a historical novel of Jurjî Zaydân.[22]

The third element of *Mountain Journey*'s birth triptych returns to the

---

[18] Tûqân, *Rihla*, p. 12.

[19] Al-Sa'dâwî, *Mudhakkirât*, p. 5; al-Sa'dawi, "Growing Up," p. 111. See, also, chapter 6 above.

[20] See, for example, Bouhdiba, *La sexualité*, pp. 259–279.

[21] I am understanding motherhood here in its traditional Arabo-Islamic sense, as combining biological maternity with early childhood nurturing. On contemporary questions of definition, see Nancy Chodorow, *The Reproduction of Mothering: Psychoanalysis and the Sociology of Gender* (Berkeley: University of California Press, 1978); Judith Kegan Gardiner, "On Female Identity and Writing by Women," in *Writing and Sexual Difference*, pp. 182ff.; Friedman, "Women's Autobiographical Selves," pp. 41–42; Sara Ruddick, *Maternal Thinking: Toward a Politics of Peace* (Boston: Beacon Press, 1989).

[22] Tûqân, *Rihla*, p. 13.

thematics of the first, the subversion of birth and motherhood. It turns out that the exact birth date of the heroine is a victim of forgetfulness. She does not know when she was born. When it is necessary for Fadwâ to get a passport, her mother is able to link the birth to a concrete event, the death of her own cousin during a war. The narrator then draws the connection between this and her own birth: "I will extract my birth certificate (*shahâda*) from the tombstone (*shâhida*) of your cousin," she tells her mother, with a deliberate play on words.[23] More is at stake than a mere birth-death connection. It is the death of a male that permits the establishment of the birth of the female.

Ignorance of the time of birth is neither sociologically odd nor without literary precedent. It is well known that Tâhâ Husayn's autobiography begins with a similar statement of nonknowledge.[24] But the reference in *al-Ayyâm* remains personal and frames the structure of memory. Fadwâ Tûqân, once again, makes of the personal reality an attack on her mother.

This conflictual relationship between mother and daughter only sets the stage for further complications. The mother figure becomes almost an obsession with the narrator of *Journey*. The portrait of the mother is generally quite negative. In addition to the attempted abortion, she is responsible for Fadwâ's unbecoming clothing as a child; she transfers her caretaking responsibilities to someone else; when she combs Fadwâ's hair, she causes her pain; she punishes her inappropriately, and so forth.[25] This maternal obsession causes the narrator nightmares about her, even after her death.[26]

But this problematic and bitter (the narrator's word)[27] relationship with the mother does not go unnoticed by the self-aware narrator, who realizes at a certain point that she must enumerate the mother's positive characteristics. However, this need only surfaces after the mother appears in the public bath. Here, she "would become without clothing more beautiful and more attractive. She would appear to my eyes like a legendary hûrî."[28] Hûrîs are the maidens promised to believers in Paradise. The mother can be a positive figure, but only outside the confines of the family and when literally and figuratively denuded of her everyday attire. It is her public persona that permits this transformation, an unrealistic one indeed, since she also turns into someone legendary. The woman can be beautiful, the mother not.

More eloquent perhaps is Fadwâ's association of her feeling of noth-

---

[23] Ibid., pp. 14–15.
[24] Husayn, *al-Ayyâm*, 1:3; Malti-Douglas, *Blindness and Autobiography*, pp. 104–105.
[25] Tûqân, *Rihla*, pp. 18, 20, 21–22.
[26] Ibid., p. 22.
[27] Ibid., p. 26.
[28] Ibid.

ingness with her mother. The narrator mentions that the mother always told her children anecdotes and entertaining stories about their childhood at which they would laugh. Fadwâ invariably awaited her turn, which never came. And when she would ask her mother to tell stories about her, she got nothing in response. "I would feel my nothingness: I am nothing, and I have no place in her memory."[29] The "nothingness" is also "non-existence" in the Arabic (lâshay'iyya), an interesting term indeed, given that the mother really did try to reduce the fetus to nonexistence in the repeated but unsuccessful attempts at abortion.

More suggestive is the link to memory. Of all literary genres, it is perhaps autobiography that relies most on the act of memory. The autobiographer relates past events, and it is memory that permits their re-creation. This literary act of creation forms a clear parallel to the biological one. And this is where Fadwâ Tûqân's subversive beginning links to her nonexistence in her mother's memory. She becomes free to create her own life story, unencumbered by any ties, biological or sentimental. The mother's desire to deny (or occult) the act of procreation turns the birth into a literary absence that has to be retrieved by the protagonist.[30] And one could argue that the creation of the autobiography represents this retrieval.

We have seen that the literary negation of the birth act is combined with the absence of the birth date. More important, it is linked with the initial absence of a proper name for the protagonist. A name gives a character identity in a text, and the first appearance of the subject's name in any autobiographical text permits the fusion among author, narrator, and central character fundamental to the autobiographical text.[31]

The appropriation of the name can only be had intertextually. The narrator's father and mother were addicted to Jurjî Zaydân's novels; they particularly liked the heroine of his story Asîrat al-Mutamahhidî and decided that they would give her name to the first female born after that.[32] The reader is not told the heroine's name (which the reader, using the autobiographical pact,[33] can conclude is Fadwâ). The reference to Zaydân's novel is problematic for a second reason. While Tûqân's text reads Asîra (Female prisoner), Zaydân's title is actually Asîr al-Mutamahhidî (The male prisoner); and the prisoner referred to in the title is, indeed, of the masculine gender.[34] Whether consciously or not, by feminizing the

[29] Ibid., p. 21.
[30] Cf. Benstock, "Authorizing," in Benstock, The Private Self, pp. 20–21.
[31] Cf. Lejeune, Le pacte, pp. 13–46.
[32] Tûqân, Rihla, p. 13.
[33] Lejeune, Le pacte, pp. 13–46.
[34] Jurjî Zaydân, Asîr al-Mutamahhidî, in Jurjî Zaydân, Mu'allafât Jurjî Zaydân al-Kâmila (Beirut: Dâr al-Jîl, 1981), 7:5–226.

title, the text substitutes the female Fadwâ for the male hero of the book. As we shall see, the image of the woman as prisoner is not without echoes in *Mountain Journey*. But something further is added also. This literary-historical substitution creates a special kind of unreliable narration, inviting the reader to examine and decode other literary-historical attributions (or misattributions).

The name Fadwâ Tûqân surfaces for the first time in *Journey* in an even more suggestive intertextual situation. After a boy gave her a flower in the street, Fadwâ was forbidden to go to school. It was after this that her brother Ibrâhîm began teaching her poetry. The poetic experience is framed by imprisonment, since it was her sequestration (the act of another brother) that cut her off from the public environment of school and permitted Ibrâhîm to be her teacher and mentor.

As a thirteen-year-old, Fadwâ looks at the cover of her study notebook and sees her bad handwriting:

The Name: Fadwâ Tûqân
The Class: (I crossed off the word and wrote instead of it: The Teacher):
    Ibrâhîm Tûqân
The Subject: Learning Poetry
The School: Home[35]

Here, for the first time, the reader encounters the name Fadwâ Tûqân. But precisely because the name is presented on a document, the cover of the notebook, it takes on a different guise. It is a written text within another text, the autobiography, which permits it to stand on its own as an independent phenomenon, detached from the entity that is the central character. And since the name in its first appearance is directly associated with poetry, the official persona to which it refers also becomes from that point on attached to, and defined through, poetry. The acquisition of the name, concomitant as it is with the acquisition of poetry, signals a type of rebirth for the heroine. It is only when she embarks on her poetic path that she acquires a name and an identity.

But the appearance of the name and its association with verse is not sufficient to establish the self-definition and identification of the character. Poetry plays a key role in this intricate game of identity. Fadwâ studies poetry with her brother and begins publishing under a pen name. She has to repeatedly fight the claims that Ibrâhîm is actually the one responsible for her verse: "Sharp tongues used to always say: 'Her brother Ibrâhîm writes her poetry for her and appends her name to it.' "[36] As Joanna Russ has amply demonstrated in her lively study, *How to Suppress Women's*

---

[35] Tûqân, *Rihla*, pp. 69–70.
[36] Ibid., p. 116. See, also, p. 82.

Writing, this is a pervasive phenomenon that a great number of women writers have been faced with.[37] (As an aside, such allegations are still rampant in the Arab world today: many an Arab has confidently declared to me that the poetry of the Kuwaitî Su'âd al-Sabâh is written by her longtime companion, the well-known Syrian poet Nizâr Qabbânî.) Clearly then, the ownership of the poetic voice in *Mountain Journey* is a major issue.

Fadwâ's situation was, of course, not made any easier by the fact that her brother Ibrâhîm Tûqân was himself one of the most, if not the most, important poets in Palestine in the early decades of this century and "was influential in modernizing the poetry of his country."[38] His poetic voice, especially its nationalist and political aspects, would prove to be in Fadwâ's autobiography a pole she would continue to resist.

There is a tension, however, on the level of the subtext in the role of poetry in Fadwâ's search for self. For the first lesson in poetry, Ibrâhîm, imbued in the classical Arabic literary tradition, turned to *al-Hamâsa*, the medieval verse collection by the ninth-century neoclassical poet Abû Tammâm. Ibrâhîm looked in the index of the book, chose a poem, and told his sister that he would read and explain the poem, and would expect her to have it memorized that same evening. The narrator then presents five verses from a poem entitled "A Woman Mourns Her Brother" ("Imra'a Tarthî Akhâhâ"). The teacher explained the verses and declared to his student that he had chosen this poem so that she could see how Arab women used to write beautiful poetry.[39]

This is first and foremost an introduction to the rich classical Arabic literary corpus (and canon). Not only is it what Fadwâ should learn (through the act of memorization) but what she should also write (through the imitation of the "beautiful poetry"—*al-shi'r al-jamîl*—written by Arab women). The choice of the word "how" (*kayf*) emphasizes this tendency. The process of education is one of imitation.

But there is more to this than meets the eye. The writing of rithâ' (elegies), especially commemorating male relatives (brothers or fathers, most often), was a task assigned to the female poetic voice, from even before the birth of Islam. Fadwâ Tûqân uses this poetic form, but in a reasonably overt manner. It is not surprising, therefore, that a modern critic, Shâkir al-Nâbulusî, should actively compare Fadwâ Tûqân to her pre-Islamic ancestor, al-Khansâ', whose elegies for her brothers have made her name

---

[37] Joanna Russ, *How to Suppress Women's Writing* (Austin: University of Texas Press, 1983).

[38] Jayyusi, *Trends and Movements*, 1:284. Ibrâhîm Tûqân's collected verse was published in Ibrâhîm Tûqân, *Dîwân* (Amman: Maktabat al-Muhtasib, 1984). See, also, 'Abd al-Latîf Sharâra, *Ibrâhîm Tûqân* (Beirut: Dâr Sâdir, 1964).

[39] Tûqân, *Rihla*, pp. 68–69.

eternal in the annals of Arabic literature.[40] Her exploitation of this typically female poetic form differs from its modern exploitation at the hands of the widow ʿAbla al-Ruwaynî. The latter's biography of her dead poet-husband functions effectively as a modern subverted marthiya.[41] Al-Hamâsa of Abû Tammâm, Ibrâhîm's source for this poem according to the narrator, contains, however, no mention of a sister-brother duo. The text simply states, "A woman recited." And lest this be understood ambiguously, the commentary explains the circumstances of the poem: it was written by a mother to mourn her murdered son.[42]

Why this transformation? Most important, the change brings to the fore the brother-sister relationship, so important in *Mountain Journey*. In fact, this is an emotional attachment (when not an obsession) that outweighs all others in the text. Ibrâhîm's return to Nablus after an educational sojourn in Beirut becomes the occasion for Fadwâ to direct her energies to serving him. He is like the ship that is there to save the drowning man, and the air which she breathes.[43] His departure, once again to Beirut, has a deep effect on her. In his room, for example, she feels the neckties he left behind and smells the shirt he had worn the previous day.[44] The replacement of the original *Hamâsa* mother-son serves as well to play down the maternal, if not to eliminate it completely. This concords with the narrator's earlier eloquent denunciations of motherhood. The maternal is sacrificed at the altar of the fraternal.

Brother-sister relations are powerful ones, indeed, in the Arabo-Islamic context, as Ibn Tufayl's philosophical allegory showed us so eloquently. There, the brother-sister duo was pitted against the heterosexual couple of Hayy's occulted father and transgressing mother. But the textual world and realities of the medieval physician-philosopher differ from that of the contemporary Palestinian poet. His problematic brother-sister duo leads to the abandonment of the infant. Woman's voice and woman's plight are seen through the lens of the male. In the twentieth century, it becomes possible for a Fadwâ Tûqân to portray brother-sister dynamics, but this time through the lens of the female. In her odyssey, as well, it is the prob-

---

[40] Shâkir al-Nâbulusî, *Fadwâ Tûqân wal-Shiʿr al-Urdunnî al-Muʿâsir* (Cairo: al-Muʾassasa al-Misriyya al-ʿAmma lil-Taʾlîf wal-Inbâʾ wal-Nashr, 1966), pp. 45–54.

[41] See chapter 8 above.

[42] Abû Tammâm, *Dîwân al-Hamâsa* (Cairo: Matbaʿat al-Saʿâda, 1927), 1:378–380. Medieval commentators on Abû Tammâm's work concur that the woman in question was a mother. See, for example, al-Tibrîzî, *Sharh Dîwân al-Hamâsa* (Beirut: ʿAlam al-Kutub, n.d.), 2:191–213; al Marzûqî, *Sharh Dîwân al-Hamâsa*, ed. Ahmad Amîn and ʿAbd al-Salâm Hârûn, vol. 2 (Cairo: Lajnat al-Taʾlîf wal-Tarjama wal-Nashr, 1952), pp. 914–918; Abû Tammâm, *Dîwân al-Hamâsa*, Riwâyat al-Jawâlîqî, ed. ʿAbd al-Munʿim Ahmad Sâlih (Baghdad: Dâr al-Rashîd lil-Nashr, 1980), pp. 258–260.

[43] Tûqân, *Rihla*, pp. 61–62.

[44] Ibid., p. 79.

lematic heterosexual couple of herself and the young man who offered
her the flower that causes her sequestration. Thus it is that she will become Ibrâhîm's student. The conflict is brought about by an exogamic
male-female couple that eventually leads to a seemingly less problematic
brother-sister couple. Fadwâ Tûqân's deep attachment to Ibrâhîm would
continue long past his death.[45] The forces informing the medieval and the
modern narratives may look identical, but their articulation most certainly is not.

Fadwâ's initial relationship with poetry is the traditional female one.
At the same time, her attachment to the rithâ' is an attachment to the
high poetic culture. Her place in the canon is laid out for her. Accepting
it means accepting her female literary role. But even the high poetic culture can give rise to ambivalent gender questions. In introducing one of
her early poems, 'Umar Farrûkh, the editor of the Beirut journal al-
Amâlî, noted that while many men were writing an effeminate and sensitive poetry, she was reviving the likes of Abû Tammâm and al-Mutanabbî
(d. 354/965).[46] These are certainly leading representatives of what one
could call the macho tradition in Arabic poetry.

Pulling at this, and in a subversive fashion, is another link made with
the poetic tradition, and that is through the pen name, Danânîr, which
Fadwâ attaches to her earliest love poems. As the narrator herself explains, Danânîr was a slave girl of one of the famous eighth-century Bar-
makid viziers, Yahyâ al-Barmakî. And since love was connected in Fadwâ's mind with disgrace and shame, she placed before her first two love
poems a quotation from the great anthologist Abû al-Faraj al-Isfahânî,
who, in his Kitâb al-Aghânî, says (according to Fadwâ): "Danânîr was
honorable and virtuous."[47]

But choosing a slave girl to exorcise the shame that might be associated
with love poetry is richly ironic. Slave girls in the Islamic Middle Ages
were trained to compose and recite poetry, as well as to entertain at social
occasions where men were present. Treatises from the classical period on
singing slave girls, such that of al-Jâhiz, make it clear that singing slave
girls were sex objects and great courtesans, whose singing and poetry had
enormous seductive power.[48] Al-Jâhiz asks himself how it is possible for
a slave girl to either avoid creating fitna, that chaos generated by the female, or be virtuous.[49] The word he uses here is 'afîfa, the very same term
Fadwâ attributes to Danânîr. Is this famous slave girl "virtuous," or is

[45] See the very interesting essay by Fadwâ Tûqân, "Akhî Ibrâhîm" (My brother Ibrâhîm),
in Ibrâhîm Tûqân, Dîwân, pp. 11–37.

[46] Tûqân, Rihla, p. 89.

[47] Ibid.

[48] Al-Jâhiz, Qiyân. See, also, chapter 2 above.

[49] Al-Jâhiz, Qiyân, p. 21.

this a virtue Fadwâ has transferred to her? Curiously enough, I have not been able to locate Fadwâ's quotation from *al-Aghânî* in that famous work. Danânîr lived during the heyday of the practices described in the medieval literary corpus on slave girls, having studied singing and music with the greatest names in music, like Ibn Jâmiʿ, Fulayh, and Ibrâhîm al-Mawsilî. It is with Ibrâhîm al-Mawsilî, however, that her special relationship appears. It was said that she imitated his singing so well that no difference could be heard. Ibrâhîm al-Mawsilî once even told Yahyâ al-Barmakî, "If you lose me and Danânîr remains, you have not lost me."[50] Should one discount the parallels of Danânîr/Fadwâ and Ibrâhîm al-Mawsilî/Ibrâhîm Tûqân? And, of course, Danânîr is still a slave, a woman without power. Even her name (the plural of *dînâr*) lacks the dignity of a typical Muslim woman's name.

A pen name ties a character to an alternative reality. More important here, it raises a question about Fadwâ Tûqân's right to romantic poetic speech. It seems that only through the identity with another established female poetic voice, the slave girl Danânîr, does the narrator feel she has a right to speak.

But the choice of a slave girl as persona has broader reverberations that tie in with poetry, politics, and women's status. After all, the Islamic Middle Ages did boast of a few liberated (for a time) female iconoclasts, like the Andalusian royal poet, Wallâda.[51] And that is just the point. *Mountain Journey* likens the oppression of the emotion of love by Eastern Arab society to the oppression of women.[52] Fadwâ eloquently bemoans her status and that of other women. Not only does the reader encounter the familiar imagery of the Arab woman's existence as prison (eloquently exploited by an earlier fiction writer, the Egyptian Ihsân Kamâl)[53] but *Journey* goes further. Her family is the prison from which she wishes to flee.[54] Her femininity "moans like a wounded animal in its cage."[55] It is finally in England that she knows the joy of the prisoner when he gets out into space and light.[56] The narrator's view of women's state is so harsh as to almost preclude sympathy for them. Women are "victims without individuality, without independent being," they are old at age twenty-five,

[50] See Abû al-Faraj al-Isfahânî, *al-Aghânî*, 16:136–139. See, also, Kahhâla, *A'lâm al-Nisâ'*, 1:417–419.

[51] See, for example, W. Hoenerbach, "Zur Charakteristik Wallâdas, der Geliebten Ibn Zaydûns," *Die Welt des Islams* 13 (1971): 20–25.

[52] Tûqân, *Rihla*, p. 139.

[53] Ihsân Kamâl, "A Jailhouse of My Own," trans. Wadida Wassef, rev. Lewis Hall, in *Arabic Writing Today: The Short Story*, ed. Mahmoud Manzalaoui (Cairo: Dar al-Maaref, 1968), pp. 304–316.

[54] Tûqân, *Rihla*, p. 59.

[55] Ibid., p. 131.

[56] Ibid., p. 174.

they have no friends, and so forth.[57] Rather than a place in which one could find social or political consciousness, the house becomes "a large coop filled with domesticated birds at whom feed was thrown" that they would swallow without discussion.[58]

Fadwâ's imprisonment, though different, recalls that of al-Saʿdâwî. The Egyptian feminist paints a more corporal enslavement. It is the specific, such as the hair that is chained and imprisoned in ribbons, that holds the narrator's attention.[59] It is "chains of my own blood that bind me to the bed so that I am unable to run and jump . . . chains from within my own body . . . that shackle me in fetters of shame and disgrace."[60] Even the general is corporal. Speaking of her mother, the Saʿdâwian narrator muses, "Can she love me while putting chains every day on my feet, on my hands, and around my neck?"[61] Nawâl al-Saʿdâwî's escape from the body is paralleled by Fadwâ Tûqân's escape from society and its confinements. It is in England that Fadwâ finally finds solace.

When the narrator of al-Saʿdâwî's *Memoirs of a Female Physician* let her dress ride up while she was sitting, her mother would throw her a sharp look and the young woman would sense her ʿawra, her shame.[62] Fadwâ would be chastised by an old religious woman, Shaykha, when she wore a short dress. Shaykha would scream at her and tell her that both she and her mother would go to Hell. The young girl takes the occasion to reflect on this deity who would send her to Hell for a short dress. He is frightening, indeed, and without any pity.[63] Relatively similar situations, which both involve some baring of the female body, lead to different results. Tûqân, unlike al-Saʿdâwî, links her experience directly to religion, redefining the entire phenomenon in the context of patriarchy. For Nawâl al-Saʿdâwî, the occasion is a source of rebellion. Is it a surprise that both young women create their own worlds, isolated from others?[64]

And the desperate state in which Fadwâ finds herself is partially a result of the tension between her imprisonment in the women's world and what she sees as the outside, inaccessible to her. After Ibrâhîm's death, Fadwâ resisted her father's attempts to steer her to political poetry, to fill the gap her brother left behind. "How and under what right or logic does my father ask me to compose political poetry, while I am a prisoner of walls,

[57] Ibid., pp. 129–130.
[58] Ibid., p. 133.
[59] Al-Saʿdâwî, *Mudhakkirât*, p. 5; al-Saʿdawi, "Growing Up," p. 111.
[60] Al-Saʿdâwî, *Mudhakkirât*, p. 8; al-Saʿdawi, "Growing Up," p. 113.
[61] Al-Saʿdâwî, *Mudhakkirât*, p. 14; al-Saʿdawi, "Growing Up," p. 116.
[62] Al-Saʿdâwî, *Mudhakkirât*, pp. 5–6; al-Saʿdawi, "Growing Up," p. 112.
[63] Tûqân, *Rihla*, p. 37.
[64] Al-Saʿdâwî, *Mudhakkirât*, p. 10; al-Saʿdawi, "Growing Up," p. 114; Tûqân, *Rihla*, p. 58.

not attending men's gatherings nor listening to the serious discussions?"[65] Her social situation does not encourage political awareness. "If I am not emancipated socially," she muses, "how can I fight with my pen for political, ideological, or national emancipation?"[66]

The tension created by the reality of the narrator's status as imprisoned female and the expectations that she should participate in the male act of writing political poetry was quite destructive. It was just at this point that she attempted suicide by swallowing a bottle of aspirin.[67] The father's death in 1948 finally releases her, and she puts pen to paper a few months later to write nationalist poetry.[68] This is again a rebirth for the female, one that comes about through the death of a male. As such, it echoes the earlier conscious link made by the narrator through the wordplay on *shahâda* and *shâhida*, expressing a male's death (the cousin of Fadwâ's mother) as concurrent with a female's birth (Fadwâ's).

But while one male death permits an establishment of a physical birth, the other signals a dual, metaphorical one. Not only is Fadwâ able after her father's demise to write nationalist poetry (literary birth), but she also becomes more conscious of political activity (political birth). She attends political meetings, hides political refugees in her home, and the like.[69] But her poetic writings remain a "prisoner" of her emotional and psychological states, and her full political literary liberation does not come about until after the June 1967 War.[70] This is perhaps not so unusual. Hamida Kazi notes, in her study of the political participation of women in the West Bank, women's more active role after 1967.[71] And this is what permits *Mountain Journey* to differ so drastically from other post-1967 autobiographical accounts, like those of Leila Khaled and Raymonda Hawa Tawil, that are more political.[72]

Politics, then, for Fadwâ is clearly connected to the male and is defined predominantly as his domain. The narrator does cite instances of feminist involvement on the part of women. Her mother, for example, was the first woman of her generation to lift off the veil in Nablus.[73] She was also

[65] Tûqân, *Rihla*, p. 131.
[66] Ibid., pp. 133–134.
[67] Ibid., p. 135.
[68] Ibid., p. 137.
[69] Ibid., pp. 142–152.
[70] See, for example, ibid., p. 152.
[71] Hamida Kazi, "Palestinian Women and the National Liberation Movement: A Social Perspective," in *Women in the Middle East*, special issue of *Khamsin* (London: Zed Books, 1987), pp. 26–39.
[72] See, for example, Leila Khaled, *Mon peuple vivra*, trans. Michel Pagnier (Paris: Gallimard, 1973); Raymonda Hawa Tawil, *My Home, My Prison* (New York: Holt, Rinehart and Winston, 1979).
[73] Tûqân, *Rihla*, p. 27.

active in a women's group that joined Hudâ Sha'râwî's General Union of
Arab Women in 1929.[74] But, to quote Fadwâ, "this does not change anything in the picture." Her mother was not permitted to travel to women's
conferences; she could not participate in women's demonstrations.[75]
Fadwâ could not have put it more eloquently: "I was afflicted with the
sickness of hatred of politics."[76] She exposes the masculinist values underlying political activity. A long, essentially heroic description of the political activities of 1936 (general strike, National Committee, etc.) leads
to the words of a popular song:

> We are the ones who defend the nation
> And kiss its wound.
And the echo comes back:
> Sell your mother and buy a rifle.
> The rifle is better than your mother.
> On the day of the revolution, it will dispel your worries.[77]

The implications of these last lines are not hard to decipher. The verses
are grammatically addressed to a male listener. The rifle as the symbol of
masculinity needs no commentary. The word for "to dispel" (*tufarrij*) is
derived from the same root as the word for "vulva" (*farj*).[78] Motherhood,
the primary life-giving act, is useless. Compared to the masculine political
act, it might as well be eliminated. The male organ is better than the female one.

   This citation reflects a tension characteristic of *Mountain Journey, Difficult Journey*. On the surface, it is yet another attack on the mother. The
crudeness of its gender politics, however, gives a feminist twist to the
whole argument, leading to a more fundamental critique of the entire refrain. In effect, Fadwâ Tûqân's autobiography moves from an unreflective
rejection of motherhood (it is not a coincidence that its heroine neither
marries nor bears children) through a critique of the subjection of
women, to a final assault on the masculine citadel of politics and power.
Not surprisingly for the autobiography of a poet, this "journey" can also
be seen in relation to the canons of Arabic literary production. If the creation of a poetic voice counteracted the metaphoric nonbeing associated
with the mother, it took the death of the father to free the heroine from

---

[74] Ibid., pp. 132–133.
[75] Ibid., p. 132.
[76] Ibid., p. 133.
[77] Ibid., p. 102.
[78] *Farj* can also take on the more general usage of "pudenda" and, as such, refer to both
male and female genitalia. Even this usage, however, concords with the refrain's paradigmatic comparison of rifle with mother. See al-Zabîdî, *Tâj al-'Arûs*, vol. 6, ed. Husayn Nassâr (Kuwait: Matba'at Hukûmat al-Kuwayt, 1969), p. 142.

the linked prisons of the house and woman's poetry. Nor is it a coincidence that the successful transition to political poetry is not completed until after the 1967 War, that is, until all the inhabitants of Nablus become, in their own way, prisoners. In an ironic way, Fadwâ's development inversely reflects that of her homeland. The year 1917 marks her birth—and the Balfour Declaration, a death threat for her country; 1948 is a rebirth and access to political activity—and the loss of two-thirds of Palestine; 1967 consummates the loss of Palestine and Fadwâ's full maturity. In literary-historical terms, the poet is no longer confined to the role of Danânîr but can take on that of Abû Tammâm.

The developing gender consciousness of the narrator permits a devastating attack on tradition, in both its maternal and paternal aspects. Fadwâ's mother used to narrate to her children the story of Moses who once, upon seeing a poor man and feeling sorry for him, went up to Jabal al-Tûr and asked God to provide the man with sustenance. God promised that good would come to him. Moses returned, happy with God's promise, and was surprised at seeing the man hanged, a corpse. He was stunned and immediately returned to the mountain and addressed the deity in a reprimanding tone, saying that he had asked God to provide for the man, not to hang him. But God answered that He had created him and knew best. The children were surprised and the mother would continue the story. It seems that the owner of the house in front of which the poor man was seeking shelter dropped a gold coin. The poor man picked it up and went to a tavern. There he got drunk and got into a fight with one of the other drinkers. With his remaining money, he then bought a knife and stabbed the other man. At this, he was taken to the ruler, who ordered his hanging.[79]

This gives the narrator ample opportunity to muse about justice. Tradition is clearly the place devoid of justice. After all, it is the ultimate patriarch, the deity, who, although He claims to know best (Father Knows Best?), has the man killed. The mother is also open to ridicule since she transmits this absurd story. But more fundamentally, this little anecdote effectively burlesques Islamic theological discussions (which Fadwâ was familiar with, as she herself notes in the same chapter). The problem of divine justice was a favored topic of argument in the medieval period between two theologico-philosophical schools, the Muʿtazilites and the Ashʿarites. Often cited was the story of the three sons: one son, who is just, goes to Heaven; another, who is wicked, to Hell, and the third dies young, because, it is explained, God knew that he would grow up to become evil. The one in Hell then asks why he was not permitted to die

---

[79] Tûqân, *Rihla*, p. 154.

young.[80] This thoroughgoing attack on the justice of the divinity transcends gender politics to become a total attack on tradition. After all, this masculine justice was already questioned when the young woman was chastised for her short dress.

Fadwâ Tûqân is perhaps the ideal female vehicle for an effective criticism and recasting of Arabo-Islamic discourse. Unlike the medieval voice, the twentieth-century scriptor is responsible for the form and means of her discourse. But more than that: Fadwâ Tûqân is first and foremost a poet. It is not accidental that it should be a poet, since poets are highly favored in the Arabic tradition, who should question the tradition in a prose text, the medium of her contemporaries.

The narrator of *Mountain Journey, Difficult Journey* is at the crossroads of the classical and the modern in Arabo-Islamic discourse. The elements of her saga relate to practically the entirety of the tradition I have analyzed. Shahrazâd's procreative body is ultimately what permitted the setting down on paper of her words. Fadwâ is fleeing from the procreative body, that of her mother. Instead, the young poet links herself directly to the sexual woman's tradition, that of the slave girls. At the same time, she attempts to redefine this sexuality (which is, after all, nothing but corporality) by insisting that the slave girl of her choice is virtuous.

A woman's recasting of the tradition has its surprises. Ibn Tufayl's brother-sister duo is transformed by Fadwâ. In a fascinating tour de force, she ties this problematic relationship to the Joseph story. Gone is the kayd of the medieval misogynists; gone is the proverbial beauty of this Muslim prophet. "The religious books say that the well in which Jacob's sons threw their brother Joseph was empty of water. So does this mean that it was empty of everything? Is it not possible that there were poisonous reptiles crouching in the corners or moving here and there on the walls of the well?" She is saved, from the dark well of her soul, by Ibrâhîm's hand.[81] In the traditional religious story, that of the male prophet, Jacob's sons cast their brother in the well. In the modern female rewriting, a brother's hand becomes the "rope of safety" that stretches out and saves the young woman. Roles are reversed, identities are created. But are we not close to that womb-well in which al-Suhrawardî threw his male protagonists?[82]

Escape is as important for Fadwâ as it was for the heroines of Nawâl al-Sa'dâwî. Simply, the modalities are different. When the young Fadwâ would raise her voice in song, the old woman Shaykha would shut her up, threatening her that she would become like the popular singers in

---

[80] W. Montgomery Watt, *Islamic Philosophy and Theology* (Edinburgh: Edinburgh University Press, 1962), pp. 67-68.

[81] Tûqân, *Rihla*, pp. 62–63.

[82] See chapter 5 above.

Nablus. But this did not sound so unpleasant to Fadwâ: it represented freedom.[83] How distant this is from the young narrator of al-Saʿdâwî's *Memoirs of a Female Physician*, for whom freedom and power are linked to the appropriation of the male role.

Al-Saʿdâwî would certainly not speak, as Fadwâ did, of coming out of "al-qumqum al-harîmî."[84] The *qumqum* is that thick, long-necked bottle from which jinnis traditionally emerge. Add to this its being a bottle defined as belonging to the harem, and one has a most fascinating image of rebirth. And imprisonment in a bottle harks back to *The Thousand and One Nights*.

Fadwâ Tûqân's relationship with the male universe of Arabo-Islamic discourse seems to run counter to that of her female contemporaries. Did she not, after all, allow Samîh al-Qâsim to introduce her personal account of her life? Is not her poetic guide and savior her brother Ibrâhîm? Does she not reject for a long time her father's push to write political poetry: in her mind, a male prerogative? Does she not set up an identification with the ultimate paragon of male beauty in Islam, the prophet Joseph? The evidence would seem overwhelming.

But the subversion of *Mountain Journey* is fundamental. Writing in Arabic, the language of the rich Arabo-Islamic textual tradition, she disassembles this very language. Speaking of "the family atmosphere which man controls," Fadwâ declares: "Woman should forget the existence of the word *no* [*lâ*] in language, except at the time of the creed ('There is no deity but God') in her ablutions and in her prayers. As for *yes* [*naʿam*], it is the parroting word that she whispers from her suckling infancy, to become thereafter a gumlike word that sticks on her lips during her entire life."[85] The body and the word have been brought together in a devastating attack on gender and the Arabic language. Woman is turned into an eternal child. The Arabic term for "word" here is *lafza*, an utterance—not the word as semiotic unit but the embodied corporeal word of speech. The Arab woman may, in Fadwâ's autobiographical vision, be restricted to *naʿam*, yes. But Fadwâ Tûqân herself has very effectively said *lâ*, no.

[83] Tûqân, *Rihla*, p. 37.
[84] Ibid., p. 132.
[85] Ibid., p. 40.

Works Cited

ʿAbd al-Wahhâb, Muhammad Fahmî. *Al-Harakât al-Nisâʾiyya fî al-Sharq wa-Silatuhâ bil-Istiʿmâr wal-Sahyûniyya al-ʿAlamiyya*. Cairo: Dâr al-Iʿtisâm, 1979.

Abrams, M. H. *A Glossary of Literary Terms*. 3d ed. New York: Holt, Rinehart and Winston, 1971.

Abû al-Faraj al-Isfahânî. *Kitâb al-Aghânî*. 20 vols. in 10. Beirut: Reprint of Bûlâq edition, 1970.

Abû Tammâm. *Dîwân al-Hamâsa*. 2 vols. in 1. Cairo: Matbaʿat al-Saʿâda, 1927.

———. *Dîwân al-Hamâsa*. Riwâyat al-Jawâlîqî. Edited by ʿAbd al-Munʿim Ahmad Sâlih. Baghdad: Dâr al-Rashîd lil-Nashr, 1980.

Accad, Evelyne. *Sexuality and War: Literary Masks of the Middle East*. New York: New York University Press, 1990.

Accad, Evelyne, and Rose Ghurayyib. *Contemporary Arab Women Writers and Poets*. Beirut: Institute for Women's Studies in the Arab World, 1985.

Ahmed, Leila. "Arab Culture and Writing Women's Bodies." *Feminist Issues* (Spring 1989): 41–55.

———. "Between Two Worlds: The Formation of a Turn-of-the-Century Egyptian Feminist." In *Life/Lines: Theorizing Women's Autobiography*, edited by Bella Brodzki and Celeste Schenck, pp. 154–174. Ithaca: Cornell University Press, 1988.

———. "Feminism and Cross-Cultural Inquiry: The Terms of the Discourse in Islam." In *Coming to Terms: Feminism, Theory, Politics*, edited by Elizabeth Weed, pp. 143–151. New York: Routledge, 1989.

Aït Sabbah, Fatna. *La femme dans l'inconscient musulman*. Paris: Albin Michel, 1986.

ʿAjâʾib al-Hind. Attributed to Buzurk ibn Shahriyâr. Edited by Yûsuf al-Shârûnî. London: Riyâd al-Rayyis lil-Kutub wal-Nashr, 1990.

Alf Layla wa-Layla. 2 vols. Cairo: Matbaʿat Bûlâq edition, 1252 A.H.

Algosaibi, Ghazi A. *From the Orient and the Desert*. London: Oriel Press, 1977.

Allard, Guy H., et al. *Aspects de la marginalité au moyen âge*. Montreal: Les Editions de l'Aurore, 1975.

al-Amîr, Daisy. "Matâr Wâq Wâq." In Daisy al-Amîr, *ʿAlâ Lâʾihat al-Intizâr*, pp. 64–71. Baghdad: Bayt Sîn lil-Kutub, 1990.

Arberry, A. J. *FitzGerald's Salâmân and Absâl*. Cambridge: Cambridge University Press, 1956.

———. *The Koran Interpreted*. 2 vols. in 1. New York: Macmillan Publishing Co., 1974.

———. *Sufism*. London: Unwin Paperbacks, 1979.

Arkoun, Mohamed, Jacques Le Goff, Tawfiq Fahd, and Maxime Rodinson. *L'étrange et le merveilleux dans l'Islam médiéval*. Paris: Editions J.A., 1978.

Ascha, Ghassan. *Du statut inférieur de la femme en Islam*. Paris: L'Harmattan, 1989.

ʿAtiyya, Naʿîm. "Kayduhunna ʿAzîm." In Naʿîm ʿAtiyya, *Nisâʾ fî al-Mahâkim*, pp. 82–88. Cairo: Dâr al-Maʿârif, 1980.

al-Atraqjî, Wâjida Majîd ʿAbd Allâh. *Al-Marʾa fî Adab al-ʿAsr al-ʿAbbâsî*. Baghdad: Dâr al-Rashîd lil-Nashr, 1981.

al-ʿAttâr, Samar. "Al-Rihla min al-Hamajiyya ilâ al-Hadâra wa-Darûrat Taqyîd Hurriyyat al-Marʾa al-Jinsiyya: Mithâlâ Imraʾat al-Sundûq wa-Shahrazâd fî *Alf Layla wa-Layla*." In *al-Fikr al-ʿArabî al-Muʿâsir wal-Marʾa*, pp. 47–59. Cairo: Dâr Tadâmun al-Marʾa al-ʿArabiyya, 1988.

Awwad, Hanan. *Arab Causes in the Fiction of Ghâdah al-Sammân 1961/1975*. Quebec: Editions Naaman, 1983.

Baconnet, Marc. *Midi, la nuit*. Paris: Gallimard, 1984.

Bâhithat al-Bâdiya [Malak Hifnî Nâsif]. *Al-Nisâʾiyyât*. Cairo: Dâr al-Hudâ lil-Tabʿ wal-Nashr wal-Tawzîʿ, n.d.

Barth, John. *Chimera*. New York: Fawcett Crest, 1972.

Barthes, Roland. *Roland Barthes*. Paris: Seuil, Ecrivains de Toujours, 1980.

Baruch, Elaine Hoffman. "Women in Men's Utopias." In *Women in Search of Utopia: Mavericks and Mythmakers*, edited by Ruby Rohrlich and Elaine Hoffman Baruch, pp. 209–218. New York: Schocken Books, 1984.

al-Bayhaqî. *Al-Mahâsin wal-Masâwî*. 2 vols. Edited by Muhammad Abû al-Fadl Ibrâhîm. Cairo: Matbaʿat Nahdat Misr, n.d.

Beauvoir, Simone de. *La cérémonie des adieux*. Paris: Editions Gallimard, 1981.

Bellamy, James A. "Sex and Society in Islamic Popular Literature." In *Society and the Sexes in Medieval Islam*, edited by Afaf Lutfi al-Sayyid Marsot, pp. 23–42. Malibu: Undena Publications, 1979.

Ben Jelloun, Tahar. *La nuit sacrée*. Paris: Editions du Seuil, 1987.

Bencheikh, Jamel Eddine. *Les Mille et Une Nuits ou la parole prisonnière*. Paris: Editions Gallimard, 1988.

———. "Le roi, la reine et l'esclave noir." Special issue on *Itinéraires d'écritures*. *Peuples méditerranéens* 30 (1985): 145–157.

Benstock, Shari. "Authorizing the Autobiographical." In *The Private Self: Theory and Practice of Women's Autobiographical Writing*, edited by Shari Benstock, pp. 10–33. Chapel Hill: University of North Carolina Press, 1988.

Benveniste, Emile. *Problèmes de linguistique générale, I*. Paris: Gallimard, 1966.

Bettelheim, Bruno. *The Uses of Enchantment: The Meaning and Importance of Fairy Tales*. New York: Vintage Books, 1977.

Bloom, Harold. *The Anxiety of Influence: A Theory of Poetry*. New York: Oxford University Press, 1973.

Boswell, John. *Christianity, Social Tolerance, and Homosexuality*. Chicago: University of Chicago Press, 1980.

Bosworth, C. E. *The Medieval Islamic Underworld: The Banû Sâsân in Arabic Society and Literature*. 2 vols. Leiden: E. J. Brill, 1976.

Bouhdiba, Abdelwahab. *La sexualité en Islam*. Paris: Presses Universitaires de France, 1979.

Boullata, Issa J. *Trends and Issues in Contemporary Arab Thought*. Albany: State University of New York Press, 1990.

Brock, D. Heyward. "An Interview with Dannie Abse." *Literature and Medicine* 3 (1984): 5–18.

Brockelmann, Carl. *Geschichte der Arabischen Litteratur*. 5 vols. Leiden: E. J. Brill, 1937–1949.

Brown, Peter. *The Body and Society: Men, Women, and Sexual Renunciation in Early Christianity*. New York: Columbia University Press, 1988.

Burdekin, Katharine. *The End of This Day's Business*. New York: The Feminist Press, 1989.

Bürgel, J. C. *Allmacht und Mächtigkeit*. Munich: Beck, forthcoming.

———. "The Lady Gazelle and Her Murderous Glances." *Journal of Arabic Literature* 20 (1989): 1–11.

———. "Love, Lust, and Longing: Eroticism in Early Islam as Reflected in Literary Sources." In *Society and the Sexes in Medieval Islam*, edited by Afaf Lutfi al-Sayyid Marsot, pp. 81–117. Malibu: Undena Publications, 1979.

Burton, Richard F. *The Book of the Thousand Nights and a Night*. 10 vols. Burton Club Edition.

Bynum, Caroline Walker. *Jesus as Mother: Studies in the Spirituality of the High Middle Ages*. Berkeley: University of California Press, 1982.

Les cent et une nuits. Presented and translated by M. Gaudefroy-Demombynes. Paris: Sindbad, 1982.

Chebel, Malek. *Le corps dans la tradition au Mahgreb*. Paris: Presses Universitaires de France, 1984.

———. *L'esprit de sérail: Perversions et marginalités sexuelles au Maghreb*. Paris: Lieu Commun, 1988.

Chedid, Andrée. *Le sommeil délivré*. Paris: Flammarion, 1976.

Chodorow, Nancy. *The Reproduction of Mothering: Psychoanalysis and the Sociology of Gender*. Berkeley: University of California Press, 1978.

Clinton, Jerome W. "Madness and Cure in *The 1001 Nights*." *Studia Islamica* 61 (1985): 107–125.

Colloque de Cerisy. *Robbe-Grillet: Analyse, théorie*. Vol. 1. Paris: Union Générale d'Editions, 1976.

Conrad, Lawrence I. "Through the Thin Veil: On the Question of Communication and the Socialization of Knowledge in *Hayy ibn Yaqzân*." In *The World of Ibn Tufayl: Interdisciplinary Perspectives on Hayy ibn Yaqzân*, edited by Lawrence I. Conrad. Oxford: Oxford University Press, forthcoming.

Cooke, Miriam. "Telling Their Lives: A Hundred Years of Arab Women's Writings." *World Literature Today* 60 (Spring 1986): 212–216.

———. *War's Other Voices: Women Writers on the Lebanese Civil War*. Cambridge: Cambridge University Press, 1987.

Corbin, Henry. *Avicenne et le récit visionnaire*. Paris: Adrien-Maisonneuve, 1954.

al-Damîrî. *Hayât al-Hayawân al-Kubrâ*. Beirut: Dâr Ihyâ' al-Turâth al-'Arabî, n.d.

Daudet, Léon. *Les morticoles*. Paris: Bernard Grasset, 1956.

Defoe, Daniel. *Robinson Crusoe*. Edited by Angus Ross. New York: Penguin Books, 1983.

Divine, Donna Robinson. " 'Difficult Journey—Mountainous Journey,' The Memoirs of Fadwa Tuqan." In *The Female Autograph: Theory and Practice of Autobiography from the Tenth to the Twentieth Century*, edited by Domna Stanton, pp. 187–204. Chicago: University of Chicago Press, 1987.

―――. "Palestinian Arab Women and Their Reveries of Emancipation." In *Women Living Change*, edited by Susan C. Bourke and Donna Robinson Divine, pp. 57–83. Philadelphia: Temple University Press, 1985.

al-Djawbarî. *Le voile arraché: L'autre visage de l'Islam*. 2 vols. Translated by René R. Khawam. Paris: Editions Phébus, 1979–1980.

Djebar, Assia. *L'amour, la fantasia*. Paris: Editions Jean-Claude Lattès, 1985.

Doane, Mary Ann. "The Clinical Eye: Medical Discourses in the 'Woman's Film' of the 1940s." In *The Female Body in Western Culture: Contemporary Perspectives*, edited by Susan Rubin Suleiman, pp. 152–174. Cambridge: Harvard University Press, 1986.

Douglas, Allen, and Fedwa Malti-Douglas. "Al-ʿAdl wal-Fann fî al-Fallâh al-Fasîh." In *Shâdî ʿAbd al-Salâm wal-Fallâh al-Fasîh*, edited by Salâh Marʿî et al. Cairo: al-Hayʾa al-Misriyya al-ʿAmma lil-Kitâb, forthcoming.

―――. "Femmes, tradition, et bandes dessinées." *Revue tunisienne de sciences sociales*, forthcoming.

―――. "Reflections of a Feminist: Conversation with Nawal al-Saadawi." In *Opening the Gates: A Century of Arab Feminist Writing*, edited by Margot Badran and Miriam Cooke, pp. 394–404. London and Bloomington: Virago and Indiana University Press, 1990.

Dunqul, Amal. *Al-Aʿmâl al-Shiʿriyya al-Kâmila*. Beirut: Dâr al-ʿAwda, 1985.

Eagleton, Terry. *The Rape of Clarissa: Writing, Sexuality and Class Struggle in Samuel Richardson*. Minneapolis: University of Minnesota Press, 1982.

El Saadawi, Nawal. *The Fall of the Imam*. Translated by Sherif Hetata. London: Methuen, 1988.

―――. *The Hidden Face of Eve: Women in the Arab World*. Translated by Sherif Hetata. Boston: Beacon Press, 1982.

―――. "The Man with Buttons." In Nawal El Saadawi, *She Has No Place in Paradise*, translated by Shirley Eber, pp. 103–111. London: Minerva, 1989.

―――. *Memoirs of a Woman Doctor*. Translated by Catherine Cobham. San Francisco: City Lights Books, 1989.

―――. "A Private Letter to an Artist Friend." In Nawal El Saadawi, *Death of an Ex-Minister*, translated by Shirley Eber, pp. 97–111. London: Methuen, 1987.

―――. *Two Women in One*. Translated by Osman Nusairi and Jana Gough. London: al-Saqi Books, 1985.

―――. *Woman at Point Zero*. Translated by Sherif Hetata. London: Zed Press, 1983.

El Samman, Ghada. "Street Walker." Translated by Azza Kararah. Revised by Lewis Hall. In *Arabic Writing Today: The Short Story*, edited by Mahmoud Manzalaoui, pp. 317–327. Cairo: Dar al-Maaref, 1968.

El-Shamy, Hasan. "The Brother-Sister Syndrome in Arab Family Life, Socio-Cultural Factors in Arab Psychiatry: A Critical Review." *International Journal of Sociology of the Family* 11 (1981): 313–323.

———. *Brother and Sister Type 872*: A Cognitive Behavioristic Analysis of a Middle Eastern Oikotype.* Folklore Monographs Series, vol. 8. Bloomington: Folklore Publications Group, 1979.

The Encyclopaedia of Islam. 2d ed. Edited by H.A.R. Gibb et al. Leiden: E. J. Brill, 1960–present.

al-Fârâbî. *Kitâb Arâ' Ahl al-Madîna al-Fâdila.* Edited by Albîr Nasrî Nâdir. Beirut: Dâr al-Mashriq, 1973.

Fawzî, Mahmûd. *Adab al-Azâfir al-Tawîla.* Cairo: Dâr Nahdat Misr lil-Tabʿ wal-Nashr, 1987.

Fenoglio-Abd el Aal, Irène. *Défense et illustration de l'Egyptienne: Aux débuts d'une expression féminine.* Cairo: Centre d'Etudes et de Documentation Economique, Juridique et Sociale, 1988.

Ferguson, Margaret W., Maureen Quilligan, and Nancy J. Vickers. *Rewriting the Renaissance: The Discourses of Sexual Difference in Early Modern Europe.* Chicago: University of Chicago Press, 1986.

Fetterley, Judith. *The Resisting Reader: A Feminist Approach to American Fiction.* Bloomington: Indiana University Press, 1978.

Foucault, Michel. *Herculine Barbin dite Alexina B.* Paris: Editions Gallimard, 1978.

———. *Histoire de la folie à l'âge classique.* Paris: Editions Gallimard, 1972.

———. *Histoire de la sexualité.* 3 vols. Paris: Editions Gallimard, 1984–1988.

———. *Naissance de la clinique: Une archéologie du regard médical.* Paris: Presses Universitaires de France, 1963.

Friedman, Susan Stanford. "Women's Autobiographical Selves: Theory and Practice." In *The Private Self: Theory and Practice of Women's Autobiographical Writings,* edited by Shari Benstock, pp. 34–62. Chapel Hill: University of North Carolina Press, 1988.

Frye, Northrop. *The Great Code: The Bible and Literature.* New York: Harcourt Brace Jovanovich, 1983.

Gardiner, Judith Kegan. "On Female Identity and Writing by Women." In *Writing and Sexual Difference,* edited by Elizabeth Abel, pp. 177–191. Chicago: University of Chicago Press, 1982.

Gates, Henry Louis, Jr. *The Signifying Monkey: A Theory of African-American Literary Criticism.* Oxford: Oxford University Press, 1988.

Gauthier, Léon. *Ibn Thofaïl, sa vie, ses oeuvres.* Paris: E. Leroux, 1909.

Genette, Gérard. *Figures III.* Paris: Editions du Seuil, 1966.

Gerhardt, Mia I. *The Art of Storytelling: A Literary Study of the Thousand and One Nights.* Leiden: E. J. Brill, 1963.

al-Ghazâlî. *Ihyâ' 'Ulûm al-Dîn.* 5 vols. Beirut: Dâr al-Qalam, n.d.

———. *Al-Munqidh min al-Dalâl.* Edited by ʿAbd al-Halîm Mahmûd. Cairo: Dâr al-Kutub al-Hadîtha, 1965.

al-Ghazâlî, Zaynab. *Ayyâm min Hayâtî.* Beirut: Dâr al-Shurûq, 1987.

Ghazoul, Ferial Jabouri. *The Arabian Nights: A Structural Analysis.* Cairo: Cairo

Associated Institution for the Study and Preservation of Arab Cultural Values, 1980.

Gide, André. *La symphonie pastorale*. Paris: Gallimard, 1925.

Gilbert, Sandra M., and Susan Gubar. *The Madwoman in the Attic: The Woman Writer and the Nineteenth-Century Literary Imagination*. New Haven: Yale University Press, 1979.

Gilman, Charlotte Perkins. *Herland*. New York: Pantheon Books, 1979.

Gómez, Emilio García. "Un cuento árabe, fuente común de Abentofáil y de Gracián." *Revista de archivos, bibliotecas y museos* 30 (1926): 1–67, 261–269.

Graham, Theodora R. "The Courage of His diversity: Medicine, Writing, and William Carlos Williams." *Literature and Medicine* 2 (1983): 9–20.

Gubar, Susan. " 'The Blank Page' and the Issues of Female Creativity." In *Writing and Sexual Difference*, edited by Elizabeth Abel, pp. 73–93. Chicago: University of Chicago Press, 1982.

Hafez, Sabry. "Intentions and Realisation in the Narratives of Nawal El-Saadawi." *Third World Quarterly* 11, no. 3 (July 1989): 188–198.

al-Hamadhânî. *Al-Maqâmât*. Edited by Muhammad ʿAbduh. Beirut: Dâr al-Mashriq, 1968.

Harlow, Barbara. "The Middle East." In *Longman Anthology of World Literature by Women*, compiled by Marian Arkin and Barbara Shollar, pp. 1163–1171. New York: Longman, 1989.

———. *Resistance Literature*. New York: Methuen, 1987.

Henri, Pierre. *Les aveugles et la société*. Paris: Presses Universitaires de France, 1958.

Heppenstall, Rayner. *The Blaze of Noon*. London: Allison and Busby, 1980.

Herrmann, Claudine. *Les voleuses de langue*. Paris: éditions des femmes, 1976.

Hetata, Sherif. *Al-ʿAyn Dhât al-Jafn al-Maʿdanî*. Cairo: Dâr al-Thaqâfa al-Jadîda, 1981.

———. *The Eye with the Iron Lid*. Translated by Sherif Hetata. London: Zed Press, n.d.

Hoenerbach, W. "Zur Charakteristik Wallâdas, der Geliebten Ibn Zaydûns." *Die Welt des Islams* 13 (1971): 20–25.

Hourani, George F. "The Principal Subject of Ibn Tufayl's *Hayy ibn Yaqzân*." *Journal of Near Eastern Studies* 15 (1956): 40–46.

Hume, Kathryn. *Fantasy and Mimesis: Responses to Reality in Western Literature*. New York: Methuen, 1984.

Hunayn ibn Ishâq. "Qissat Salâmân and Absâl." Translated from the Greek. In Ibn Sînâ, *Tisʿ Rasâ'il*, pp. 158–168. Cairo: Maktabat Hindiyya, 1908.

Husayn, Suzanne Tâhâ. *Maʿak*. Translated by Badr al-Dîn ʿArûdakî. Cairo: Dâr al-Maʿârif, 1964.

Husayn, Tâhâ. *Al-Ayyâm*. Vol. 1. Cairo: Dâr al-Maʿârif, 1971.

———. *Al-Ayyâm*. Vol. 2. Cairo: Dâr al-Maʿârif, 1971.

———. *Al-Ayyâm*. Vol. 3. Cairo: Dâr al-Maʿârif, 1973.

———. *A Passage to France*. Translated by Kenneth Cragg. Leiden: E. J. Brill, 1976.

al-Husrî. *Jamᶜ al-Jawâhir fî al-Mulah wal-Nawâdir.* Edited by ᶜAlî Muhammad al-Bijâwî. Beirut: Dâr al-Jîl, 1987.

Hussein, Taha. *An Egyptian Childhood.* Translated by E. H. Paxton. Washington, D.C.: Three Continents Press, 1981.

———. *The Stream of Days.* Translated by Hilary Wayment. London: Longman, 1948.

Huston, Nancy. "The Matrix of War: Mothers and Heroes." In *The Female Body in Western Culture: Contemporary Perspectives,* edited by Susan Rubin Suleiman, pp. 119–136. Cambridge: Harvard University Press, 1986.

Ibdâᶜ 1, no. 10 (1983). Special issue in memory of Amal Dunqul.

Ibn ᶜAbd Rabbihi. *Al-ᶜIqd al-Farîd.* Edited by Ahmad Amîn et al. 7 vols. Cairo: Matbaᶜat Lajnat al-Ta'lîf, 1949–1965.

Ibn Abî Tâhir [Tayfûr]. *Balâghât al-Nisâ' wa-Tarâ'if Kalâmihinna wa-Mulah Nawâdirihinna wa-Akhbâr Dhawât al-Ra'y minhunna wa-Ashᶜâruhunna fî al-Jâhiliyya wal-Islâm.* Edited by Ahmad al-Alfî. Tunis: al-Maktaba al-ᶜAtîqa, 1985.

Ibn Bâjja. *Kitâb Tadbîr al-Mutawahhid.* Edited by Maᶜn Ziyâda. Beirut: Dâr al-Fikr al-Islâmî, 1978.

Ibn al-Batanûnî. *Kitâb al-ᶜUnwân fî Makâyid al-Niswân.* MS. Cairo Adâb 3568.

Ibn Hanbal, Ahmad. *Ahkâm al-Nisâ'.* Edited by ᶜAbd al-Qâdir Ahmad ᶜAtâ. Beirut: Dâr al-Kutub al-ᶜIlmiyya, 1986.

———. *Musnad al-Imâm Ahmad ibn Hanbal.* 6 vols. Beirut: al-Maktab al-Islâmî lil-Tibâᶜa wal-Nashr, n.d.

Ibn al-Jawzî. *Ahkâm al-Nisâ'.* Beirut: Dâr al-Kutub al-ᶜIlmiyya, 1985.

———. *Akhbâr al-Adhkiyâ'.* Edited by Muhammad Mursî al-Khawlî. Cairo: Matâbiᶜ al-Ahrâm al-Tijâriyya, 1970.

———. *Akhbâr al-Zirâf wal-Mutamâjinîn.* Edited by Muhammad Anîs Muharât. Damascus and Beirut: Dâr al-Hikma, 1987.

———. *Dhamm al-Hawâ.* Beirut: Dâr al-Kutub al-ᶜIlmiyya, 1987.

Ibn Kamâl Bâshâ. *Kitâb Rujûᶜ al-Shaykh ilâ Sibâh.* Marrakech(?): n.p., n.d.

Ibn Khurradâdhbih. *Al-Masâlik wal-Mamâlik.* Edited by M. J. De Goeje. Bibliotheca Geographorum Arabicorum. Leiden: E. J. Brill, 1889.

Ibn Mâja. *Sunan Ibn Mâja.* Edited and commentated by Muhammad Fu'âd ᶜAbd al-Bâqî. 2 vols. Beirut: al-Maktaba al-ᶜIlmiyya, n.d.

Ibn Manzûr. *Lisân al-ᶜArab.* 20 vols. in 10. Cairo: al-Dâr al-Misriyya lil-Ta'lîf wal-Tarjama, n.d.

Ibn al-Muᶜtazz. *Tabaqât al-Shuᶜarâ'.* Edited by ᶜAbd al-Sattâr Ahmad Farrâj. Cairo: Dâr al-Maᶜârif, 1968.

Ibn al-Nafîs. *The Theologus Autodidactus of Ibn al-Nafîs.* Edited with an introduction, partial translation, and notes by Max Meyerhof and Joseph Schacht. Oxford: The Clarendon Press, 1968.

Ibn Qayyim al-Jawziyya. *Akhbâr al-Nisâ'.* Edited by Nizâr Ridâ. Beirut: Manshûrât Dâr Maktabat al-Hayât, 1982.

———. *Hukm al-Nazar lil-Nisâ'.* Cairo: Maktab al-Turâth al-Islâmî, 1982.

Ibn Qutayba. *Al-Shiᶜr wal-Shuᶜarâ'.* 2 vols. in 1. Beirut: Dâr al-Thaqâfa, 1969.

———. *ᶜUyûn al-Akhbâr.* 4 vols. in 2. Cairo: Dâr al-Kutub, 1963.

Ibn Sîda. *Al-Muhkam wal-Muhît al-A'zam fî al-Lugha*. Edited by 'Abd al-Sattâr Ahmad Farrâj, Husayn Nassâr, et al. 7 vols. to date. Cairo: Matba'at Mustafâ al-Bâbî al-Halabî, 1958–present.

Ibn Sînâ. *Hayy ibn Yaqzân*. In *Hayy ibn Yaqzân*. Edited by Ahmad Amîn. Cairo: Dâr al-Ma'ârif, 1952.

———. *Al-Ishârât wal-Tanbîhât*. With commentary by Nasîr al-Dîn al-Tûsî. Edited by Sulaymân Dunyâ. 4 vols. Cairo: Dâr al-Ma'ârif, 1957–1968.

———. "Risâlat Hayy ibn Yaqzân." In Ibn Sînâ, *Rasâ'il* (*Traités Mystiques*), edited by M.A.F. Mehren. Leiden: E. J. Brill, 1899.

———. "Risâlat al-Qadr." In Ibn Sînâ, *Rasâ'il* (*Traités Mystiques*), edited by M.A.F. Mehren. Leiden: E. J. Brill, 1899.

Ibn Tufayl. *Hayy ibn Yaqzân*. Edited by Fârûq Sa'd. Tripoli, Libya: al-Dâr al-'Arabiyya lil-Kitâb, 1983.

———. *Hayy ibn Yaqzân*. Edited by Léon Gauthier. Beirut: Imprimerie Catholique, 1936. Published as Léon Gauthier, *Hayy ben Yaqdhân, roman philosophique d'Ibn Thofaïl*, texte arabe et traduction française.

———. *Hayy ibn Yaqzân*. In *Hayy ibn Yaqzân*, edited by Ahmad Amîn. Cairo: Dâr al-Ma'ârif, 1952.

———. *The Journey of the Soul: The Story of Hai bin Yaqzân as Told by Abu Bakr Muhammad bin Tufail*. Translated by Riad Kocache. London: The Octagon Press, 1982.

Ibn al-Wardî. *Kharîdat al-'Ajâ'ib wa-Farîdat al-Gharâ'ib*. Cairo: Mustafâ al-Bâbî al-Halabî, n.d.

al-Ibshîhî. *Al-Mustatraf fî Kull Fann Mustazraf*. Edited by Mufîd Muhammad Qumayha. 2 vols. Beirut: Dâr al-Kutub al-'Ilmiyya, 1986.

Idrîs, Yûsuf. "'Alâ Waraq Sîlûfân." In Yûsuf Idrîs, *Bayt min Lahm*, pp. 31–51. Cairo: Dâr Misr lil-Tibâ'a, 1982.

———. "In Cellophane Wrapping." Translated by Roger Allen. In *In the Eye of the Beholder: Tales of Egyptian Life from the Writings of Yusuf Idris*, edited by Roger Allen, pp. 169–189. Minneapolis and Chicago: Bibliotheca Islamica, 1978.

al-Idrîsî. *Nuzhat al-Mushtâq fî Ikhtirâq al-Afâq*. 2 vols. Beirut: 'Alam al-Kutub, 1989.

Irigaray, Luce. *Spéculum de l'autre femme*. Paris: Les Editions de Minuit, 1974.

'Itânî, Samîra. *Hal Sahîh anna Akthar Ahl al-Nâr Hum al-Nisâ'*? Beirut: Dâr al-Fath lil-Tibâ'a wal-Nashr, 1979(?).

al-Jâhiz. *Al-Bukhalâ'*. Edited by Tâhâ al-Hâjirî. Cairo: Dâr al-Ma'ârif, 1971.

———. *Al-Hayawân*. Edited by 'Abd al-Salâm Muhammad Hârûn. 8 vols. Cairo: Matba'at Mustafâ al-Bâbî al-Halabî, 1965–1969.

———. *Risâlat al-Qiyân*. Edited and translated by A.F.L. Beeston as *The Epistle on Singing-Girls of Jâhiz*. Warminster, England: Aris & Phillips, 1980.

Jardine, Alice. "Death Sentences: Writing Couples and Ideology." In *The Female Body in Western Culture: Contemporary Perspectives*, edited by Susan Rubin Suleiman, pp. 84–96. Cambridge: Harvard University Press, 1986.

Jayyusi, Salma Khadra. *Trends and Movements in Modern Arabic Poetry*. 2 vols. Leiden: E. J. Brill, 1977.

Jean, Raymond. *La lectrice*. Paris: Actes Sud, 1986.

————. *Lectures du désir*. Paris: Editions du Seuil, 1977.

Kahhâla, 'Umar Ridâ. *A'lâm al-Nisâ'*. 5 vols. Beirut: Mu'assasat al-Risâla, n.d.

Kamâl, Ihsân. "A Jailhouse of My Own." Translated by Wadida Wassef. Revised by Lewis Hall. In *Arabic Writing Today: The Short Story*, edited by Mahmoud Manzalaoui, pp. 304–316. Cairo: Dar al-Maaref, 1968.

Kanafani, Ghassan. *All That's Left to You*. Translated by May Jayyusi and Jeremy Reed. Austin: University of Texas Center for Middle Eastern Studies, 1990.

————. *Mâ Tabaqqâ lakum*. In Ghassân Kanafânî, *Al-Athâr al-Kâmila*. 4 vols. Beirut: Dâr al-Talî'a lil-Tibâ'a wal-Nashr, 1980.

Kattan, Naïm. "Du récit du désir dans les Mille et une Nuits." In *La séduction*, edited by Maurice Olender and Jacques Sojcher, pp. 173–179. Paris: Editions Aubier Montaigne, 1980.

Kazi, Hamida. "Palestinian Women and the National Liberation Movement: A Social Perspective." In *Women in the Middle East*, pp. 26–39. Special issue of *Khamsin*. London: Zed Books, 1987.

Keller, Helen. *The Story of My Life*. New York: Airmont Publishing Company, 1965.

Keuls, Eva C. *The Reign of the Phallus: Sexual Politics in Ancient Athens*. New York: Harper & Row, 1985.

Khaled, Leila. *Mon peuple vivra*. Translated by Michel Pagnier. Paris: Gallimard, 1973.

al-Khatîb al-Baghdâdî. *Al-Bukhalâ'*. Edited by Ahmad Matlûb, Khadîja al-Hadîthî, and Ahmad al-Qaysî. Baghdad: Matba'at al-'Anî, 1964.

————. *Al-Tatfîl wa-Hikâyât al-Tufayliyyîn wa-Akhbâruhum wa-Nawâdir Kalâmihim wa-Ash'âruhum*, edited by Kâzim al-Muzaffar. Najaf: al-Maktaba al-Haydariyya, 1966.

Khatibi, Abdelkebir. *La blessure du nom propre*. Paris: Denoël, 1986.

————. "De la mille et troisième nuit." In *La séduction*, edited by Maurice Olender and Jacques Sojcher, pp. 131–147. Paris: Editions Aubier Montaigne, 1980.

Kilito, Abd el-Fattah. "Le genre 'Séance': une introduction." *Studia Islamica* 43 (1976): 25–51.

Kirtley, Donald D. *The Psychology of Blindness*. Chicago: Nelson-Hall, 1975.

Kitâb Alf Layla wa-Layla. Edited by Muhsin Mahdi. 2 vols. Leiden: E. J. Brill, 1984.

Kolodny, Annette. "A Map for Rereading: Gender and the Interpretation of Literary Texts." In *The New Feminist Criticism: Essays on Women, Literature and Theory*, edited by Elaine Showalter, pp. 46–62. New York: Pantheon Books, 1985.

Kurpershoek, P. M. *The Short Stories of Yûsuf Idrîs*. Leiden: E. J. Brill, 1981.

Leach, Edmund, and D. Alan Aycock. *Structural Interpretations of Biblical Myth*. Cambridge: Cambridge University Press, 1983.

Lees, Susan H. "Motherhood in Feminist Utopias." In *Women in Search of Uto-*

pia: Mavericks and Mythmakers, edited by Ruby Rohrlich and Elaine Hoffman Baruch, pp. 219–232. New York: Schocken Books, 1984.

Lefebvre, Gustave. *Romans et contes égyptiens de l'époque pharaonique*. Paris: Adrien-Maisonneuve, 1949.

Lejeune, Philippe. *Le pacte autobiographique*. Paris: Editions du Seuil, 1975.

———. "Le pacte autobiographique (bis)." *Poétique* 56 (1983): 416–434.

Lévi-Strauss, Claude. *Anthropologie structurale*. Paris: Librairie Plon, 1974.

Lewis, Bernard. *The Muslim Discovery of Europe*. New York: W. W. Norton & Co., 1982.

Lichteim, Miriam. *Ancient Egyptian Literature*. Vol. 1: *The Old and Middle Kingdoms*. Berkeley: University of California Press, 1975.

Mahdi, Muhsin. "Exemplary Tales in the *1001 Nights*." In *The 1001 Nights: Critical Essays and Annotated Bibliography*. Special issue of *Mundus Arabicus* 3 (1983): 1–24.

———. "Philosophy." In *The Cambridge History of Arabic Literature*, Cambridge: Cambridge University Press, forthcoming.

———. "Remarks on the *Theologus Autodidactus* of Ibn al-Nafîs." *Studia Islamica* 31 (1970): 197–209.

Mahfûz, Najîb. "Kayduhunna." In Najîb Mahfûz, *Hams al-Junûn*, pp. 79–89. Beirut: Dâr al-Qalam, 1973.

Mahmûd, Muhyî. *Nubû'a Shârida*. Cairo: Matâbiʿ Dâr al-Shaʿb, 1978.

Malti-Douglas, Fedwa. "Al-ʿAnâsir al-Turâthiyya fî al-Adab al-ʿArabî al-Muʿâsir: al-Ahlâm fî Thalâth Qisas." Translated by ʿI. al-Sharqâwî. *Fusûl* 2, no. 2 (1982): 21–29.

———. *Blindness and Autobiography: al-Ayyâm of Tâhâ Husayn*. Princeton: Princeton University Press, 1988.

———. "Blindness and Sexuality: Traditional Mentalities in Yûsuf Idrîs' 'House of Flesh.' " In *Critical Pilgrimages: Studies in the Arabic Literary Tradition*, edited by Fedwa Malti-Douglas. *Literature East and West* 25 (1989): 70–78.

———. "The Classical Arabic Detective." *Arabica* 35 (1988): 59–91.

———. "An Egyptian Iconoclast: Nawal el-Saadawi and Feminist Fiction." *The American Book Review* 11, no. 3 (July–August 1989): 5, 8.

———. "*Mentalités* and Marginality: Blindness and Mamlûk Civilization." In *The Islamic World from Classical to Modern Times: Essays in Honor of Bernard Lewis*, edited by C. E. Bosworth et al., pp. 211–237. Princeton: Darwin Press, 1989.

———. "Playing with the Sacred: Religious Intertext in *Adab* Discourse." In *Medieval and Renaissance Humanism*, edited by George Makdisi and Giles Constable, forthcoming.

———. "Shahrazâd Feminist." In *The Thousand and One Nights in Arabic Literature and Society*, edited by Fedwa Malti-Douglas and Georges Sabagh. Cambridge: Cambridge University Press, forthcoming.

———. "Structure and Organization in a Monographic *Adab* Work: *Al-Tatfîl* of al-Khatîb al-Baghdâdî." *Journal of Near Eastern Studies* 40, no. 3 (1981): 227–245.

————. *Structures of Avarice: The Bukhalâ' in Medieval Arabic Literature*. Leiden: E. J. Brill, 1985.

————. "Views of Arab Women: Society, Text, and Critic." *Edebiyât* 4 (1979): 256–273.

al-Maqdisî. *Al-Bad' wal-Ta'rîkh*. 6 vols. in 3. Beirut: Maktabat Khayyât, n.d.

Marzolph, Ulrich. *Der Weise Narr Buhlûl*. Wiesbaden: Kommissionsverlag Franz Steiner GMBH, 1983.

al-Marzûqî. *Sharh Dîwân al-Hamâsa*. 4 vols. Edited by Ahmad Amîn and ʿAbd al-Salâm Hârûn. Cairo: Lajnat al-Taʾlîf wal-Tarjama wal-Nashr, 1951–1953.

al-Maydânî. *Majmaʿ al-Amthâl*. 2 vols. Beirut: Dâr Maktabat al-Hayât, n.d.

Mazaheri, Aly. *La vie quotidienne des musulmans au moyen âge, Xᵉ au XIIIᵉ siècle*. Paris: Librairie Hachette, 1951.

Mehta, Ved. *Vedi*. New York: Oxford University Press, 1981.

Mernissi, Fatima. *Beyond the Veil: Male-Female Dynamics in a Modern Muslim Society*. Cambridge, Mass.: Schenkman Publishing Company, 1975.

————. *Chahrazad n'est pas marocaine*. Casablanca: Editions Le fennec, 1988.

————. *Le harem politique: Le Prophète et les femmes*. Paris: Editions Albin Michel, 1987.

Les merveilles de l'Inde. Translated by L. Marcel Devic. Paris: Alphonse Lemerre, 1878.

Miles, Margaret R. *Carnal Knowing: Female Nakedness and Religious Meaning in the Christian West*. Boston: Beacon Press, 1989.

Millett, Kate. *Going to Iran*. New York: Coward, McCann & Geoghegan, 1982.

Minh-ha, Trinh T. *Woman, Native, Other: Writing Postcoloniality and Feminism*. Bloomington: Indiana University Press, 1989.

Miquel, André. *La géographie humaine du monde musulman jusqu'au milieu du 11ᵉ siècle*. 2 vols. Paris: Mouton, 1967–1975.

————. "Mille nuits, plus une." *Critique, littératures populaires* 36 (March 1980): 240–246.

Moi, Toril. *Sexual/Textual Politics: Feminist Literary Theory*. London: Methuen, 1985.

More, Thomas. *Utopia*. Edited and translated by H.V.S. Ogden. Arlington Heights, Ill.: Harlan Davidson, 1949.

al-Munajjid, Salâh al-Dîn. *Al-Hayât al-Jinsiyya ʿind al-ʿArab*. Beirut: Dâr al-Kitâb al-Jadîd, 1958.

————. *Jamâl al-Marʾa ʿind al-ʿArab*. Beirut: Dâr al-Kitâb al-Jadîd, 1969.

Musallam, Basim F. *Sex and Society in Islam*. Cambridge: Cambridge University Press, 1983.

al-Muwaylihî, Muhammad. *Hadîth ʿIsâ ibn Hishâm*. Cairo: Matbaʿat al-Maʿârif, 1907.

al-Nâbulusî, Shâkir. *Fadwâ Tûqân wal-Shiʿr al-Urdunnî al-Muʿâsir*. Cairo: al-Muʾassasa al-Misriyya al-ʿAmma lil-Taʾlîf wal-Inbâʾ wal-Nashr, 1966.

al-Nafzâwî, Mouhammad. *La prairie parfumée où s'ébattent les plaisirs*. Translated by René R. Khawam. Paris: Editions Phébus, 1976.

————. *Al-Rawd al-ʿAtir fî Nuzhat al-Khâtir*. Marrakech(?): n.p., n.d.

Nasr, Seyyed Hossein. *Three Muslim Sages: Avicenna—Suhrawardî—Ibn ʿArabî.* Cambridge: Harvard University Press, 1964.

Nefzawi. *The Perfumed Garden of the Shaykh Nefzawi.* Translated by Sir Richard F. Burton. Secaucus, N.J.: Castle Books, 1964.

Nicholson, R. A. *A Literary History of the Arabs.* Cambridge: Cambridge University Press, 1969.

al-Nisâʾî. *Sunan al-Nisâʾî.* With commentary by Jâlal al-Dîn al-Suyûtî. 8 vols. in 4. Beirut: al-Maktaba al-ʿIlmiyya, n.d.

al-Nuwayrî. *Nihâyat al-Arab fî Funûn al-Adab.* 25 vols. to date. Cairo: Tabʿat Dâr al-Kutub, n.d.

Pagels, Elaine. *Adam, Eve, and the Serpent.* New York: Vintage Books, 1989.

Park, Heong-Dug. "Nawâl al-Saʿadâwî [sic] and Modern Egyptian Feminist Writings." Ph.D. diss., University of Michigan, 1988.

Pastor, Antonio. *The Idea of Robinson Crusoe.* Watford: The Gongora Press, 1930.

Paulson, William R. *Enlightenment, Romanticism, and the Blind in France.* Princeton: Princeton University Press, 1987.

Phelps, Ethel Johnston. *The Maid of the North: Feminist Folk Tales from Around the World.* New York: Henry Holt and Company, 1981.

Phillips, John A. *Eve: The History of an Idea.* San Francisco: Harper & Row, 1984.

Poe, Edgar Allan. "The Thousand-and-Second Tale of Scheherazade." In *Edgar Allan Poe, Greenwich Unabridged Library Classics,* pp. 491–502. New York: Chatham River Press, 1981.

Pratt, Annis. *Archetypal Patterns in Women's Fiction.* Bloomington: Indiana University Press, 1981.

Qattân, Munâ. *Ayyâm maʿa Salâh Jâhîn.* Cairo: Maktabat Madbûlî, 1987.

al-Qazwînî. *ʿAjâʾib al-Makhlûqât wa-Gharâʾib al-Mawjûdât.* Edited by Fârûq Saʿd. Beirut: Dâr al-Afâq al-Jadîda, 1981.

———. *Athâr al-Bilâd wa-Akhbâr al-ʿIbâd.* Beirut: Dâr Sâdir, 1960.

———. *Mufîd al-ʿUlûm wa-Mubîd al-Humûm.* Edited by Muhammad ʿAbd al-Qâdir ʿAtâ. Beirut: Dâr al-Kutub al-ʿIlmiyya, 1985.

Qumayha, Jâbir. *Al-Turâth al-Insânî fî Shiʿr Amal Dunqul.* Cairo: Hajar lil-Tibâʿa wal-Nashr wal-Tawzîʿ, 1987.

al-Qurʾân. Cairo: Mustafâ al-Bâbî al-Halabî, 1966.

al-Qurtubî. *Bahjat al-Majâlis wa-Uns al-Mujâlis.* Edited by Muhammad Mursî al-Khawlî. Beirut: Dâr al-Kutub al-ʿIlmiyya, 1982.

———. *Al-Jâmiʿ li-Ahkâm al-Qurʾân.* 20 vols. in 10. Cairo: Dâr al-Kitâb al-ʿArabî lil-Tibâʿa wal-Nashr, 1967.

al-Qushayrî. *Latâʾif al-Ishârât.* Edited by Ibrâhîm Basyûnî. 3 vols. Cairo: al-Hayʾa al-Misriyya al-ʿAmma lil-Kitâb, 1981.

al-Râghib al-Isfahânî. *Muhâdarât al-Udabâʾ wa-Muhâwarât al-Shuʿarâʾ wal-Bulaghâʾ.* 4 vols. in 2. Beirut: Dâr Maktabat al-Hayât, n.d.

Ramadân, Sumayya. "Al-Radd ʿalâ Kitâb *Unthâ Didd al-Unûtha.*" In *al-Fikr al-ʿArabî al-Muʿâsir wal-Marʾa,* pp. 125–131. Cairo: Dâr Tadâmun al-Marʾa al-ʿArabiyya, 1988.

Rank, Otto. *The Myth of the Birth of the Hero: A Psychological Interpretation of Mythology.* Translated by Dr. F. Robbins and Dr. Smith Ely Jelliffe. New York: Robert Brunner, 1957.

al-Râzî. *'Ismat al-Anbiyâ'.* Edited by Muhammad Hijâzî. Cairo: Maktabat al-Thaqâfa al-Dîniyya, 1986.

Richter-Bernburg, Lutz. "Towards an Anatomy of Ibn Tufayl's Medicine." In *The World of Ibn Tufayl: Interdisciplinary Perspectives on Hayy ibn Yaqzân,* edited by Lawrence I. Conrad. Oxford: Oxford University Press, forthcoming.

Riffaterre, Michael. "Intertextual Scrambling." *Romanic Review* 68 (1977): 197–206.

Rosenthal, Franz. "Sources for the Role of Sex in Medieval Muslim Society." In *Society and the Sexes in Medieval Islam,* edited by Afaf Lutfi al-Sayyid Marsot, pp. 3–22. Malibu: Undena Publications, 1979.

Ruddick, Sara. *Maternal Thinking: Toward a Politics of Peace.* Boston: Beacon Press, 1989.

Russ, Joanna. *How to Suppress Women's Writing.* Austin: University of Texas Press, 1983.

al-Ruwaynî, 'Abla. *Al-Janûbî: Amal Dunqul.* Cairo: Maktabat Madbûlî, n.d.

al-Sa'dâwî, Nawâl. *'An al-Mar'a.* Cairo: Dâr al-Mustaqbal al-'Arabî, 1988.

———. *Al-Ghâ'ib.* Cairo: Maktabat Madbûlî, n.d.

———. "Growing Up Female in Egypt." Translated by Fedwa Malti-Douglas. In *Women and the Family in the Middle East: New Voices of Change,* edited by Elizabeth Warnock Fernea, pp. 111–120. Austin: University of Texas Press, 1985.

———. *Hanân Qalîl.* Beirut: Dâr al-Adâb, 1986.

———. *Imra'a 'ind Nuqtat al-Sifr.* Beirut: Dâr al-Adâb, 1979.

———. *Imra'atâni fî-Mra'a.* Cairo: Maktabat Madbûlî, 1983.

———. *Izîs.* Cairo: Dâr al-Mustaqbal al-'Arabî, 1986.

———. *Kânat Hiya al-Ad'af.* Cairo: Maktabat Madbûlî, 1979.

———. *Al-Khayt wa-'Ayn al-Hayât.* Cairo: Maktabat Madbûlî, 1972.

———. *Lahzat Sidq.* Beirut: Dâr al-Adâb, 1986.

———. *Al-Mar'a wal-Jins.* Cairo: Maktabat Madbûlî, 1983.

———. *Al-Mar'a wal-Sirâ' al-Nafsî.* Cairo: Maktabat Madbûlî, 1983.

———. *Mawt Ma'âlî al-Wazîr Sâbiqan.* Cairo: Maktabat Madbûlî, 1980.

———. *Mudhakkirât Tabîba.* Beirut: Dâr al-Adâb, 1980.

———. *Qadiyyat al-Mar'a al-Misriyya al-Siyâsiyya wal-Jinsiyya.* Cairo: Dâr al-Thaqâfa al-Jadîda, 1977.

———. *Al-Rajul wal-Jins.* Beirut: al-Mu'assasa al-'Arabiyya lil-Dirâsât wal-Nashr, 1980.

———. *Suqût al-Imâm.* Cairo: Dâr al-Mustaqbal al-'Arabî, 1987.

———. *Ta'allamt al-Hubb.* Cairo: Maktabat al-Nahda al-Misriyya, 1961.

———. *Al-Unthâ Hiya al-Asl.* Maktabat Madbûlî, 1983.

———. *Al-Wajh al-'Arî lil-Mar'a al-'Arabiyya.* Beirut: al-Mu'assasa al-'Arabiyya lil-Dirâsât wal-Nashr, 1977.

al-Safadî. *Nakt al-Himyân fî Nukat al-'Umyân.* Edited by Ahmad Zakî Bâshâ. Cairo: al-Matba'a al-Jamâliyya, 1911.

al-Sakhâwî. *Al-Daw' al-Lâmi' li-Ahl al-Qarn al-Tâsi'*. 6 vols. Beirut: Manshûrât Dâr Maktabat al-Hayât, n.d.

Sâlih, Madanî. *Ibn Tufayl: Qadâyâ wa-Mawâqif*. Baghdad: Dâr al-Rashîd lil-Nashr, 1980.

al-Sammân, Ghâda. "Ghajariyya bi-lâ Marfa'." In Ghâda al-Sammân, *Lâ Bahr fî Bayrût*, pp. 71–81. Beirut: Manshûrât Ghâda al-Sammân, 1981.

Schimmel, Annemarie. "Eros—Heavenly and Not So Heavenly—in Sufi Literature and Life." In *Society and the Sexes in Medieval Islam*, edited by Afaf Lutfi al-Sayyid Marsot, pp. 119–141. Malibu: Undena Publications, 1979.

———. *Mystical Dimensions of Islam*. Chapel Hill: University of North Carolina Press, 1975.

Sedgwick, Eve Kosofsky. *Between Men: English Literature and Male Homosocial Desire*. New York: Columbia University Press, 1985.

Selzer, Richard. *Rituals of Surgery*. New York: Harper's Magazine Press, 1974.

Seurat, Marie. *Les corbeaux d'Alep*. Paris: Gallimard, 1988.

Shaarawi, Huda. *Harem Years: The Memoirs of an Egyptian Feminist*. Translated and introduced by Margot Badran. London: Virago, 1986.

Sharabi, Hisham. *Neopatriarchy: A Theory of Distorted Change in Arab Society*. New York: Oxford University Press, 1988.

Sharâra, 'Abd al-Latîf. *Ibrâhîm Tûqân*. Beirut: Dâr Sâdir, 1964.

Shattuck, Roger. *The Forbidden Experiment: The Story of the Wild Boy of Aveyron*. New York: Farrar Straus Giroux, 1980.

Shaykh al-Rabwa al-Dimashqî. *Nukhbat al-Dahr fî 'Ajâ'ib al-Barr wal-Bahr*. Edited by A. Mehren. Leipzig: Otto Harrassowitz, 1923.

Snow, C. P. *The Two Cultures and A Second Look*. Cambridge: Cambridge University Press, 1986.

Somekh, Sasson. "Al-'Alâqât al-Nassiyya fî al-Nizâm al-Adabî al-Wâhid." *Al-Karmil* 7 (1986): 109–129.

———. *Dunyâ Yûsuf Idrîs min Khilâl Aqâsisihi*. Tel Aviv: Dâr al-Nashr al-'Arabî, 1976.

———. *Lughat al-Qissa fî Adab Yûsuf Idrîs*. Acre: Matba'at al-Sarûjî, 1984.

Sontag, Susan. *Illness as Metaphor*. New York: Farrar, Straus and Giroux, 1978.

Spellberg, Denise. "Nizâm al-Mulk's Manipulation of Tradition, 'A'isha and the Role of Women in the Islamic Government." *The Muslim World* 78 (1988): 111–117.

Stanton, Domna. "Autogynography: Is the Subject Different?" In *The Female Autograph: Theory and Practice of Autobiography from the Tenth to the Twentieth Century*, edited by Domna Stanton, pp. 3–20. Chicago: University of Chicago Press, 1987.

Stetkevych, Suzanne Pinckney. "Intoxication and Immortality: Wine and Associated Imagery in al-Ma'arrî's Garden." In *Critical Pilgrimages: Studies in the Arabic Literary Tradition*, edited by Fedwa Malti-Douglas. *Literature East and West* 25 (1989): 29–48.

Stowasser, Barbara Freyer. "The Status of Women in Early Islam." In *Muslim Women*, edited by Freda Hussain, pp. 11–43. New York: St. Martin's Press, 1984.

al-Suhrawardî. *Hayy ibn Yaqzân*. In *Hayy ibn Yaqzân*, edited by Ahmad Amîn. Cairo: Dâr al-Maʿârif, 1952.

Suhrawardi. *The Mystical and Visionary Treatises of Shihabuddin Yahya Suhrawardi*. Translated by W. M. Thackston, Jr. London: The Octagon Press, 1982.

al-Suyûtî. *Al-Ashbâh wal-Nazâʾir fî Qawâʿid wa-Furûʿ Fiqh al-Shâfiʿiyya*. Cairo: ʿIsâ al-Bâbî al-Halabî, n.d.

——. *Nuzhat al-Julasâʾ fî Ashʿâr al-Nisâʾ*. Edited by ʿAbd al-Latîf ʿAshûr. Cairo: Maktabat al-Qurʾân, 1986.

al-Tabarî. *Jâmiʿ al-Bayân ʿan Taʾwîl al-Qurʾân*. 30 vols. in 12. Cairo: Mustafâ al-Bâbî al-Halabî, 1968.

Tâmir, Zakariyyâ. "Al-ʿUrs al-Sharqî." In Zakariyyâ Tâmir, *al-Raʿd*, pp. 71–79. Damascus: Manshûrât Maktabat al-Nûrî, 1978.

al-Tanûkhî. *Nishwâr al-Muhâdara*. Edited by ʿAbbûd al-Shâlijî. 8 vols. Beirut: Dâr Sâdir, 1971–1973.

Tarabishi, Georges. *Woman against Her Sex: A Critique of Nawal el-Saadawi*. Translated by Basil Hatim and Elisabeth Orsini. London: Saqi Books, 1988.

Tarâbîshî, Jûrj. *Unthâ Didd al-Unûtha*. Beirut: Dâr al-Talîʿa, 1984.

Tawil, Raymonda Hawa. *My Home, My Prison*. New York: Holt, Rinehart and Winston, 1979.

al-Thaʿâlibî. *Latâʾif al-Lutf*. Edited by ʿUmar al-Asʿad. Beirut: Dâr al-Masîra, 1980.

——. *Qisas al-Anbiyâʾ*. Beirut: Dâr al-Qalam, n.d.

——. *Al-Tamthîl wal-Muhâdara*. Edited by ʿAbd al-Fattâh Muhammad al-Hulw. Cairo: ʿIsâ al-Bâbî al-Halabî, 1961.

——. *Thimâr al-Qulûb fî al-Mudâf wal-Mansûb*. Edited by Muhammad Abû al-Fadl Ibrâhîm. Cairo: Dâr al-Maʿârif, 1985.

Thompson, Stith. *Motif-Index of Folk-Literature*. 6 vols. Bloomington: Indiana University Press, 1955–1958.

al-Tibrîzî. *Sharh Dîwân al-Hamâsa*. 4 vols. Beirut: ʿAlam al-Kutub, n.d.

al-Tîfâchî, Ahmad. *Les délices des coeurs*. Translated by René R. Khawam. Paris: Editions Phébus, 1981.

al-Tirmidhî. *Al-Jâmiʿ al-Sahîh—Sunan al-Tirmidhî*. Edited by Ahmad Muhammad Shâkir, Muhammad Fuʾâd ʿAbd al-Bâqî et al. 5 vols. Beirut: Dâr al-Kutub al-ʿIlmiyya, 1987(?).

Todorov, Tzvetan. "Les hommes-récits." In Tzvetan Todorov, *Poétique de la prose*, pp. 78–91. Paris: Editions du Seuil, 1971.

——. "Style." In Oswald Ducrot and Tzvetan Todorov, *Dictionnaire encyclopédique des sciences du langage*, pp. 383–388. Paris: Editions du Seuil, 1972.

Tolmacheva, Marina. "The African Wâq-Wâq: Some Questions Regarding the Evidence." *Fontes Historiae Africanae: Bulletin d'information*. Nos. 11/12 (1987/1988): 9–15.

Torgovnick, Marianna. *Closure in the Novel*. Princeton: Princeton University Press, 1981.

Trible, Phyllis. *Texts of Terror: Literary-Feminist Readings of Biblical Narratives*. Philadelphia: Fortress Press, 1985.

Tûqân, Fadwâ. "Akhî Ibrâhîm." In Ibrâhîm Tûqân, *Dîwân*, pp. 11–34. Amman: Maktabat al-Muhtasib, 1984.

———. *ʿAlâ Qimmat al-Dunyâ Wahîdan*. Beirut: Dâr al-Adâb, 1973.

———. *Amâm al-Bâb al-Mughlaq*. Acre: Matbaʿat al-Jalîl, 1968.

———. *Aʿtinâ Hubban*. Beirut: Dâr al-ʿAwda, 1974.

———. "Difficult Journey—Mountainous Journey." Translated by Donna Robinson Divine. In *Opening the Gates: A Century of Arab Women's Writing*, edited by Margot Badran and Miriam Cooke, pp. 26–40. London and Bloomington: Virago and Indiana University Press, 1990.

———. *Al-Layl wal-Fursân*. Beirut: Dâr al-Adâb, 1969.

———. *A Mountainous Journey: An Autobiography*. London: The Women's Press, 1990.

———. *Rihla Jabaliyya, Rihla Saʿba*. Amman: Dâr al-Shurûq lil-Nashr wal-Tawzîʿ, 1985

———. *Tammûz wal-Shayʾ al-Akhar*. Amman: Dâr al-Shurûq, 1987.

———. *Wahdî maʿa al-Ayyâm*. Beirut: Dâr al-ʿAwda, 1974.

———. *Wajadtuhâ*. Beirut: Dâr al-ʿAwda, 1974.

Tûqân, Ibrâhîm. *Dîwân*. Amman: Maktabat al-Muhtasib, 1984.

Ullmann, Manfred. *Islamic Medicine*. Edinburgh: Edinburgh University Press, 1978.

Watt, W. Montgomery. *The Faith and Practice of al-Ghazâlî*. Chicago: Kazi Publications, 1982.

———. *Islamic Philosophy and Theology*. Edinburgh: Edinburgh University Press, 1962.

Weber, Edgard. *Le secret des Mille et une nuits: L'inter . . . dit de Shéhérazade*. Toulouse(?): Eché, 1987.

Wehr, Hans. *A Dictionary of Modern Written Arabic*. Edited by J. Milton Cowan. Ithaca: Spoken Languages Services, 1976.

Williams, William Carlos. *The Doctor Stories*. Compiled by Robert Coles. New York: New Directions Books, 1984.

Wittig, Monique. *Les guerillères*. Paris: Les Editions de Minuit, 1969.

Yâqût. *Muʿjam al-Buldân*. 5 vols. Beirut: Dâr Sâdir, 1979.

Yohannan, John D. *Joseph and Potiphar's Wife in World Literature*. New York: New Directions Books, 1968.

al-Zabîdî. *Tâj al-ʿArûs*. 10 vols. Beirut: Dâr Sâdir, n.d. Reprint of Cairo edition.

———. *Tâj al-ʿArûs*. Edited by ʿAbd al-Sattâr Ahmad Farrâj et al. 22 vols. to date. Kuwait: Matbaʿat Hukûmat al-Kuwayt, 1965–present.

Zaki, H. M. "Utopia and Ideology in *Daughters of a Coral Dawn* and Contemporary Feminist Utopias." Special issue on "Feminism Faces the Fantastic." *Women's Studies* 14, no. 2 (1987): 119–133.

al-Zamakhsharî. *Al-Mustaqsâ fî Amthâl al-ʿArab*. 2 vols. Beirut: Dâr al-Kutub al-ʿIlmiyya, 1977.

Zaydân, Jurjî. *Asîr al-Mutamahhidî*. In Jurjî Zaydân, *Muʾallafât Jurjî Zaydân al-Kâmila*. 21 vols. Beirut: Dâr al-Jîl, 1981.